# KNOW-HOW

Illustrated by Etti de Laczay

# KNOW-HOW

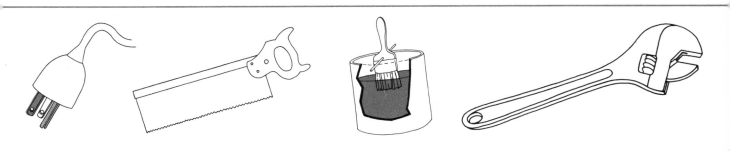

A Fix-It Book for the Clumsy but Pure at Heart

by Guy Alland, Miron Waskiw, and Tony Hiss

Little, Brown and Company — Boston —Toronto

First Edition

T 04/75


The authors are grateful to the following manufacturers and organizations for their assistance:

Adjustable Clamp Company
Albert Constantine & Son Inc.
American Hardboard Association
American Standard Inc.
American Walnut Manufacturers Association
Appalachian Hardwood Manufacturers, Inc.
Borden Inc.
Fine Hardwoods Association
Hardwood Plywood Manufacturers Association
Maple Flooring Manufacturers Association
National Oak Flooring Manufacturers Association
Southern Forest Products Association
Western Red Cedar Lumber Association

Special acknowledgment is made to:

American Plywood Association
California Redwood Association
National Paint, Varnish and Lacquer Association
Stanley Tool Company

The authors are also grateful to the Division of Architecture of The Cooper Union for the Advancement of Science and Art for permission to reproduce drawings of the Villa Savoie by Daniel Libeskind, and to the Octagon Press Ltd. for permission to reprint "King Without a Trade" from *Reflections* by Idries Shah. Copyright © 1971 by Idries Shah.


LIBRARY OF CONGRESS CATALOGING IN PUBLICATION DATA

Alland, Guy.
    Know-how: the fix-it book for the clumsy but pure at heart.

    1. Repairing—Amateurs' manuals. I. Waskiw, Miron, joint author. II. Hiss, Anthony, joint author.
III. Title.
TT151.A44  1975          643'.7          74-23429
ISBN 0-316-03140-2
ISBN 0-316-03141-0 pbk.


Designed by Barbara Bell Pitnof

*Published simultaneously in Canada by Little, Brown & Company (Canada) Limited*

Printed in the United States of America

Contents

Everything in this book is easy to understand and easy to do. The only reason we have written the book is to let you in on this secret. Two years ago, two of the authors, Guy Alland and Miron Waskiw, founded a school in New York City — The Knowhow Workshop (motto: "Even if you never held a hammer before") — to impart this secret in a classroom. One of their students was a klutz named Tony Hiss, who, after the secret had been passed to him, went home and changed all the light switches in his house to dimmers. Hiss later became the third author of this book. Alland is an architect who has been an acoustical engineer, a space planner, a furniture designer, an architect of gas stations in New York's West-chester County and of a house in the Bahamas, a cabinetmaker, a carpenter, and a motorcycle freak. Waskiw is also an architect; he has been a construction engineer for the Getty Oil Company, a contractor, a lifeguard, a cook, a chemical researcher for International Flavors & Fragrances, a hotel designer, a motel designer, an architect of apartment houses, and a technical writer. His greatest love in the world is horse racing. Hiss is a staff writer for *The New Yorker* and himself the publisher of a magazine, *The Real World* (The Magazine of Special Interest Consciousness). He is the author of a children's book, *The Giant Panda Book*; he is the co-author of *All Aboard with E. M. Frimbo, World's Greatest Railroad Buff*; he is writing a book about city politics with former New York Mayor Robert F. Wagner; and he is also working on two more children's books — one about sleep and dreaming, the other about magic. Etti de Laczay, the illustrator of this book, has degrees in fine arts and philosophy and is completing a Ph.D. in sociology. She has been a book editor, a book designer, a painter, a photographer, an etcher, a translator, the designer of educational film strips, and is the author of two books, *Gandhi* and *Loneliness*.

We think the only reason people have trouble with the things we write about in this book, or find them mysterious, is that nobody has ever explained to them, in the right way, that all these things are simple. Other books try to explain things to you by giving you an endless stream of facts. This book doesn't. This book explains things the right way. It makes things simple by explaining why they work the way they do. In the case of, for instance, plumbing, we tell you why there are such things as plumbing systems, and then we give you a little history, a little physics, a little hydraulics, a little systems engineering, a few stories, and, finally, some plain, old everyday recipes for working with the pipes, valves, and wrenches that are the result of all this engineering and science. The point is: Once you know why something is done the way it is, you can then do everyday stuff on your own. More important, when you come across something new, you can sit down and, by going through the process you've already come to know, figure out what's going on and what needs to be done.

Second secret: The concepts of all the systems we write about — plumbing, electricity, building a house — are simplicity itself, and they're all related. All systems are organized in similar ways — they have to be, because men's minds work in certain ways. The vacuum cleaner's not working, the plumbing's not working, the marriage isn't working — they're all similar.

The only other thing we need to tell you at this point is that people try to guard what they know by making up fancy words about it that only they can understand. This familiar process, known as *jargon,* is dealt with effectively in this book. All the hard words are in red when they make their first appearance. They are then translated into English. And then they are explained even more completely in the glossary at the end of the book.

What use are skills, anyway? There is a very old story, which dates from the early days of mankind, that answers that question. It is called "The King Without a Trade," and it appears in this book as the introduction.

There was once a king who had forgotten the ancient advice of the sages that those who are born into comfort and ease have greater need for proper effort than anyone else. He was a just king, however, and a popular one.

Journeying to visit one of his distant possessions, a storm blew up and separated his ship from its escort. The tempest subsided after seven furious days, the ship sank, and the only survivors of the catastrophe were the king and his small daughter, who had somehow managed to climb upon a raft.

After many hours, the raft was washed upon the shore of a country which was completely unknown to the travelers. They were at first taken in by fishermen, who looked after them for a time, then said:

"We are only poor people, and cannot afford to keep you. Make your way inland, and perhaps you may find some means of earning a livelihood."

Thanking the fisherfolk, and sad at heart that he was not able to enlist himself among them, the king started to wander through the land. He and the princess went from village to village, from town to town, seeking food and shelter. They were, of course, no better than beggars, and people treated them as such. Sometimes they had a few scraps of bread, sometimes dry straw in which to sleep.

Every time the king tried to improve his condition by asking for employment, people would say: "What work can you do?" And he always found that he was completely unskilled in whatever task he was required to perform, and had to take to the road again.

In that entire country there were hardly any opportunities for manual work, since there were plenty of unskilled laborers. As they moved from place to place, the king realized more and more strongly that being a king without a country was a useless state. He reflected more and more often on the proverb which the ancients have laid down:

"That only may be regarded as your property which will survive a shipwreck."

After years of this miserable and futureless existence, the pair found themselves, for the first time, at a farm where the owner was looking for someone to tend his sheep.

He saw the king and the princess and said: "Are you penniless?"

They said that they were.

"Do you know how to herd sheep?" asked the farmer.

"No," said the king.

"At least you are honest," said the farmer, "and so I will give you a chance to earn a living."

He sent them out with some sheep, and they soon learned that all they had to do was to protect them against wolves and keep them from straying.

The king and the princess were given a cottage, and as the years passed the king regained something of his dignity, though not his happiness, and the princess blossomed into a young woman of fairylike beauty. As they only earned enough to keep themselves alive, the two were unable even to plan to return to their own country.

It so happened that one day the sultan of that country was out hunting when he saw the maiden and fell in love with her. He sent his representative to ask her father whether he would give her in marriage to the sultan.

"Ho, peasant," said the courtier who had been sent to see him, "the sultan, my lord and master, asks for the hand of your daughter in marriage."

"What is his skill, and what is his work, and how can he earn a living?" asked the former king.

"Dolt! You peasants are all alike," shouted the grandee. "Do you not understand that a king does not need to have work, that his skill is in managing kingdoms, that you have been singled out for an honor such as is ordinarily beyond any possible expectation of commoners?"

"All I know," said the shepherd-king, "is that unless your master can earn his living, sultan or no sultan, he is no husband for my daughter. And I know a thing or two about the value of skills."

The courtier went back to his royal master and told him, adding: "We must not be hard on these people, sire, for they know nothing of the occupations of kings."

The sultan, however, when he had recovered from his surprise, said:

"I am desperately in love with this shepherd's daughter, and I therefore am prepared to do whatever her father may direct in order to win her."

So he left the empire in the hands of a regent, and apprenticed himself to a carpet-weaver. After a year or so, he had mastered the art of simple carpet making. Taking some of his handiwork to the shepherd-king's hut, he presented it to him and said:

"I am the sultan of this country, desirous of marrying your daughter, if she will have me. Having received your message that you require a future son-in-law to possess useful skills, I have studied weaving, and these are examples of my work."

"How long did it take you to make this rug?" asked the shepherd-king.

"Three weeks," said the sultan.

"And when sold, how long could you live on its profit?" asked the shepherd-king.

"Three months," answered the sultan.

"You may marry my daughter, if she will accept you," said the father.

The sultan was overjoyed, and his happiness was complete when the princess agreed to marry him. "Your father, though he may be only a peasant, is a wise and shrewd man," he told her.

"A peasant may be as clever as a sultan," said the princess, "but a king, if he has had the necessary experiences, may be as wise as the shrewdest peasant."

The sultan and the princess were duly married, and the king, borrowing some money from his new son-in-law, was able to return to his own country, where he became known for evermore as the benign and sagacious monarch who never tired of encouraging each and every one of his subjects to learn a useful trade.

— A Sufi tale told by Idries Shah
in his book, *Reflections*

One

# Tools

Partly because we like them, partly to get your attention, and a little because it's important, the first thing we are going to talk about in this book is bodies. This will not be just another Saturday night at home alone. This book will be an *experience*.

Bodies are great. They get us around; they're lovely to look at, delightful to hold. There are many things you can do with your body. And there are many things you would like to do with your body, but shouldn't.

You could screw a screw with your fingernail, or nail a nail with your fist — once. For these sorts of things, the ones you wouldn't use your body for, use a tool. (Oh, well, you knew it wouldn't last.)

A tool is a specialized, durable, long-lasting hand. Tools concentrate forces in small areas. Most tools make use of the principles of leverage to increase your strength. Tools are tougher than your skin and perform specialized tasks.

There is a critical difference between good tools and bad tools. If you like good bodies you will love good tools. They have similar properties. Good tools get the job done quickly, enjoyably and with a minimum of effort. It is, in fact, the *tool* that does the work. This is so important that we will call it the first principle of fixing.

### First Principle of Fixing

A good tool does work for you.
A bad tool makes work for you.

Be lazy! Use good tools.

A good tool is well made and well designed. To be well made it must be made with good materials.

A tool has two ends: the end you hold (the social end), and the end that does the work (the business end). Tools' social ends (handles) have traditionally been made out of wood, because wood is comfortable and has a nice feel. The wood used is heavy, hard, strong, close-grained, and tough — woods like white ash, beech, and hickory.

The business end of tools is usually made out of steel, a metal whose main qualities are hardness, toughness, and the ability to retain a cutting edge. Steel is an alloy of iron and contains a small amount of carbon, and even smaller amounts of manganese, silicone, phosphorous, sulfur, and oxygen. Many tools are made out of tool steel, which is even harder and tougher and sharper than ordinary steel.

If you heat up a piece of steel and let it cool slowly, it is quite soft when it cools. If you heat it up and cool it off quickly, by plunging it into water or oil, the cold steel will be much harder. This process is known as tempering. Tool steel is generally tempered.

Tools are also often drop-forged: a big heavy weight is dropped on the steel when it is still molten, compressing the metal to make it stronger and harder. High-speed steel is a hard steel used in metal cutting because it retains its hardness even when red hot, which makes it very useful for high-speed lathes and drills. Carbide steel is one of the hardest steels. It is steel with a high carbon content which is used to get cutting edges that last ten to forty times as long as high-speed cutting edges. Carbide steel is also very brittle, and chips or breaks when dropped.

If the tools are made out of good materials it is likely they will be put together well. Tool manufacturers usually make two lines of tools, one brand for the "handyman" and one brand for the "professional." The handyman brand gets poor materials and craftsmanship. The professional tool usually gets good everything. Go to a store and stare at tools the way you would at bodies. Then pick them up and feel them, and go through the motions of using them. All lovers of good bodies will like the pleasing weight and balance of good tools in their hands. Good tools last a long time, make jobs easier, and require only some care.

The first tool you should learn how to use is your eye. Always look at what you're doing — and keep looking at what you're doing as you work. Tools allow for a degree of precision not otherwise obtainable, but the basis for that precision is always your own eye.

Always use a tool with the least amount of effort necessary to accomplish a task. Hold a tool with just enough pressure to keep it from dropping out of your hand, and increase that pressure only when necessary. Practice with a tool until you know how to use it. When you practice with a hammer, hammer nails into a scrap piece of wood until you're using just enough force to send the nails into the wood — and using all the force you are using on the nails themselves, and not on the wood or on your thumb.

## The Basic Tool Kit

The basic kit is made out of the fewest tools possible. But because we like tools we describe about twice as many as we have to. For this reason, all the tools in this chapter have been rated with either a ★, a ●, or a ♥.

★ tools are necessary tools.
● tools are good tools to have around.
♥ tools are tools owned by people who love tools — by fanatics.

The tools are presented in roughly the order that you will use them. We have also grouped them. We have also presented only tools that might take their place in a basic tool kit. For instance, we are about to describe a measuring tape, and one of the things we're going to say about it is that it is 12 feet long. Now, in fact, measuring tapes are available in any number of different lengths, and 12 feet is only one of the eight most common lengths (the others are 6, 10, 16, 20, 25, 50, and 100 feet). However, only the 12-foot-long tape is both large enough to handle most jobs and small and compact enough for you to use easily. It's a case of This-porridge-is-too-hot, This-porridge-is-too-cold, and This-porridge-is-just-right. We've left out *almost* all the porridges that aren't just right.

## Instructions for Buying Tools

1. Tools should be bought as you need them.
2. Read the appropriate section in this chapter just before buying the tool. It will remind you of the things to look for.
3. Buy the best tool you can afford.

Note: You cannot do any work without a set of tools.
A 4-ounce hammer, a pair of pliers, a 24-cent screwdriver, and a bottle of booze is *not* a set of tools.

## Measuring Tools

★ You

The human body is the basic measuring tool, and it's free. Most of the familiar units of measure are based on sizes of various components of the body. The middle joint of a finger is approximately an inch long. A foot is approximately a foot long. A stride is approximately a yard long. It makes sense to get to know some of your own measurements, since you are the one measuring tool you always have with you. A spread hand is approximately 8½ inches long — from thumbtip to little fingertip. Your palm is approximately 3½ to 4 inches wide. Your armspread approximates your height.

When you familiarize yourself with your own measurements

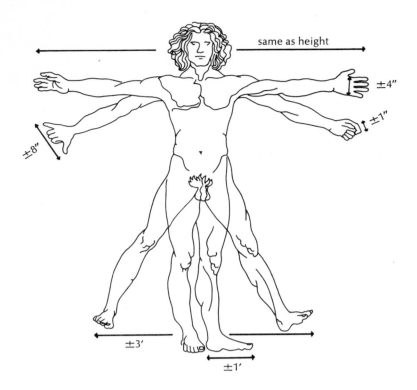

same as height

±4"

±1"

±8"

±3'

±1'

(and you should check our approximations against a calibrated tool), you find that you're developing a different awareness of distances and dimensions. Interesting thing. You see, you now have an instant size reference to the things around you, so pretty soon you get to notice things like how wide streets are, how big doorways are, how big buildings are — all the things around you. And when you notice how big things are, why, then you begin to notice how things are made, and what they're like. You develop a sense of scale and an awareness of your environment.

★   Tape Measure
  — Twelve feet long.
  — Made out of steel coated with mylar (a clear plastic stuff that keeps it nice and smooth and un-gummed-up, and also keeps the inch marks from wearing away).
  — Shows inches and feet on one edge and centimeters on the other edge (the metric system is the coming thing, you know, and just because it's so much easier to use than our system is no reason for us not to get used to it).

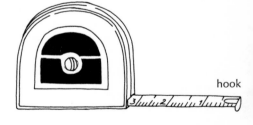

hook

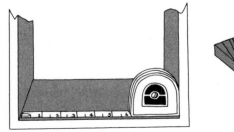

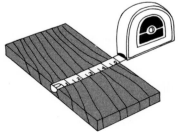

— Lives in a little metal case that is exactly and conveniently 2 inches long for inside dimensions.

— Has a lock to keep tape in place while you're using it, and also a spring return to slurp it back into the case like spaghetti when you're finished with it.

— Has a little hook on the very end that slides its own width and allows for precise measuring. Careful — don't bend the blade too sharply or it'll get a crease in it, and then it could break.

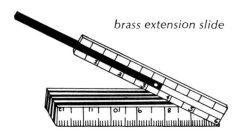

*brass extension slide*

● Folding Rule

— 8 feet long.

— 6-inch extending brass rule at one end (inside dimension again).

— Less accurate than tape measure because its joints make for imprecision.

— Can't measure curves.

— Can measure straight-up distances better than tape.

— Can measure distances across space better than tape. You would measure the Grand Canyon with a folding rule, because if you used a tape measure you'd have to have another person on the other side to hold the end to keep the tape from sagging.

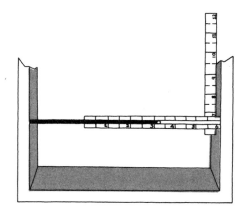

## Guidelines for Measuring

"Measure once, cut twice. Measure twice, cut once." (Lee Bolton, summer of '72.)

It's better to cut a little big than a little little. (You can always shave a little off if it turns out that you did cut a little big, but it's hard to grow a thing back if it turns out you cut it a little little.)

## Marking and Guiding Tools

★ Pencil

You have to tilt pencils when you use them to mark lines, otherwise the line a pencil draws is always $\frac{1}{16}$ inch away from the line you want it to draw.

*scratch awl*

● Scratch Point of an Awl

See Cutting, Boring, and Shaping Tools for the definition of an awl.

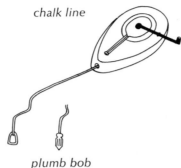

*chalk line*

*plumb bob*

● Chalk Line

It comes out of a little box, and gets a chalk coat as it comes out, and you twang it against something, like a bowstring, to make your mark.

★ Combination Square

There are four types of squares talked about here. You'll want at least this one.

— The combination square is a versatile instrument. It includes a one-foot ruler which can be used as a cutting-along edge, a scratch awl for marking, and a level for short spaces.

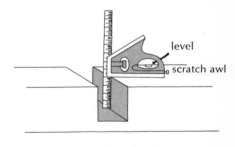

*level*

*scratch awl*

*measuring depth*

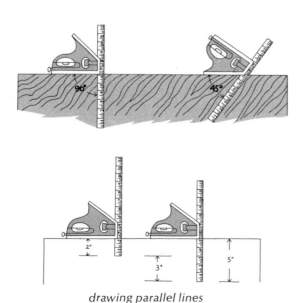

*drawing parallel lines*

— Combination squares can make 90-degree and/or 45-degree angles
— Or can be used to draw parallel lines.

### ♥ Try Square

A fixed square — and a more accurate square.
  Used for checking inside and outside corners and for marking lines perpendicular to the face of anything.

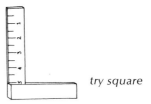

*try square*

### ● Framing Square

Just a large steel square useful for checking larger pieces. One of a carpenter's three key tools; with a saw, a hammer, and a framing square (maybe a few materials), you can build a house.

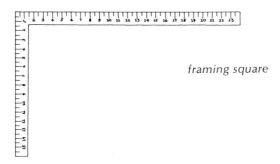

*framing square*

— The markings in the middle are a guide to the pitches of roofs, used to help put up rafters (Chapter Two).
— Also used to prepare stringers for stairs (stringers are the sides of stairs).
— Fascinating tool, a chapter in itself (another time, maybe).

### ♥ Sliding Bevel Square

For transferring angles other than 90 or 45 degrees. Loosen nut; adjust metal piece to angle; tighten nut; transfer the angle to the piece of wood that's to be marked.

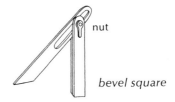

nut

*bevel square*

## Testing Tools

### ● Level

For checking true horizontal (level) and true vertical (plumb).

— Made of wood or some lightweight metal like aluminum or magnesium. Get a metal one if you can.

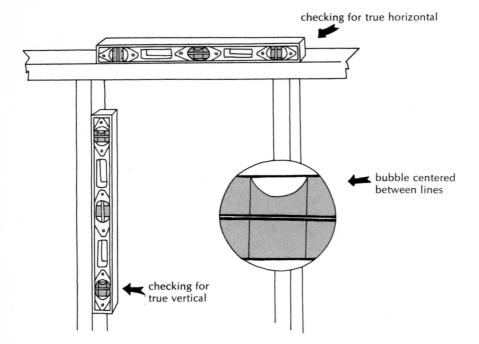

checking for true horizontal

bubble centered
between lines

checking for
true vertical

— Has three pairs of vials (one at each end, one in the middle). Vials are usually filled with alcohol, which freezes only at very low temperatures.
— The bubble in a vial has to be between the two black lines on the side of that vial to mark an exact horizontal or vertical line. For plumb, make sure by checking the vial at the top and the vial at the bottom at the same time.
— Particularly useful for hanging shelves (if you measure from a floor, a ceiling, or a door, assuming them to be level or plumb, you need to be told that they're usually not).

● Plumb Line

A line with a weight, called a plumb bob, used to mark an exact vertical line. See chalk line illustration on page 8.

— Use it against a wall, but it has to hang free of the wall to be accurate.
— Available with a chalk line for marking.

## Cutting, Boring, and Shaping Tools

★ Crosscut Saw

For cutting wood across the grain (Chapter Three).

— Has either eight or ten points (teeth) per inch.

— The more teeth per inch, the smoother the cut the saw makes and the harder the work for you. The point number is stamped into the blade, up near the handle.

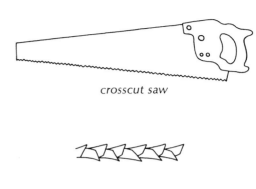

*crosscut saw*

The blade of a good saw is made of spring steel — how to tell? Hold the handle, bend the blade, and then let go. If it springs back into place, it's spring steel. If it stays bent, don't buy the saw.

A good saw blade is taper ground (or hollow ground), meaning the blade is tapered: thin at the top, thick down where the teeth are. Wood, you see, has a tendency to close back on itself after it's been cut. (If the blade isn't tapered the wood will bind the saw, that is, close back on itself and grab the saw.)

The saw cut, the kerf, is even wider than the widest part of the blade (how come? because sawteeth are set pointing outward, first to one side, then to the other). This set is actually the primary way of preventing binding during cutting, and it also provides a space for pushing sawdust out of the way.

set

kerf

— All American saws cut on the push stroke only; that's the only way the teeth can cut: they're facing away from the handle.
— But saw blades are made of a thin piece of metal, so don't push too hard, or the blade'll bend and quiver.

You'd think, wouldn't you, that the saw would work better if you could pull on it, instead of pushing on it, because pulling would tend to straighten the blade out. Well, Japanese saws, and very fine saws they are, are made that way — they cut only on the pull stroke. I guess you'd have to say Japanese saws are ♥ ♥ tools, probably, but they are certainly most attractive, well-designed, and well-thought-out tools.

— The handle of the saw you buy has to be firmly attached to the blade — this means it has to be attached with a ferrule (a metal band) and at least five rivets that go all the way through.
— Before sawing always check the blade to see if the teeth in the center are as sharp as the teeth in the toe and the heel. Just run your thumb lightly along the teeth from toe to heel. If the center incisors are dull, don't use the saw. You see, in a good saw, the teeth themselves do the cutting with their sharpness, not with the weight you put on them.
— The easiest way to sharpen a saw is to send it out to the hardware store for a trim. Cost: $1–$2.
— Saws should be lubricated before use. Wipe the whole blade with machine oil. Wipe the oil off. A residue will remain. (Wood has resins in it — all right, sap — that will bind a saw and gum it up unless it has been lubricated.)

An important thing: Wood should not move around when you cut it. So see that it doesn't.

Wood should be supported on both sides of a cut, otherwise it will splinter when you're just barely almost through and already thinking happy thoughts.

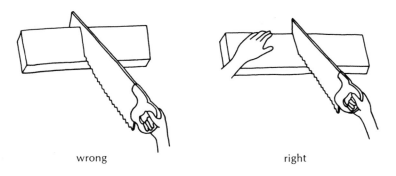

wrong      right

*hold unsupported end to prevent splitting*

Put the good side of a piece of wood (that is, the side you like best) *up* when using a handsaw; the cut is being pushed through the wood, so the down side will splinter more than the up side.

— Cut perpendicular to the length of the wood.
— And, with a crosscut saw, cut at a 45-degree angle to the wood — except for the first few strokes. For starters, you do everything differently: hold the saw vertically on the line, and pull on the saw just until the groove is started.
— Saw so that your sawing arm has free movement — just like the piston on the drive wheels of a choo-choo train. If your elbow keeps knock, knock, knocking against your side, and your arm keeps moving in and out, guess what the saw blade will do.

Remember the Little Engine That Could: I *think* I can, I *think* I can, I *think* I can, I thoughtIcould, I thoughtIcould, I thoughtIcould.

♥ Ripsaw

A saw for cutting with the grain of wood.

*ripsaw*

— Six points.

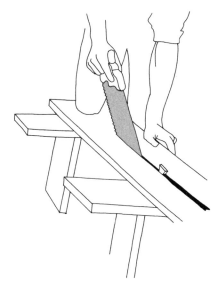

A wedge in the saw cut (kerf) will prevent the wood from closing and binding the saw.

— Hold saw at a 60-degree angle to the wood you're cutting (a little closer to vertical than with the crosscut saw).

● Backsaw

A crosscut saw with a back on it, meaning a spine of metal along the top.

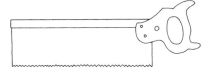

*backsaw*

— Use for fine work — picture frames, miters.
— Ten to sixteen points. More points means it's harder to use than other saws. The back makes it stiff, and so it always makes very straight, very accurate cuts.
— Hold saw horizontally, not at any angle to the wood you're cutting. A backsaw can't cut any deeper than the width of the blade below the back. (The back is wider than the rest of the blade.)

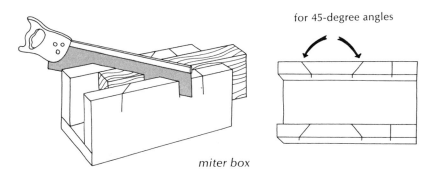

for 45-degree angles

*miter box*

— Use with a miter box; a device used to get perfect cuts.

♥ Coping Saw

A hand-operated jigsaw; a small saw used to cut shapes, curved lines, scrollwork.

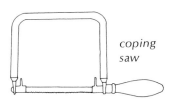

*coping saw*

### ♥ Compass Saw

Another small saw.

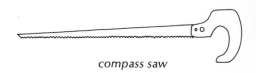

*compass saw*

— Blade comes to a point and turns easily, so it is used to cut circles.
— You have to drill a hole first, before beginning to saw.

### ♥ Keyhole Saw

An even smaller saw; kid brother to the compass saw. Cuts even smaller circles (keyholes, get it?).

### ★ Hacksaw

The metal-cutting saw. Cuts ferrous (iron, steel) and nonferrous (bronze, copper, aluminum) metals.

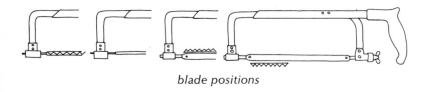

*blade positions*

— You can attach the blades in various ways for strange places so that you can always cut down. This is something you always want to do. Gravity is your friend, old chum.
— Cuts on the push stroke, not the pull stroke, just like American wood saws.
— The Important Thing: The blades are replaceable. They have to be; they break and wear out.
— You have to use different blades for different materials (the blades are labeled in stores).
— If a hacksaw blade breaks while you're cutting, you have to make a new cut with the new blade from the other side. Why? Because new blades are always thicker than old blades, so the new blade will bind if you put it in the cut of the old blade.
— Use a file to start a hacksaw cut.

*Select proper blade so that at least two teeth are in contact with the work to prevent breakage.*

### ● Saber Saw/Bayonet Saw/Jigsaw

A power saw. The nice thing about it is that, by changing blades, it can take the place of all the saws mentioned already. It can also take the place of a lot of saws unmentioned.

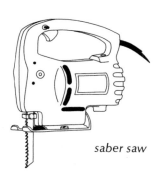

*saber saw*

— It can cut wood, metal, fiberglass, rubber, etc.
— When cutting curves, use the narrowest possible blade. The radius of a curve is limited by the width of the saw blade.

Generally speaking, buy heavy-duty power tools. They cost about twice the price of so-called homeowner, or cheap, power tools, but a homeowner tool can only be used once or twice. And if you are going to use a thing once or twice, why are you buying a power tool?

The way a jigsaw works:

— The blade goes up and down.
— The blade cuts on the UP stroke (its teeth point up).

So if you're cutting wood, put the good side of the wood down.

— The jig is up.
— The blade should be moving before it comes into contact with its work, otherwise the blade may break.

Don't go too fast. When you use a reciprocating saw (generic term for up-and-down-cutting saws) you should use it at a speed that doesn't make the motor slow down excessively, and overheat, and get irritated. The saw will just eat its way through its work if you push at the right speed.

The shoe of the saw (guard rail, guide rail) should rest on the thing you're cutting, otherwise the thing will chatter, that is, oscillate like windup false teeth, and then the blade may break.

★   Wire Cutters

For cutting wire and stripping off insulation.

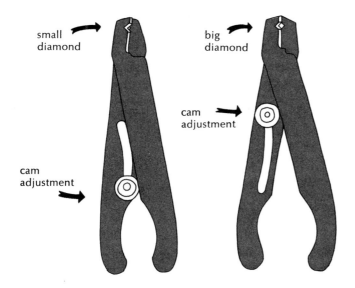

— The diamond shape in the middle is the insulation-stripping dingus. It is controlled by a sliding cam (a cam is an eccentric circle — a not-exactly-perfect circle).
— Size the diamond, as best you can, to the diameter of the

copper in the wire you want to strip. Then put the wire in the diamond and close the wire cutters and pull.

— The diamond will cut through the insulation, but not the wire, and just strip the stuff off.

♥ Side Cutters

For cutting coat hangers, metal rods, and heavy-duty wires.

*side cutters*

★ Wood Chisels

For removing wood, shaving wood, for cutting holes or slots in wood. Most common use: morticing for hinges or special wood joints. Morticing means cutting slots or grooves in wood (usually with a chisel) so that other pieces of wood, or hinges, or locks, or anything, can fit in nice and neatly. Hinges are morticed in so that they don't stick out and leave a crack in the door for the hawk to get in.

— Wood chisels are also called butt chisels.
— Get two: a ¼-inch and a ¾-inch chisel.

*butt chisel*

They should have:

*mortise chisel*

— Steel caps on top of the handles, so you can tap them with a metal hammer — though this is something that is frowned on for metallurgical reasons. It would be best to hit them with a plastic or wood or leather hammer and not with a metal hammer, because it is a principle of metallurgy that the softer material breaks first. If the chisel broke, the hammer would use your hand as a chisel (not recommended!).

*tang paring, or bevel edge, chisel*

— Chisels should be kept sharp, because a dull chisel is a waste of time. It's dull if it won't shave a soft piece of wood when you just push the chisel across with hand power. And it's dull if the cutting edge is shiny — paradox — or if you can see nicks and burrs on the knife edge. Keep all fingers out of the path of a chisel. It's *very* easy to cut yourself with these implements.

*socket firmer chisel*

— There are two sides to a wood chisel, one beveled, one flat. When you shave along a surface, put the beveled side down. When you're cutting perpendicularly into a piece of wood, put the bevel side to the part you're taking out.
— Never use a wood chisel on metal, because it necessitates a trip to the hardware store for a new chisel.

● Cold Chisels

For cutting through masonry and metal. Most common use: cutting off a frozen nut or bolt. Also good for punching holes in metal cans.

— Get a ½-inch cold chisel.

— You only need one.

You can hit a cold chisel with a sledge, which is made out of softer metal than a regular metal hammer. If you hit a cold chisel with a regular metal hammer, the hammerhead will mushroom.

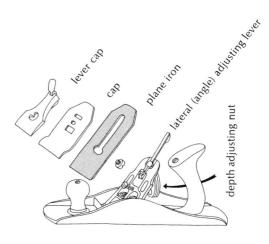

- ## Plane

A plane is a wood chisel in a metal or wood box. Its specific purpose is shaving, and there's no tool better at giving you a smooth, flat surface — you just run it across a piece of wood, and you get a smooth, flat surface.

> — Get a block plane — about 6 inches long, with the blade set at a low angle. It's a good size for smoothing both the faces and edges of a piece of wood.
> — Planes have to be put down on their sides, not their bottoms, when not in use, for the sake of the cutting surface.

- ## Rasp

A file with big teeth used for roughly shaping wood into something other than a flat surface. It's a good tool, hard to get, fallen into disfavor, old-fashioned; these days people mostly use a *Surform multiblade plane.*

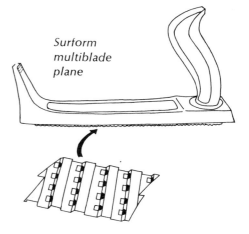

*Surform multiblade plane*

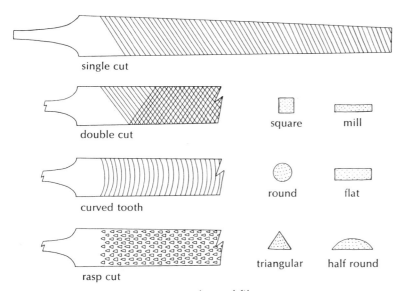

single cut

double cut

square     mill

curved tooth

round     flat

rasp cut

triangular     half round

*cross sections of files*

- ## File

Used to shape metal. Cuts on push stroke, much like a saw.

There are thousands of files. You want: 10-inch single-cut bastard with one safe edge tapered toward the end. "Bastard" means not too coarse, not too smooth — technical term. "Single-cut" means the file lines run in one direction. There are no teeth on one of the file edges — the safe edge.

● Sandpaper

Shapes wood; differentiated by grit number, a measure of the type and density of sand used, and by type of paper used. Papers available, in ascending order of quality, are flint, garnet, aluminum oxide. Also: carborundum, a waterproof paper you have to use when sanding metal since metal must be sanded wet.

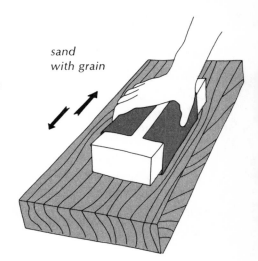

*sand with grain*

— Go ahead, get good paper, it lasts a lot longer.
— Three grit numbers to remember: 60, 100, 150. They refer to rough, medium, and fine. You start with rough and finish off with fine.
— For plywood you gotta use carborundum paper, 280 grit, and nothing else, or you will lift up the grains in the veneers.
— Other gottas: Always whenever possible sand *with* the grain. Always, always use a sanding block; that is, always wrap the sandpaper around a block of wood and don't just sand by hand. Your fingers, you see, are soft, so if you sand by hand, you will just be sanding the soft grain of the wood and leaving the hard grain — wood always has both — which makes for ridges.

♥ Electric Sander

Electric sanders are nice because they do a good deal of the work for you. There are basically two types: a belt sander and an oscillating sander.

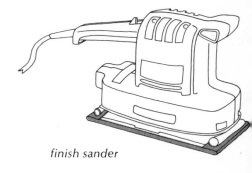

*finish sander*

— The belt sander is a fast and therefore less accurate way of sanding (errors come easily here). Buy an oscillating sander if you decide to buy a power sander.
— Oscillating sanders have an adjustment that lets you choose between back-and-forth sanding or circular sanding. Choose back-and-forth sanding whenever possible as it gives a smoother finish. Circular sanding tends to leave swirls in the grain of the wood. It is for this reason that sander attachments for electric drills are *not* recommended. Power drills are coming up.

● Scraper

You take paint off with it. (See Chapter Four: Painting.)

● Taping Knife

You smooth on putty or taping compound with it. (Also see Chapter Four: Painting.)

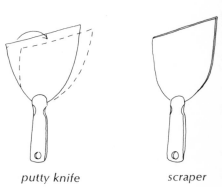

*putty knife*          *scraper*

- Awl, also called Scratch Awl

A preboring tool, used to make starter holes — in wood — for boring tools. Without starter holes, high-speed drills tend to wander. Their motion is circular, and they don't want to do this:

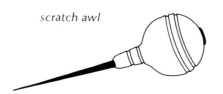

*scratch awl*

●

They want to do this:

ᖇᖇᖇᖇᖇᖇᖇᖇᖇᖇᖇᖇ

A good awl has a wooden handle and a steel shaft that continues through the handle and comes out the back, so you can hit the thing with a hammer. . . .

Also used for picking teeth, cleaning fingernails.

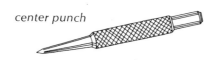

*center punch*

♥ Center Punch

Makes starter holes in metal.

♥ ♥ ♥ Egg-Beater Drill

Mentioned only for precautionary purposes. We dislike this tool enough to tell you not to buy it. Slow, inaccurate, very little lever advantage. Phooey.

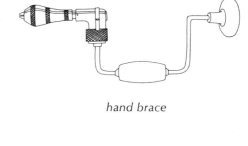

*hand brace*

● Bit Brace

A less objectionable drill, whose best use happens to be as a power screwdriver. So we'll get back to it.

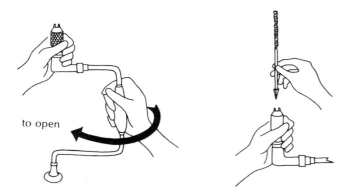

to open

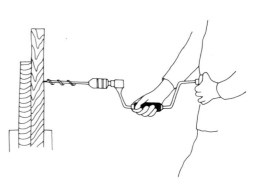

*scrap wood in back will prevent splintering*

The best bit braces have a reversible ratchet so that they can drill, or screw, in both directions.

★ Electric Drill

The only way to drill a hole, and the one power tool you ought to have.

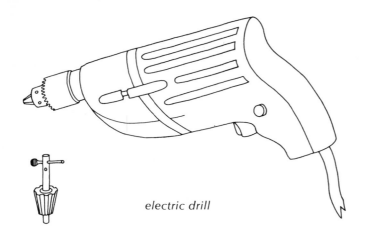

*electric drill*

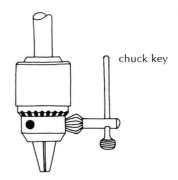

chuck key

Things it should have or be:

— Double-insulated, that is, without a metal body.
— Variable speed, with an adjusting trigger to turn it faster or slower (you have to drill more slowly through harder materials).
— A ⅜-inch drive — meaning that the maximum size bit the chuck will accept is a ⅜-inch bit. And — you can always drill twice the chuck size in wood. You can also get an adjustable bit that drills holes for wood screws. This is truly a labor-saving gadget, because in one operation it drills a small hole for the threaded part of the screw, a slightly larger hole for the shank of the screw, and a much larger hole, up top, for the head of the screw — so that you can countersink the screw.

★　Drill Bits

Many types of specialty and general purpose bits are available for both power and hand drills, including the countersink bit described above.

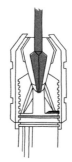

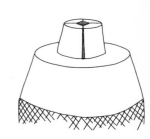

♥ *Auger bit.* For clean, large, hand-drilled holes in wood.
♥ *Spade bit.* For drilling large and fairly rough holes in wood. Note the difference in the bits between hand brace and electric drill.
● *Screwdriver bit.* For power insertion and extraction of wood screws with the bit brace.
★ *High-speed steel bits. The* correct bit for drilling relatively smaller holes in both metal and wood with the electric drill.
★ *Masonry bit.* A carbide-tipped bit which is the only thing to use when drilling in masonry (see Chapter Three).
♥ *Wire brush "bit"* (not pictured). Used to remove paint, rust, and generally prepare surfaces (see Chapter Four).

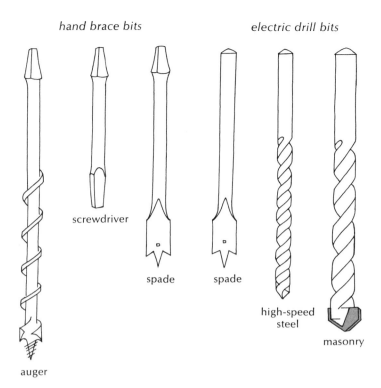

hand brace bits    electric drill bits

screwdriver

spade    spade

high-speed
steel

masonry

auger

♥ *Sanding and buffing "bit."* Do *not* use this attachment to an electric drill for sanding. It does, however, make an excellent elbow grease conserver when polishing all that paste wax you'll be using after reading Chapter Two.

Miscellaneous bits: The list of power drill attachments is as long as the Dead Sea Scrolls, single-spaced, and many of them are at least marginally useful. We will particularly caution you against the power screwdriver and the circular saw adapters; they seem to need more than a little development.

★ Utility Knife, aka Sheetrock Knife, aka Mat Knife (or Mat the Knife), aka Shop Knife

This is a metal or plastic razor-blade holder. Use for any cutting purpose. Most common use: cutting Sheetrock/plasterboard.

*utility knife*

— Has a penny-sized screw in the handle, meaning a screw you can unscrew with a penny, and space inside the unscrewed handle for an extra blade.
— Some utility knives come equipped with retractable blades, which is a good safety feature for the kiddos.

♥ Tin Snips

Big scissors with long handles used for cutting sheet metal, thin bar stock, and thin drawn metal, i.e., wire.

The long handles are for maximum leverage — it's hard to cut metal.

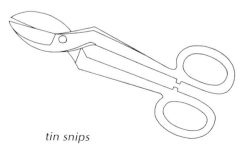

*tin snips*

★ Slip-Joint Pliers

— 8 inches long.
— Used for holding things your thumb and forefinger would hold, but better than t. and f. because metal fingers get a better grip.

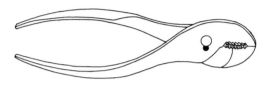

*slip-joint pliers*

The slip joint is like the jaws on most snakes in that it slides to open more, and gives the pliers a better grip on larger items.
Telegram for Mr. Plier User:

PLIERS *NOT* USED AS FASTENING TOOL STOP GRINDS UP NUTS WHEN USED AS FASTENING TOOL STOP YOU WANT WRENCH STOP SEE: WRENCH (UNDER FASTENING TOOLS) STOP WE GET QUITE UPSET ABOUT THIS STOP STOP DOING IT STOP.

● Channel Pliers

Variation of the slip-joint pliers, with several channels for expanding the jaws instead of a single joint. The jaws are curved to one side.

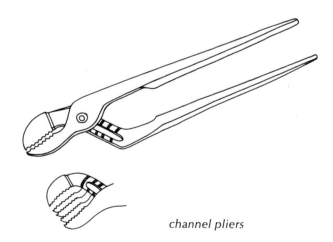

*channel pliers*

Make sure that the jaws are parallel and hold together at the tip. You can't get a good grip otherwise.

♥  Long-Nose Pliers

Used for getting into tight places.

*long-nose plier*        *curved-nose plier*

♥  Curved-Nose Pliers

Ditto.

●  Metal C Clamps

— Normally need two of 'em.
— Look like a C. (Another of those clever names.)
— Used for holding things down.

If you use them on wood, put some scrap wood between the wood and the clamps for the wood's sake. Metal compresses wood.

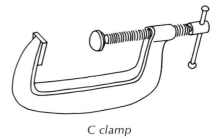

*C clamp*

♥  Wood Clamps

Made of wood. For wood; need two of them, too.

— The jaws have large surface areas, and wood clamps are used to clamp wood together when you're working on it — cutting, drilling, gluing, sanding.
— The jaws are supposed to be tightened so that they are parallel, because otherwise you just get point contact between clamp and wood which is not so efficient. Using them is a tricky business and can lead to Excedrin headache no. 10,753.

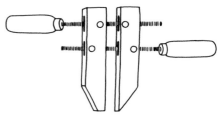

*adjustable wood clamp*

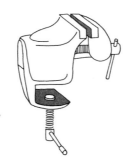

*portable wood-working vise*

●  Portable Wood-Working Vise

Clamps onto things with its jaws. It's important that its insides are made of soft stuff, so that it can't damage wood when it has it in its grip.

★ Vise Grips

A locking pliers which locks with considerable force. A third hand.
  You can lock down on something with vise grips and go away
for days; vise grips won't give up. Not until you push the little
spring release.

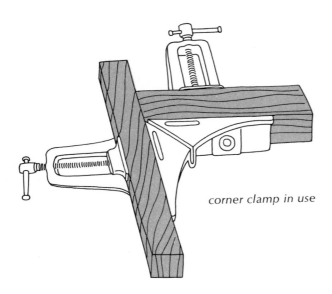

— A knurled knob/screw adjusts the size of the jaw openings.
— Available with flat jaws, curved jaws, smooth jaws, toothy
  jaws; all are great, but teeth leave marks.
— The way to remove that nut which has been stripped by
  pliers — shame!

*vise grips*

♥ Corner Clamps

For holding pieces of wood at right angles to one another for purposes of gluing, nailing, screwing, and marking.

*corner clamp in use*

— One corner clamp sufficient if you never use stock over 2
  inches wide; otherwise you will need two.
— Just the right tool if you have ever tried to hold wood at
  right angles while trying to nail/screw/glue it. Remember
  how awful it was? Now it's going to be a piece of chocolate
  cake. (See the Universal Box, page 63.)

♥ ♥   1/8-Inch Pin Punch

Used for driving out bolts. (You could use an old nail.)

*pin punch*

♥ Propane Torch

A heat source. Used for heating up metal to bend it, for melting
frozen pipes, for loosening a stuck nut, for soldering, for sweating

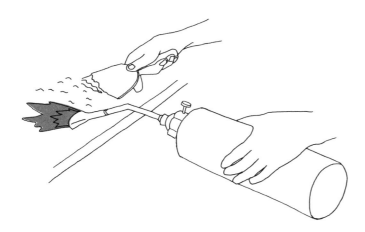

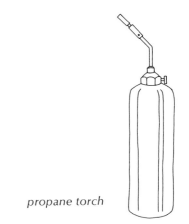

*propane torch*

(a type of soldering used in plumbing, not . . . although it could be . . .), and, with a flame spreader, the fastest paint remover in the West; and East; and . . .

● Nail Set

A very useful tool used for driving finish nails below the surface of a piece of wood so they won't scratch you or anything else.

*nail set*

— $1/16$ inch across the point.
— Also can remove nails that have come out the side of the piece we have tried to nail into. Very useful.

## Fastening Tools

★★ Hammer

*The* tool. General characteristics of the hammer you want:

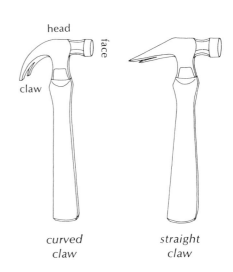

*curved claw*          *straight claw*

— The head weighs *16 ounces*.
— It has a *curved claw* for pulling nails.
— The hammer is *all steel* (it is unbreakable, and also the head can't fly off as it could off a wooden handle — but wooden handles feel better).
— It is *drop-forged* — the head has a *rounded edge* and can't chip like a square head.
— It also has a *crowned head,* meaning that the face is rounded, so that the head has a greater hitting range.
— The face has also been *rim-tempered;* that is, it's been through a toughening process, and now the hammer is a little harder than the nails it will hit.
— This hammer has no other function than driving nails. If you try to hit anything harder than a nail with it you can chip or dent the surface of the hammer, and the chip could

wind up in your eye. You're supposed to hit nails with it.

Grip the hammer near the far end of the handle for best action. Gripping it near the head is wrong for two reasons. One, you hit the nail at the wrong angle that way. Two, you have to work too hard. You don't get full advantage of the swing of the hammer. Mass × lever arm = punch. It's the weight of the head of the hammer that drives a nail, not the force of your swing.

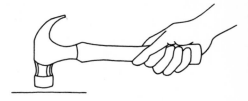

*correct use of hammer*

♥ Ball-Peen Hammer

A hammer used for hitting metal and automotive equipment.

— The head should weigh 12 ounces.
— This hammer has no claw. Instead it has a rounded end called a *peen,* which is used in riveting. Rivets are metal rods that have their ends rounded so that they look like dumbbells. They are used to hold pieces of metal together. Many bridges are riveted together. When a rivet is installed it looks like somebody has put in a screw with a head on both ends and forgot to put in the slot for the screwdriver.

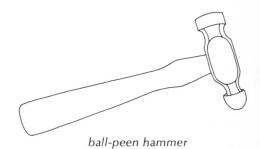

*ball-peen hammer*

★ Screwdrivers

Plural. One tool you can't have enough of. Why? Because screwdrivers are essentially made incorrectly these days. Screw heads are made with a square slot. But screwdrivers are made with tapered blades. Tapered blades fit uneasily into square slots. What happens is that, as you turn it, the screwdriver tends to rotate right

*straight-blade screwdriver with square shank*

*wrong,*
*but common*

*right,*
*but not readily available*

out of the screw. This means you have to maintain force on the screwdriver with the palm of your hand. This pushing, plus the twisting-up-and-out action, tends to ruin the slots of screws and the heads of screwdrivers and the palms of hands. Screws come in so many sizes that if you have a lot of screwdrivers, then you have a better chance of finding a somewhat better fit.

— There is one use for a ruined screwdriver: opening paint cans (see Chapter Four).

— Try to get *cross-ground* screwdrivers. They have little horizontal lines or grooves on the tips of their blades, which kind of help to keep the blades tucked into screw heads.

— The handle of a good screwdriver feels good in your hand. It is fat but not too fat to hold, and it is not full of prickly sharp edges. Some screwdriver handles have rubber grips, which is nice.

● Phillips Head Screwdriver

For screws slotted with a rounded cross. The invention of Mr. Phillips. A Phillips head screwdriver is generally more accurate than an ordinary screwdriver, being sized rather accurately to fit Phillips head screws.

Phillips head screws come in five sizes, which are 0, 1, 2, 3, and 4 (4 is bigger than 3, etc.). The screwdrivers are similarly sized. 0, 1, and 2 are the only sizes you will need.

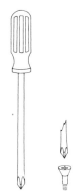

*Phillips screwdriver*

♥ Cabinet Bit Screwdriver

A screwdriver whose blade is the same width all the way. It's used for sinking screws into wood without gouging the wood.

♥ Square-Shank Screwdriver

For heavy-duty work. The purpose of the square shank is so that you can put a wrench on the screwdriver and get extra torque, the word for twisting power.

● Bit Brace

We've seen this bird before. You can get screwdriver bits for a brace and they work. (See Drill Bits in Cutting, Shaping, and Boring Tools.)

It's easy to put screws in with the bit brace, or take them out. You get mucho torque. Screwdrivers, we remember from just a little way back, tend to lift out and therefore we must apply a lot of pressure down with our palms. This turns the screwdriver into yet another tool, a palm-blister machine. The bit brace with screwdriver bit allows one to lean his/her body (or her/his body) against the screw and thus prevent lifting while permitting additional torque and cutting down on censored refrains. TRY IT. YOU'LL LIKE IT.

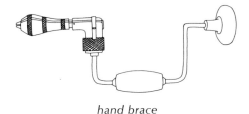

*hand brace*

★ Adjustable Open-End Wrench

This is the tool (not pliers) made for tightening square nuts and bolts, and hexagonal nuts and bolts. It works really well.

— 10 inches long. Should be drop-forged.
— Keep jaws adjusted tight against a nut so that you won't

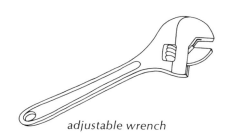

*adjustable wrench*

right

wrong

round off the corners on the nut or break the little teeth on the adjusting part of the wrench. (At last we can tell you what it means to *strip*. To round off corners with the wrong tool or technique is to strip.)

● Pipe Wrench

For pipes, rods, and other things that do not have straight sides (where *stripping* is not a consideration).

— 18 inches long.
— Only wrench mentioned here that has teeth in its jaws.

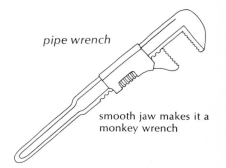

pipe wrench

smooth jaw makes it a monkey wrench

General note: You usually need two wrenches to do any sort of job. One to hold one side of a nut or pipe and another to open or close it.

● Monkey Wrench

Similar to pipe wrench mentioned above, but has no teeth, as you would expect from the old codger that it is. It is, in fact, the first kind of adjustable wrench invented. Another similarity to the pipe wrench is that in the pipe wrench, the upper jaw moves; in the monkey wrench, the lower jaw moves. See how easy it all is if you pay attention. *Another* similarity to the adjustable wrench is that it also tightens and loosens straight-sided things; but . . . the monkey wrench has a bigger capacity than the adjustable wrench, up to 3 inches.

— 18 inches long.
— For bigger capacities see Chapter Five under Spud Wrenches; seriously!

♥ Allen Wrench

For special screws and bolts with hexagonal heads.

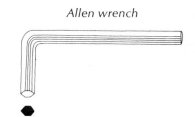

Allen wrench

- All-Purpose Glue

(Not pictured; can't imagine why not.)

- — The white glues — Elmer's, Sobo, etc.
- — For porous materials like wood.
- — Makes a joint between two pieces of wood stronger than either piece of wood.
- — Permanent but not waterproof.

★ Vise Grips

We've seen *this* bird before.
They're also an emergency fastening tool for when you've stripped a nut by using pliers or the wrong wrench. Double shame!

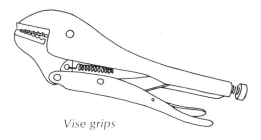

*Vise grips*

## Special Tools

Described later in this book.

## Plumbing Tools

★ Plumber's Helper

● Snake

♥ Spud Wrenches

See Chapter Five: Plumbing.

## Painting Tools

★ Paintbrush

● Roller, Roller Cage, Roller Pan, Roller Extension Handle

● Spin Cleaner

See Chapter Four: Painting.

Two

# Wood

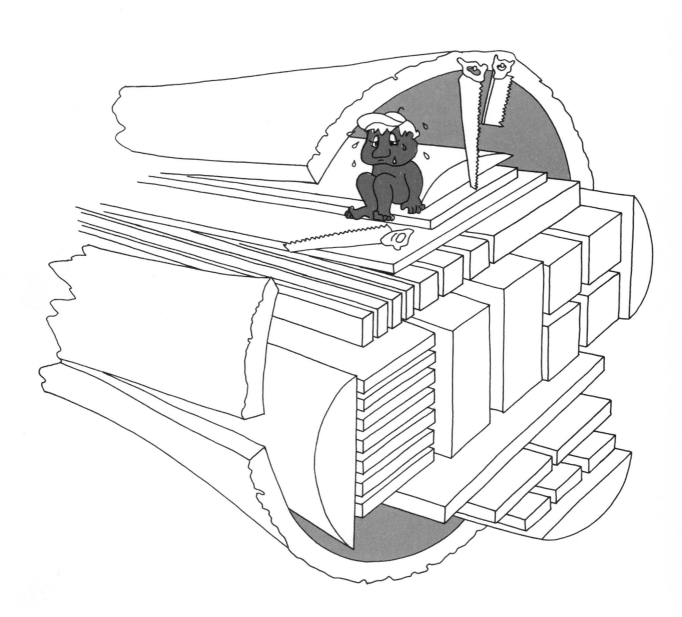

Wood is a nice material and was once plentiful. Most things that men make are made out of wood, which explains, partially, why wood was *once* plentiful. There are usually good reasons why things get to be popular — good ad campaigns, lots of media exposure, slick packaging, etc., or, in very rare cases, because the things have good qualities.

Wood has good qualities. Wood is strong, beautiful, is easy to cut and shape, holds up under adverse conditions such as wind, rain, locusts, and feels good to touch. (I think I'm in love.)

Other materials such as stone, metals, plastics, and fiberglass are either heavy or hard to cut and shape, or rust, or are cold to the touch, or are difficult to fasten, or something bad like that.

Wood is wonderful. Where would we be without wood? Nowhere! Imagine if Noah had built a granite ark.

There are two different kinds of wood in the world: hardwood and softwood. They come from the two different kinds of trees in the world: deciduous and conifers. Deciduous trees give us hardwood. They are the kind of trees that lose their leaves every winter. It's a seasonal business for them. They take their time growing. They grow quite short and rather crooked, and there isn't all that much wood in them. Hardwood, as a result, is very expensive and is primarily used these days for fine furniture. Hardwood has a dense grain pattern and is admired for its beauty. Some common hardwoods are oak, maple, cherry, mahogany, walnut, and black walnut.

Softwood comes from conifers. Conifers have cones and they almost never lose any leaves, which accounts for their nickname: evergreens. They do lose leaves, but they never lose their leaves all at once. They grow up straight, tall, and quickly, as a rule, so the wood we get from them is — also expensive. There just isn't any cheap wood right now. The best that can be said for the price of softwood is that it is lower than the price of hardwood. Softwood is used for construction. The two most common softwoods in the country are pine and Douglas fir.

Wood is baked tree slices. Let's harvest a tree and see how this

delicacy is prepared. The tree we have decided to harvest is a great big giant sequoia. The best wood in it is in the trunk from the line of the branches down to about two or three feet off the ground, so our procedure will be to lop off the top and then chop it down. A man called a topper climbs up the tree and he cuts off the top. He gets paid very well, but his life span is very short.

The top falls off, the tree whips back and forth, and the topper, if he survives, climbs back down again. Then a man called a sawyer cuts the tree at the bottom, yells "Timber!" and the tree falls down. On the ground it gets chopped into pieces 33 feet long. Most lumber comes in 16-foot lengths, and if you get it in other sizes it's because it's been cut to those sizes from 16 feet. Trees get cut into 33-foot pieces because that is a manageable length and because it is a foot longer than twice sixteen. The extra foot is because they make a lot of mistakes. Or they do a rough job, at least at first.

The 33-foot pieces of tree are sent to the mill. The people at the mill strip the bark off the pieces with high-pressure water sprays and put each piece on a track that runs by the saws that will slice it up into either lumber or plywood, if Dudley Doright can get Sweet Sue out of the way in time.

At right is a drawing of a 33-foot-long piece of wood. It appears round because we are looking at it on end, and we are looking at it on end because you can learn a lot about wood and trees when you look at them on end.

The dark wood in the middle is old heartwood from the sequoia's salad days. It is full of resin, and it is not very good wood; it is the core, or pith, of the tree. Then there are all those rings. They are annual rings that we've all seen; we also know that if you count them you will know how old the tree is. They can also tell us other things, because what they actually are is the measure of the tree's growth — they are the tree's autobiography.

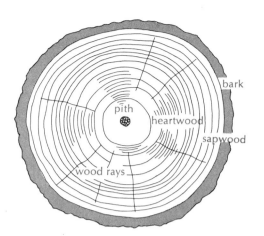

The light rings are the tree's spring growth. That is when a tree does most of its growing. A lot of water is available in the spring, and a tree grows very fast and gets ready for that long hot summer. The dark wood — the dark rings — are summer growth. The wood cells in the summer growth are more compact, having been constructed with less water, than the light spring cells, so the wood in the dark rings is harder. That's very important to remember when working with wood because if you sand the wood unduly you will sand away the soft part but leave the summer growth. That begins to make ridges in wood and it is a process that, once begun, is very difficult to correct.

What else can we read in the rings about the tree's life? Well, if there's been a drought, these rings are closer together. There are knots in the heartwood suggesting a great thunderstorm in the tree's early days. Knots are the stumps of old branches that have broken off, and a lot of missing branches at one point indicates a natural disaster. But the tree grew up after the branches broke, and as you can see the tree grew right around the knots. That is because trees don't grow up. They grow out. They add on on top and they get fatter. So if you carved your initials — H. A. Loves Annie — four feet up on a tree trunk, they'll still be in that tree at exactly the same height whenever you and Annie come back.

But it's now time to slice the barkless piece of tree we've been looking at and turn it into lumber. Lumber is a term to be used correctly; there is lumber and there is plywood. Plywood is a different business, and we'll turn another piece of wood into plywood in a few pages.

We cut the tree pieces with a very big saw with big teeth on it —

one tooth every inch or so. This saw makes big, rough, and very fast cuts, which is the sensible thing to do at this point.

There are two ways the saw can slice up a piece of tree. The more common of the ways is called flat sawing and it's very simple.

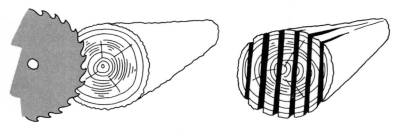

*flat slicing*

The saw just saws through the piece in parallel swathes. This leaves us a big piece with curved ends which we trim off and, presto-fixo, we have a piece of rough-sawn lumber.

This flat-sawn piece of lumber has a curvy sort of grain pattern in it that, looked at on end, looks like so:

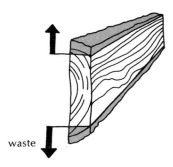

waste

Flat sawing is a relatively cheap process. It uses almost all of the wood in a piece of tree. The only wood wasted is the little bits trimmed off the ends of each piece of lumber.

Now there is also a much better way of slicing trees called quartersawing — it's better for the lumber and better for you, but

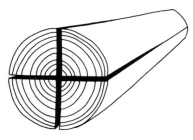

*quartersawn*

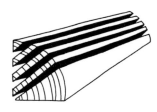

*slicing quartersawn*

worse for the lumberman's profits. Guess which is the most common way. Flat sawing, of course!

To quartersaw you first saw the log into quarters, lengthwise. It is cut in half one way first and then the other way. This leaves four long triangular pieces of wood. We then cut through this triangular piece at 45 degrees to either or both initial cuts. This leaves us a piece of wood with a very straight and regular grain pattern.

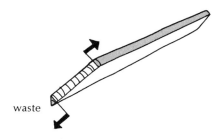

waste

The reason the lumberman doesn't like this is because he has to waste more lumber trimming the quartersawn pieces.

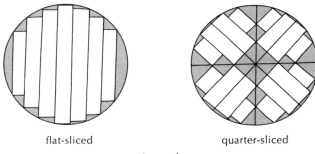

flat-sliced          quarter-sliced

*comparison of wastes*

Additionally, part of what we're wasting in quartersawing is good lumber from the outside of the tree. The outside is the best lumber because it has the fewest knots, and the lumber company can sell it for more money.

But what makes quartersawing a better way to cut lumber is that straight grain pattern it produces. As it happens, finished wood, which is called lumber, has a lot of natural problems, mostly caused by the grain patterns. The short of it is that wood tends to *warp*.

Wood warps because the grain in the wood wants to be straight. So if it is already straight, as in quartersawn lumber, well and good. But if it is curvy, as in the flat-sawn piece, then it will do a funny thing. It will straighten out the grain at the cost of curving the lumber.

One of the ways a flat-sawn piece will warp is to cup. Cupping is deformation *across the width* of the piece of lumber. Here is an end view of flat-sawn lumber just after it comes out of the mill.

fresh wood

Some time later it will look like

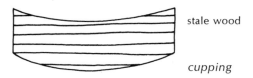

stale wood

*cupping*

because the grain has straightened out. This makes for very wavy floors, for example.

Another way wood can warp is to bow. Bowing is deformation *along the length* of the lumber. Here is another comparison between fresh wood and stale wood.

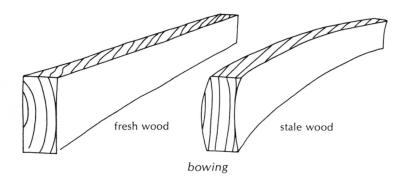

fresh wood          stale wood

*bowing*

What is even worse is that wood can also warp *along its thickness* (another type of bowing). Further it can twist, bow, and cup all at the same time. These factors make a house suitable only for a crooked man.

As we said, warping is a result of grain patterns. A quartersawn piece has a grain pattern which is very straight lengthwise and across and hence doesn't warp as much.

So of course we like to get quartersawn lumber, when we can. You can specify quartersawn when you order lumber. It does cost more, though, so you will probably only want to use it for something whose dimensional stability matters to you.

But before you can buy any lumber we have to finish making it. Here are the two stages of lumber. The board on the left has just come out of the big saw and it looks it. Remember big sawteeth cut quickly, but leave a rough cut.

The board on the right is a little smaller, but it is nice and

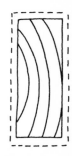

rough-sawn          planed

smooth. The two illustrations are of the same board at different times. What has happened? The board on the right has grown up! Curiously, when lumber grows up it gets smaller.

After the lumber was rough-cut, it was planed. A planer is a device for smoothing wood. It's just a great big drum with a lot of little knives all the way around. And it spins on its axis very fast and as a board goes through the little knives shave it smooth.

People used to shave their own wood, years ago. Then came the mechanical planer which not everyone could afford, so the lumber mills started doing the work. Now, planing slices bits off wood and reduces its size. So lumber rough-cut to 2 inches by 4 inches turns into something smaller when planed and sold under the name 2 x 4. And, as the years passed, the planed size — the actual size — of lumber began shrinking because some unscrupulous mill men took to scraping off more than they had to. Eventually the government stepped in and fixed the actual size at only slightly less than 2 inches by 4 inches. So then the lumber companies, instead of just reducing actual sizes, petitioned the government to do this and, permission granted, reduced actual sizes! What happens now is that mills rough-cut lumber to something smaller than 2 inches by 4 inches and then plane it to 1½ inches by 3½ inches. And you pay for it as if it were still 2 inches by 4 inches. Much the same thing has been happening to Three Musketeers bars and Kleenex.

After planing comes drying. There are two ways of drying lumber: in a kiln and in the open air. Kiln drying takes three days, air drying three to six months. Kiln-dried lumber is more expensive, but lumber sitting in the open air has a tendency to warp as it dries.

Table 1, "Standard Dimensions of Surfaced Lumber," under "Size to Order" tells you what you have to say when ordering lumber and reminds you, under "Surfaced (Actual) Size Dry," what you will really receive. (Surfaced means planed.)

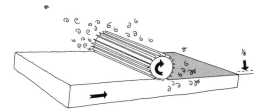

*planing rough-sawn lumber*

| For Board Lumber Size to Order | Surfaced (Actual) Size Dry | For Board Lumber Size to Order | Surfaced (Actual) Size Dry |
| --- | --- | --- | --- |
| 1 × 3 | ¾ × 2½ | 2 × 3 | 1½ × 2½ |
| 1 × 4 | ¾ × 3½ | 2 × 4 | 1½ × 3½ |
| 1 × 6 | ¾ × 5½ | 2 × 6 | 1½ × 5½ |
| 1 × 8 | ¾ × 7¼ | 2 × 8 | 1½ × 7¼ |
| 1 × 10 | ¾ × 9¼ | 2 × 10 | 1½ × 9¼ |
| 1 × 12 | ¾ × 11¼ | 2 × 12 | 1½ × 11¼ |

Thicknesses of 3- and 4-inch lumber are the same as respective widths above.

*Table 1. Standard Dimensions of Surfaced Lumber*

When you go to a lumberyard to order wood there are a number of things that you should look for Unseasoned wood is green. Dried wood is white. You can distinguish between the two colors with just a little effort. Unseasoned lumber is offered for sale, but we don't think you will want to buy it, because it will, of course, season in your house or wherever you put it up. And as it seasons it cups and bows and does everything you don't want it to do. Contractors buy a lot of unseasoned lumber because it costs half as much as dried lumber, and they use it to build partition walls and ceilings and the like. They don't much care what happens to it, because nobody's going to strip down a wall to look at the lumber inside it. So they save money. But it's still not a good idea. Unseasoned lumber is part of what causes squeaks in a house when the floors get walked around on. And, if unseasoned lumber is used as a structure for a floor, that floor will eventually start to bulge. Most of the bulge will be due to water or dampness and things like uneven heat, but at least a little will be from unseasoned lumber.

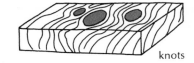
knots

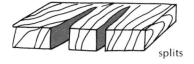
splits

You should look out for cupping and bowing. And you should look for splits, checks, shakes, pecks. There are plenty of things that can go wrong with wood. Wood tends to split *along* the grain. It also tends to split *across* the grain — that's a *check*. Little bits tend to split off the ends of boards along the grain — known as *shakes*. *Pecks* are decay or insect damage. Then there are little pieces of decay without names, and worn-away pieces of wood, and pieces of wood that can only be called crummy.

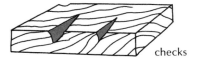
checks

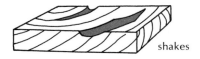
shakes

*lumber imperfections*

Partly to help you avoid some of these things, wood is graded. Three different grades of wood are being commonly offered for sale in most parts of the country nowadays. The best grade, clear wood, has no visible defects. No checks, no splits, and no knots. Number two, the next grade, has knots. Esthetic opinion is divided

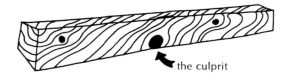
the culprit

about knots; some people go for them, others don't.

Structurally, a knot is a defect, and a big knot is a major defect. Knots are separate units and they do nothing to hold a piece of wood together. If you put any load on this particular board it will crack at the knot. Knots themselves are like heartwood, dense, filled with resin, very hard to work with, impossible to cut, impossible to nail through, impossible to do anything with. People who like to look at knots buy knotty pine, which is number two pine. Number two lumber also has shakes and pecks and things like that.

It's time for a little truth-in-advertising here. Clear wood is usually so-called sapwood from the outside of a tree that has the fewest knots. Remember, knots are stumps of branches which fell off. The stumps stayed in the same place (like the initials) and the tree grew around them. However, this wood has some defects too. It is porous (less dense), which makes it softer and easier to damage and stain (good if you intended, bad if not). It is also more likely to decay and warp.

|  | New Grades | |
| Previous Grades Douglas Fir | Douglas Fir–Larch | Southern Pine |
| Select Structural | Select Structural | Select Structural |
| Construction | No. 1 | No. 1 |
| Standard | No. 2 | No. 2 medium grain |
| Utility | No. 3 | No. 3 |

Table 2. Grades for Structural Lumber (in descending order of strength)

Then there's something called construction grade, which is the pretty crummy stuff. It comes full of the worst qualities of all the grades. There are several tables here. Refer to them *before* buying lumber. Table 2 lists the current official name for the grades of the major structural softwoods. Table 3 gives information about the grades of lumber. Tables 4 and 5 describe the properties of hardwoods and softwoods respectively.

| Grade | Defects Allowed | Finishes |
| --- | --- | --- |
| A-Select or Clear or Premium | No knots, one or two checks $1/32'' \times 3''$ per $5\ 1/4'' \times 8'$ piece. | Clear |
| B-Select or Select or Custom | None, or one $1/4''$ or $5/8''$ diameter knot, 2 or 3 checks $1/32'' \times 5''$ per $4\ 1/2'' \times 8'$ piece. | Clear |
| C-Select or Sound or Custom | 1 or 2 knots $1/2''$ diameter knot, 3 or 4 checks $3/64'' \times 6''$ per $3\ 1/2'' \times 8'$ piece. | Clear or Paint |
| D-Select | Lowest of finishing grades, suitable for painting. | |
| #1 Common | Small tight knots. No waste. | |
| #2 Common | More knots, some may not be sound. Very little waste. | |
| #3 Common | Larger knots; pitch pockets. Not as strong as #2. | |
| #4 Common | Decays quickly, much waste. Best use for temporary structures or firewood (what with the oil shortage). | |

Table 3. Grades of Lumber: Hardwoods and Softwoods

| Name | Use | Color: Sap to Heart | How Does It Work with Hand Tools? | Grain Characteristics | Remarks |
|---|---|---|---|---|---|
| Ash *white* | Tool handles, bent frames, paneling | White to reddish brown | Glue — very good<br>Nail — good<br>Work — good | Medium grain<br>Hard surface<br>Resists warping | Springy and tough, hard to nail when dry, heavy. Medium cost. |
| Birch *yellow* | Furniture, interior trim, paneling | White to light brown to reddish brown | Glue — good<br>Nail — poor<br>Work — fair | Close grain<br>Hard surface<br>Sometimes warps | Often confused with Maple. Considerable abrasion resistance, very strong. Medium cost. |
| Cherry | Cabinet-making, furniture, handles | Light reddish brown | Glue — good<br>Nail — fair<br>Work — difficult | Close grain<br>Hard surface<br>Resists warping | Light, strong. Medium cost. |
| Gum (red) *heartwood* | Furniture, paneling, cabinets | Reddish brown | Glue — very good<br>Nail — very good<br>Work — good | Close grain<br>Medium-hard surface<br>Warps | Grain looks nice. Not very strong. Used as a substitute for Walnut — usually stained. Medium cost. |
| Gum (sap) *sapwood* | Furniture, paneling, cabinets | White | Glue — very good<br>Nail — very good<br>Work — good | Medium grain<br>Medium-hard surface<br>Warps | More defects than Red Gum, not as strong, inexpensive. |
| Mahogany *tropical American* | Furniture, boats, veneers | Light reddish to reddish brown | Glue — very good<br>Nail — good<br>Work — good | Open grain<br>Medium-hard surface<br>Sometimes warps | Great variety of grain patterns and figures. Decay resistant. Inexpensive to medium cost. |
| Maple *hard sugar* | Floors, butcher blocks, furniture | White to mild brown | Glue — good<br>Nail — poor<br>Work — difficult | Close grain<br>Very hard surface<br>Sometimes warps | Usually straight grained, excellent resistance to indentation and abrasion. Medium cost to expensive. |
| Maple *soft red/silver* | Furniture | White to mild brown | Glue — very good<br>Nail — fair<br>Work — good | Medium grain<br>Medium-hard surface<br>Sometimes warps | Look for dark streaks to distinguish from Hard Maple, lots of defects. Inexpensive to medium cost. |
| Red Oak | Flooring, heavy duty furniture, construction | Light brown with mild reddish tinge | Glue — good<br>Nail — good<br>Work — good | Open grain<br>Hard surface<br>Resists warping | Not as resistant as White, durable under exposure. Great wear resistance. Tannic acid makes it fungi and insect resistant. Medium cost. |
| White Oak | Same as Red Oak, also watertight containers | Light tan to light brown | Glue — good<br>Nail — good<br>Work — good | Open grain<br>Hard surface<br>Resists warping | Same as Red Oak, but also water resistant. Medium cost. |
| Red Laun *Philippine Mahogany* | Furniture, doors, cabinets | Light red to dark brown | Glue — good<br>Nail — good<br>Work — poor | Open grain<br>Very soft surface<br>Sometimes warps | Much sanding required for good finish, not stable. Inexpensive to medium cost. |
| White Laun *Philippine Mahogany* | Same as Red Laun | Light grayish to light reddish brown | Same as Red Laun | Open grain<br>Soft surface<br>Sometimes warps | Same as Red Laun, inexpensive. |
| Yellow Poplar | Siding, interior trim, furniture (painted) | White to yellowish brown | Glue — very good<br>Nail — good<br>Work — easiest | Medium grain<br>Soft surface<br>Resists warping | Not structural, extreme discolorations (red, green, blue), takes paint beautifully. Inexpensive. |
| Rosewood *East Indian* | Fine furniture, paneling | Dark purple to ebony, streaks of red or yellow | Glue — good<br>Nail — poor<br>Work — difficult | Close grain<br>Hard surface<br>Resists warping | Takes a beautiful finish, stands up well under most conditions. Costly. |
| Teak | Furniture, floors, ship decking | Tawny yellow to dark brown | Glue — poor<br>Nail — good<br>Work — good | Open grain<br>Hard surface<br>Resists warping | Much like Walnut, except naturally oily. Insect resistant. Shellac not compatible. Costly. |
| Walnut | Quality furniture, paneling, cabinets, gunstocks | White to dark brown | Glue — good<br>Nail — good<br>Work — good | Medium grain<br>Hard surface<br>Resists warping | Greatest variety of grain pattern, very stable. Medium cost to expensive. |

*Table 4. Hardwoods*

| Name | Use | Color: Sap to Heart | How Does It Work with Hand Tools? | Grain Characteristics | Remarks |
|------|-----|---------------------|-----------------------------------|-----------------------|---------|
| Cedar *Eastern red* | Storage chests, closet lining, fence posts | White to bright red | Glue — fair<br>Nail — fair<br>Work — fair | Medium grain<br>Medium-hard surface<br>Resists warping | Durable wood for contact with ground. Smells good, said to repel moths, extremely rot resistant. Lots of natural defects — brittle. |
| Cedar *Western red* | Shingles, siding, boats | White to light brown | Glue — good<br>Nail — good<br>Work — easy | Close grain<br>Soft surface<br>Resists warping | Extremely rot resistant, needs no finish indoors or out, holds paint well, heartwood resists. Use blunt-tip rust-resistant nails. |
| Cypress *Southern* | Exterior trim, siding, decking | White to salmon | Glue — very good<br>Nail — good<br>Work — easy | Close grain<br>Medium-hard surface<br>Resists warping | Heartwood is the most durable wood for contact with soil, holds paint well, heartwood naturally termite resistant. Use blunt-tip rust-resistant nails. |
| Douglas Fir | Construction, plywood | Light cream to orange red | Glue — good<br>Nail — fair<br>Work — poor | Medium grain<br>Soft surface<br>Warps | Strong grain pattern. Summer wood much harder than spring wood. Splintery, splits easily, difficult to finish, strong. |
| Pine (hard) *Southern yellow* | Construction | Cream to light brown | Glue — good<br>Nail — poor<br>Work — poor | Medium grain<br>Hard surface<br>Warps | Strong, paints poorly. |
| Pine (soft) *Ponderosa, sugar, white* | Light construction | Cream to light brown | Glue — good<br>Nail — good<br>Work — easily | Close grain<br>Soft surface<br>Resists warping | Paints well. |
| Redwood | Siding fences, posts, interior trim | White to reddish brown | Glue — very good<br>Nail — good<br>Work — easily | Close grain<br>Soft surface<br>Resists warping | Heartwood resists decay and termite attack. Durable, decay resistant, resists fire, needs no finish. Use blunt-tip rust-resistant nails. |
| Spruce | Light construction, siding | Light cream to light reddish brown | Glue — good<br>Nail — good<br>Work — easily | Close grain<br>Soft surface<br>Warps | Splits easily, paints moderately well. |

*Table 5. Softwoods*

The best advice we can give you about what grade or type of wood to buy is: Match the material to the use intended. If you are building something you are going to look at, it may matter to you what it looks like. If something has to be strong all the way and needn't be gorgeous, you should probably buy number two. Why not have a knothole in the back of a cabinet? Mice need a way to get from one place to another, you know. Number two wood is considerably cheaper. Clear wood costs twice as much as number two, four times as much as construction grade.

Which brings us to board feet. Board feet are the way you order lumber, and they are the second confusing part of lumber buying (standard dimensions of surfaced lumber being the first). So we are printing Table 6, "Converting Lineal Feet to Board Feet," on the next page.

A board foot is an arbitrary measurement of wood, 1 inch thick by 1 foot wide by 1 foot long. It is all that a lumber merchant bothers to remember. He's selling a whole lot of different kinds of sizes of lumber, and the prices of all of them are always changing

| Lumber Dimensions | Lineal Feet | | | | | | | | |
|---|---|---|---|---|---|---|---|---|---|
| | 8 | 10 | 12 | 14 | 16 | 18 | 20 | 22 | 24 |
| 1 × 2 | Sold by lineal foot | | | | | | | | |
| 1 × 3 | Sold by lineal foot | | | | | | | | |
| 1 × 4 | 2⅔ | 3⅓ | 4 | 4⅔ | 5⅓ | 6 | 6⅔ | 7⅓ | 8 |
| 1 × 6 | 4 | 5 | 6 | 7 | 8 | 9 | 10 | 11 | 12 |
| 1 × 8 | 5⅓ | 6⅔ | 8 | 9⅓ | 10⅔ | 12 | 13⅓ | 14⅔ | 16 |
| 1 × 10 | 6⅔ | 8⅓ | 10 | 11⅔ | 13⅓ | 15 | 16⅔ | 18⅓ | 20 |
| 1 × 12 | 8 | 10 | 12 | 14 | 16 | 18 | 20 | 22 | 24 |
| 2 × 2 | Sold by lineal foot | | | | | | | | |
| 2 × 3 | Sold by lineal foot | | | | | | | | |
| 2 × 4 | 5⅓ | 6⅔ | 8 | 9⅓ | 10⅔ | 12 | 13⅓ | 14⅔ | 16 |
| 2 × 6 | 8 | 10 | 12 | 14 | 16 | 18 | 20 | 22 | 24 |
| 2 × 8 | 10⅔ | 13⅓ | 16 | 18⅔ | 21⅓ | 24 | 26⅔ | 29⅓ | 32 |
| 2 × 10 | 13⅓ | 16⅔ | 20 | 23⅓ | 26⅔ | 30 | 33⅓ | 36⅔ | 40 |
| 2 × 12 | 16 | 20 | 24 | 28 | 32 | 36 | 40 | 44 | 48 |
| 3 × 6 | 12 | 15 | 18 | 21 | 24 | 27 | 30 | 33 | 36 |
| 4 × 4 | 10⅔ | 13⅓ | 16 | 18⅔ | 21⅓ | 24 | 26⅔ | 29⅓ | 32 |

Formula for computing board feet: thickness in *inches* × width in *feet* × length in *feet*.

Table 6. *Converting Lineal Feet to Board Feet*

— up — so what he learns and will tell you is board foot prices. Prices all over the lumber industry have gone up in the neighborhood of 200 percent in the last few years, and in another year they will be in another neighborhood, because they are continuing to go up at the same rate. The whole matter is being investigated by the government — but that might make them go up even more.

So don't call up a lumberyard and say, "How much are 1 × 2s and 1 × 10s and 2 × 4s and 2 × 6s?" Use the chart. Because the guy at the lumberyard will say, "Number two lumber is 60 cents a foot," and he will be talking board feet, not lineal feet, because that's the way lumberyard guys talk. He pays for three truckloads of lumber every week full of all different sizes and all different grades of lumber, and he knows he paid so much per board foot. And he knows what his markup is. So what's on his mind? Board feet.

What you have in mind is maybe 6 feet of number two 2 × 4. You won't assume that it will cost you $3.60. Being intelligent, you'll use the chart. The chart says 6 lineal feet of 2 × 4 equals 4 board feet of 2 × 4, so 6 feet of number two 2 × 4 will cost you $2.40.

How did the chart arrive at its answer? Easy. Multiply thickness in *inches* by width in *feet* by length in *feet* (because a board foot is 1 inch thick, 1 foot wide, and 1 foot long). A 6-foot 2 × 4 is 2 inches thick, ⅓ foot wide, and 6 feet long. $6 \times ⅓ = 2$; $2 \times 2 = 4$. Four board feet. See? Easy.

The chart is easier.

The price of lumber keeps rising because the number of people that want to buy wood keeps rising. And the supply of lumber can't keep rising. A big long piece of hardwood is next to impossible to come by, and the quality of available lumber is declining. Much of the lumber sold today was burned twenty to thirty years ago as scrap.

Q. What is to be done?

A. Use plywood instead of lumber. It is cheaper than lumber and more durable.

Plywood is a Dagwood Bumstead sandwich of tree peelings. It is a way of making boards that was invented shortly before World War II. There is a lingering prejudice against plywood in some minds. These minds conceive it to be less real than lumber. Well, there is nothing fake about plywood. It is real wood all the way through. It's just different pieces of real wood all the way through instead of the same piece of real wood all the way through.

There are only two disadvantages to plywood that we can think of. The first one is not so very important. It is called the problem of *edge grain*. The edge of plywood does not look like the *face* of plywood. Hence, if you are joining pieces of plywood together, as shown below, you will have to do some tricky things: like mitered corners (in picture frames, for example) or *veneers*.

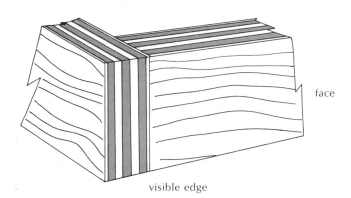

face

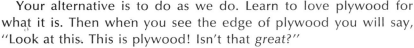

visible edge

Your alternative is to do as we do. Learn to love plywood for what it is. Then when you see the edge of plywood you will say, "Look at this. This is plywood! Isn't that *great?*"

The other disadvantage of plywood is real. If you make a fine chair out of plywood and put it on display in your living room, beware of sharpness. The first person that comes along and says, "What a nice piece of wood!" and scrapes it with his thumbnail and/or the first small child with a hammer and/or the first big dog will scrape off the top peel on the plywood, and that will be that. Because the peel underneath is different wood. It's real wood but it's not the same, so you can't sand it down and refinish it, as you could with a piece of lumber.

To make plywood we take a big piece of tree trunk just like the piece we sliced up into lumber at the beginning of the chapter. This one we peel.

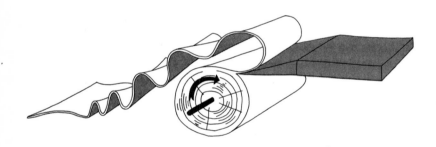

We put a big knife right next to the piece of tree, spin the tree rapidly, and the wood peels away. It's just like peeling an onion. The first layers of wood that we get are pretty good. After a while some knots turn up — not so good. But we take long sheets of all the layers, flatten them out, and put them away. And when we're ready we take several of these sheets of peelings (we call them veneers, or plies, not peelings) and spread glue on them, clap them together, and subject them to heat and high pressure. After that we have a piece of plywood.

Now, one of the things we watch out for is the grain of the veneers. The first veneer we chose very carefully as it was to be a very good piece of wood, and when we put it down we noticed that its grain ran lengthwise toward the top of the sheet. The next piece we chose was not so pretty, as it would not be visible, but we carefully chose one whose grain ran *perpendicular* to the grain of the first piece we chose. The third piece has grain perpendicular to the second. The fourth — well, you get the picture. We kept

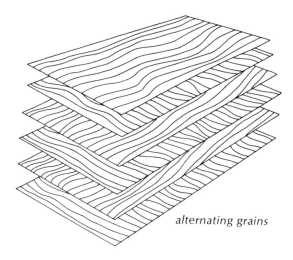

*alternating grains*

alternating the direction of the grains until we reached the thickness we were looking for.

What all this turning around achieved was a considerable amount of dimensional stability. The top veneer has a tendency to bow up. The second veneer, however, has a tendency to bow across. The third has a tendency to bow down. Just look at this diagram; it's much simpler.

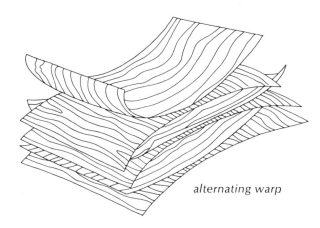

*alternating warp*

The short of this story is that each alternating grain wants to do the opposite of the grains on either side and the result is they arm wrestle to a draw. That's the theory. In real life it means that if a piece of plywood is kept to a reasonable size and is reasonably thick it will be very stable.

There are three different ways of putting together a plywood sandwich. The surface veneers, as we've said, are generally very good pieces of wood, the inside veneers are not so good. The surface veneers are generally somewhere between $1/28$ to $1/32$ inch thick. The inside veneers vary and range from about $1/16$ up to about $1/4$ inch.

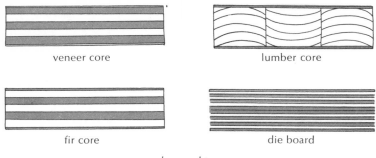

veneer core

lumber core

fir core

die board

*plywood types*

**Veneer-core plywood** is plywood all of whose veneers are the same kind of wood. A piece of birch veneer-core plywood has birch on the outside and birch all the way through (better birch on the outside, of course). Fir-core plywood is filled with layers of fir veneer. A piece of birch plywood–fir core would have two outside plies of birch with fir plies inside. The third possibility is lumber core. Lumber core means small pieces of lumber stacked side by side with veneers glued to either side. The lumber used is kiln-dried pine. The grains of the strips of lumber are alternated to help a little with the warp, but lumber-core plywood does tend to warp a little. A piece of birch plywood–lumber core has two outside plies of birch and nothing but pieces of kiln-dried pine inside. Lumber-core plywood, and a kind of plywood called die board, are the two kinds of plywood used to make fine furniture. The edge conditions are handsome, and you can fasten into the edges of lumber-core plywood. Ordinary plywood does not hold screws in its edges. Lumber-core plywood is also delightful to work with — the interior pine is very soft, so it's easy to saw, easy to glue, and easy to match together.

Die board is a special strong plywood imported from Europe. It is made with a lot of very thin veneers, which are what gives it its strength. The more plies you have in the plywood the better it will be in a given thickness, because there will be fewer defects in each ply. Die board is very solid, dimensionally stable, and doesn't change much with temperature changes. It is used to make shoes and is most often seen these days in platform shoes, which are ever so much stronger than the ankles they support. Did you ever notice all those little lines in a platform heel? Well, that's die board.

The three domestic plywoods, veneer core, fir core, and lumber core, are all available in two varieties: interior and exterior. This refers to the two kinds of glue they are squeezed together with: interior glue and exterior glue. The only difference between them is that exterior glue is more resistant to moisture, and that means that the only difference between interior and exterior plywood is that exterior plywood is more resistant to moisture. Exterior plywood is not nicer than interior plywood. Of course, if you use a piece of interior plywood outside, very soon it will start to bubble up and the veneers will peel away, and there will be less niceness in that piece of plywood. Exterior plywood costs more — the glue is more expensive. There are also fewer defects in the interior plies

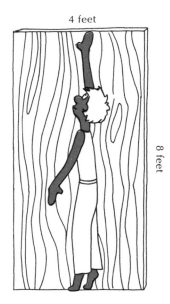

4 feet

8 feet

of the exterior plywood, and this adds to the expense. And there is a hidden expense, too. Exterior plywood tends to ruin saw blades faster than interior plywood, because the glue is harder.

What else do we need to know about plywood? Five things.

1. Plywood comes in only two standard sizes: 4 feet by 8 feet sheets and 5 feet by 9 feet sheets; very often 4 × 8 is all that a lumberyard has in stock. There is one exception to this rule: die board and certain other very, very special plywoods with lots of veneers come in different only-two standard sizes: You can get die board in 5 feet by 5 feet sheets and in 4 feet by 6 feet sheets, and in no other way. The reason die board and the special plywoods are not available in bigger sheets is that they weigh too much.

2. There are seven different thicknesses of plywood: ¼, ⅜, ½, ⅝, ¾, 1-inch, and 1¼-inch, known as ⁵⁄₄ ("five-quarters"). In general, the thicker the plywood, the more plies it has, but you can specify more plies to the inch if you are looking for greater strength. Ordinary plywood, for instance, has seven plies in a ¾-inch piece; die board has fourteen plies in a ¾-inch piece. Incidentally, the number of plies in a sheet of plywood is always an odd number, except in a case of ¾-inch die board, and the only reason it's got fourteen plies is because it's two seven-ply ⅜-inch die boards glued together.

*die board*

3. Plywood sizes are real sizes. Plywood is a machine-made product, start to finish, so it is exactly what it says it is. Corners can't be cut. Three-quarter-inch plywood is ¾ inch thick, and a 4 feet by 8 feet sheet of plywood is exactly 8 feet long and 4 feet wide.

4. The wood in the veneers is graded into five different categories of quality — N, A, B, C, and D — and you can specify which grade you want. N is special orders. A is no visible defects. B, C, and D get worse and worse. You can have different grades on the outside and on the inside (except that you can't buy plywood with a bad grade on the outside and a good grade on the inside). You can get a good grade on the front and a worse grade on the back. Table 7, "Guide to Appearance Grades of Plywood and General Information," has been prepared by the American Plywood Association to help you choose the plywood you want. Table 8, "Types of Plywood," gives you general information about plywood.

As in lumber buying, it's a question of ordering what you will need for what you will want. The NN, the NA, and the ND woods are probably best ignored. They are very, very expensive, and unless you are doing some cabinetwork, or getting in someone else to do some cabinetwork for you, you won't need them. INT is the abbreviation for interior glue, EXT is the abbreviation for exterior glue. DFPA you don't need to know about — it's just the quality stamp from the American Plywood Association. Plyron and MDO *are* worth knowing about. MDO stands for Medium Density Overlaid plywood. It is ordinary Douglas fir plywood (the most common kind of plywood, incidentally) with a kind of paper coating on it that is perfect for paint. It is perfectly smooth. You can also put a fancy veneer on MDO plywood. You can buy strips of fancy veneer

Plywood is manufactured in two types — exterior type with 100 percent waterproof glue and interior type with highly moisture resistant glue. Veneers in the inner plies of exterior type have fewer defects than in interior type.

Interior type is also made with exterior glue. It can be used where excessive moisture may occur occasionally. However, it is not an adequate substitute for true exterior-type plywood.

Within each type there are a variety of appearance grades determined by the grade of the veneer used in the face and back. These grades (see below) may range from A and B veneers, which are used when the finish surface is important, to the C and D veneers, which are used in plywood designed primarily for structural applications.

### Veneer Grades

| | |
|---|---|
| A | Smooth and paintable. Neatly made repairs permissible. Also used for natural finish in less demanding applications. |
| B | Solid surface veneer. Circular repair plugs and tight knots permitted. |
| C | Knotholes to 1". Occasional knotholes ½" larger permitted providing total width of all knots and knotholes within a specified section does not exceed certain limits. Limited splits permitted. Minimum veneer permitted in exterior-type plywood. |
| C Plugged | Improved C veneer with splits limited to ⅛" in width and knotholes and borer holes limited to ¼" by ½". |
| D | Permits knots and knotholes to 2½" in width and ½" larger under certain specified limits. Limited splits permitted. |

*Table 7. Guide to Appearance Grades of Plywood and General Information*

and glue them onto something when you've finished making it. Plyron has something called hardboard on the front and back, and hardboard, aka Masonite, is a form of wood pulp that has been pressed together to make it very hard. It's a fair to middling board that has its specific uses.

Sheething, or Plyscore, which you won't find on the chart, is also worth knowing about. It is the cheapest form of plywood there is — DD, actually — and it's good for a floor that won't be seen because it has a rug or some finished flooring on top of it.

Texture III is a grooved plywood which is sometimes used as a siding but is also great for the sides of shelf units as the grooves make great shelf rests.

Panel 15 is plywood covered with an aluminum sheet that comes with a baked painted surface and is good for trim, for the eaves of a building, etc.

There are many specialized types of plywood and more types coming out weekly. Keep your eyes open.

### Match the Material to the Use Intended.

The little rectangular boxes on Table 8 (listed under "Typical Grade-Trademarks") are the symbols stamped on every sheet of

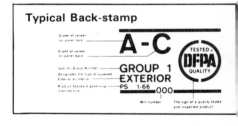

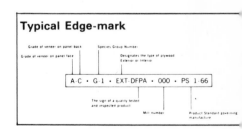

## Table 8. Guide to Appearance Grades of Plywood[1]

| Use These Terms When You Specify Plywood[2] | Description and Most Common Uses | Typical Grade-Trademarks | Face | Back | Inner Plies | Most Common Thicknesses (inch)[3] |
|---|---|---|---|---|---|---|
| **Interior Type** | | | | | | |
| N-N, N-A, N-B INT-APA | Cabinet quality. For natural finish furniture, cabinet doors, built-ins, etc. Special order items. | [N N G1 INT APA PS 1 74] [N A G2 APA PS 1 74] | N | N, A, or B | C | 3/4 |
| N-D-INT-APA | For natural finish paneling. Special order item. | [N D G1 INT APA PS 1 74] | N | D | D | 1/4 |
| A-A INT-APA | For applications with both sides on view. Built-ins, cabinets, furniture and partitions. Smooth face; suitable for painting. | [AA G4 INT APA PS 1 74] | A | A | D | 1/4  3/8  1/2  5/8  3/4 |
| A-B INT-APA | Use where appearance of one side is less important but two smooth solid surfaces are necessary. | [AB G4 INT APA PS 1 74] | A | B | D | 1/4  3/8  1/2  5/8  3/4 |
| A-D INT-APA | Use where appearance of only one side is important. Paneling, built-ins, shelving, partitions, and flow racks. | A-D GROUP INTERIOR APA | A | D | D | 1/4  3/8  1/2  5/8  3/4 |
| B-B INT-APA | Utility panel with two smooth sides. Permits circular plugs. | [BB G1 INT APA PS 1 74] | B | B | D | 1/4  3/8  1/2  5/8  3/4 |
| B-D INT-APA | Utility panel with one smooth side. Good for backing, sides of built-ins. Industry: shelving, slip sheets, separator boards and bins. | B-D GROUP INTERIOR APA | B | D | D | 1/4  3/8  1/2  5/8  3/4 |
| DECORATIVE PANELS — APA | Rough-sawn, brushed, grooved, or striated faces. For paneling, interior accent walls, built-ins, counter facing, displays, and exhibits. | [DECORATIVE BD G1 INT APA PS 1 74] | C or btr. | D | D | 5/16  3/8  1/2  5/8 |
| PLYRON INT-APA | Hardboard face on both sides. For counter tops, shelving, cabinet doors, flooring. Faces tempered, untempered, smooth, or screened. | [PLYRON INT APA PS 1 74] | | | C & D | 1/2  5/8  3/4 |
| **Exterior Type[7]** | | | | | | |
| A-A EXT-APA[4] | Use where appearance of both sides is important. Fences, built-ins, signs, boats, cabinets, commercial refrigerators, shipping containers, tote boxes, tanks, and ducts. | [AA G1 EXT APA PS 1 74] | A | A | C | 1/4  3/8  1/2  5/8  3/4 |
| A-B EXT-APA[4] | Use where the appearance of one side is less important. | [AB G1 EXT APA PS 1 74] | A | B | C | 1/4  3/8  1/2  5/8  3/4 |
| A-C EXT-APA[4] | Use where the appearance of only one side is important. Sidings, soffits, fences, structural uses, boxcar and truck lining, farm buildings. Tanks, trays, commercial refrigerators. | A-C GROUP EXTERIOR APA | A | C | C | 1/4  3/8  1/2  5/8  3/4 |
| B-B EXT-APA[4] | Utility panel with solid faces. | [BB G1 EXT APA PS 1 74] | B | B | C | 1/4  3/8  1/2  5/8  3/4 |
| B-C EXT-APA[4] | Utility panel for farm service and work buildings, boxcar and truck lining, containers, tanks, agricultural equipment. Also as base for exterior coatings for walls, roofs. | B-C GROUP EXTERIOR APA | B | C | C | 1/4  3/8  1/2  5/8  3/4 |
| HDO EXT-APA[4] | High density overlay plywood. Has a hard, semi-opaque resin-fiber overlay both faces. Abrasion resistant. For concrete forms, cabinets, counter tops, signs and tanks. | [HDO AA G1 EXT APA PS 1 74] | A or B | A or B | C or C plgd | 5/16  3/8  1/2  5/8  3/4 |
| MDO EXT-APA[4] | Medium density overlay with smooth, opaque, resin-fiber overlay one or both panel faces. Highly recommended for siding and other outdoor applications, built-ins, signs, and displays. Ideal base for paint. | [MDO BB G4 EXT APA PS 1 74] | B | B or C | C | 5/16  3/8  1/2  5/8  3/4 |
| 303 SIDING EXT-APA[6] | Proprietary plywood products for exterior siding, fencing, etc. Special surface treatment such as V-groove, channel groove, striated, brushed, rough-sawn. | 303 SIDING 16 oc GROUP EXTERIOR APA | [5] | C | C | 3/8  1/2  5/8 |
| T 1-11 EXT-APA[6] | Special 303 panel having grooves 1/4 inch deep, 3/8 inch wide, spaced 4 or 8 inches o.c. Other spacing optional. Edges shiplapped. Available unsanded, textured, and MDO. | 303 SIDING 16 oc T1-11 GROUP EXTERIOR APA | C or btr. | C | C | 5/8 |
| PLYRON EXT-APA | Hardboard faces both sides, tempered, smooth or screened. | [PLYRON EXT APA PS 1 74] | | | C | 1/2  5/8  3/4 |
| MARINE EXT-APA | Ideal for boat hulls. Made only with Douglas fir or western larch. Special solid jointed-core construction. Subject to special limitations on core gaps and number of face repairs. Also available with HDO or MDO faces. | [MARINE AA EXT APA PS 1 74] | A or B | A or B | B | 1/4  3/8  1/2  5/8  3/4 |

[1] Sanded both sides except where decorative or other surfaces specified.
[2] Available in Group 1, 2, 3, 4, or 5 unless otherwise noted.
[3] Standard 4 × 8 panel sizes, other sizes available.
[4] Also available in Structural I (all plies limited to Group 1 species) and Structural II (all plies limited to Group 1, 2, or 3 species).
[5] C or better for 5 plies; C Plugged or better for 3-ply panels.
[6] Stud spacing is shown on grade stamp.
[7] For finishing recommendations, see form V307.

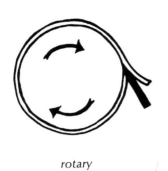

*rotary*

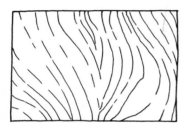

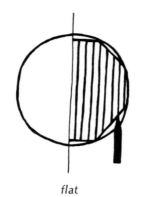

*flat*

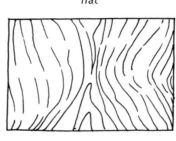

*quarter slice*

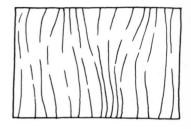

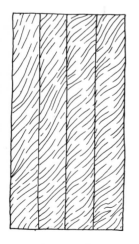

*slip match*

*"V"*

*book match*

*herringbone*

plywood. If the sheet has a D face the box will be stamped on that face. If it doesn't the box will appear on the edge of the sheet.

5. The final thing we need to know about plywood has to do with the grain on the surface veneers. When plywood is made by peeling a tree like an onion the grain on the veneer produced has a tigerish quality. We talked about light spring wood and dark summer wood at the beginning of this chapter, and we know that spring wood is soft, summer wood hard. What happens when you paint or stain a piece of plywood with a tigerish grain is that the softwood absorbs more paint or stain than the hardwood and the grain pattern stands out in bolder relief than ever before. So this kind of plywood is primarily used for structural purposes.

There are other kinds of plywood with different grains, because, although we haven't mentioned it before, peeling is not the only way of making plywood. You can cut a piece of tree trunk into very thin slices or layers. These thinly sliced veneers come out looking like zebras, and have the name *zebra wood*. Sliced veneers have a variety of appearances as shown at left.

A General and Important Point about Buying Wood, Lumber, or Plywood: It pays to go down to the lumberyard to see what you're getting. Otherwise you're faced with the problem of "Have it delivered at two," and it doesn't come till four; and, if it does come, maybe it has some defects or isn't suitable for you, and then you have to send it back, and wait until four o'clock the next afternoon. If you go down to the lumberyard you can pick out exactly what you want — you're allowed to do that. You're allowed to say, "I don't want that piece, it's full of defects." And then you don't have to take it. Anything you'll take, they'll sell to you. Not that they're trying to put anything over on you. It's simply you have to *match the material to the use intended*.

## Wood Finishing, or Finishing the Wood Off

Q. Why do we finish wood?

A. To protect it from water, people, alcohol, dogs, and the like. It's a matter of morality.

Wood is prey to a lot of problems. Water does a good deal of damage — stains it, warps it, and the like. Dogs and kids and people tend to scratch it and beat up on it. Insects and fungi and various microorganisms like to live in it and eat it.

If the wood is not subject to these abuses it does not need to be finished. It will, like leather, turn silver or golden brown and develop its own patina if you can wait two or three years.

Some woods, notably teak, cypress, cedar heartwood, and redwood heartwood, contain their own finishes and are best left to their own devices. They are naturally resistant to decay, insects, weather, and people. If it works, why mess with it?

There are all sorts of things you can do to wood to finish it, so we'll begin by stating our own preferences and then explain them as we outline all the possibilities. Furniture — we like to leave it natural or oil it. It's the easiest thing you can do. Floors — two coats of penetrating resin sealer and then two coats of paste wax on top of that. It's also the easiest thing you can do.

Hardwoods and softwoods come with close grain, open grain, and medium grain. Close-grain woods (maple, cherry, birch) have their pores very close together and feel smooth. Open-grain woods have their pores relatively far apart and feel bumpy and rough. Medium-grain woods are medium-grain woods.

Open-grain wood has to be filled before it can be finished. Use a clear wood filler, which comes as either a paste or a liquid. Wood filler tends to yellow the wood slightly, but the color changes vary with the type of wood and the brand of filler. If you don't fill an open-grain wood it will accept any other finish unevenly and it will always have a coarse feel to it.

Medium-grain woods will benefit somewhat from filling, but it is not really necessary except for the most critical work. Fussbudgets take note!

For grain type of a particular wood see Tables 4 and 5 on pages 42 and 43.

## Sandpaper

Before applying anything to a piece of wood it must be sanded and so you must know a little about sandpaper. There are several types of minerals used as abrasives for wood: Flint, garnet, aluminum oxide, and silicone carbide are the most common.

Flint is tan in color, cheap, and wears out quickly. Use flint paper for hand sanding woods and removing paint. Garnet is orange and, together with aluminum oxide (grayish-red), is the best for wood. Aluminum oxide can also be used for metal. Silicon carbide is black and is the hardest abrasive; 280-grit silicon carbide paper is used to remove the fuzz from the face of plywood.

| Use | Grit Number | Grade Number | Word Description |
|---|---|---|---|
| Rough sanding and shaping | 80 | 1/0 | Medium |
| Preparatory sanding on hardwoods and softwoods | 120 | 3/0 | Fine |
| Finish sanding on hardwoods | 220 to 280 | 6/0 to 8/0 | Very fine Extra fine |
| Finish sanding on softwoods | 220 | 6/0 | Very fine |

Table 9. Sandpaper Selection Chart

Grit number (coarseness) ranges from 12 to 600. The higher the grit number, the finer and slower the sanding. Generally, 60 to 280 grit paper is used on wood.

Table 9, "Sandpaper Selection Chart," is a guide to the proper use of the various sandpaper grits.

There are two families of finishes for wood regardless of grain type. *In-the-surface finishes* are the easiest to apply and can be likened to a sponge soaking up water. Wood is like a sponge and soaks up things like oil. *On-the-surface finishes* are the *hardest* to apply and can be likened to dipping an apple into sugar syrup and getting a candy-coated apple.

## In-the-Surface Finishes

*Stains:* You may want to change the color of a piece of wood. Wood produces itself in an incredible variety of colors. Ebony is black, pine is almost white, and there are browns, reds, greens, and everything in between. You can usually find a veneer to fit your desires, but you may just want to turn the wood you have another color, and in that case you are looking for a stain.

Table 10, "Types of Stain," lists the major types and properties among the stains.

| Name | Base | Wood Type Best Used On | Ease of Application | Colors | Compatible On-the-Surface Finishes | Remarks |
|---|---|---|---|---|---|---|
| Water | Water | Mahogany, cherry, walnut; medium- to open-grained woods | Dissolve packet in quart of water that is close to boiling, flood surface, remove any puddles and let dry. Use wide soft brush. Do not overlap brush strokes. Apply quickly. A protective coat of shellac, lacquer, or varnish is absolutely necessary. | Black, red, green, wood tones | Shellac, lacquer, varnish | Inexpensive, brilliant colors tend to raise the grain. See recipes for solution. Use diluted stain on end grain to prevent it from becoming too dark. |
| N.G.R. *Non–Grain Raising* | Alcohol | Maple, birch; hard close-grain wood | Brush on with wide soft brush. Avoid over-lapping brush strokes. A protective coat of shellac, lacquer, or varnish is absolutely necessary. | Wood tones, black | Shellac, lacquer, varnish | Does not raise the grain of the wood. Dries in about four hours. Not recommended for pine, spruce, and fir. |
| Pigmented Wiping Stains | Oil | Pine, fir, spruce; open- to medium-grained woods | Mix or stir well. Wipe on, wipe off excess. | Wood tones, black, white | Shellac, varnish | Actually a thin paint, it leaves pigment in pores of wood. It accentuates the grain pattern and blemishes. |

*Table 10. Types of Stain*

*Oils:* Oil keeps wood clean, lets it breathe, and doesn't let it dry out. And an oil finish, we believe, is the most natural finish there is. There are various kinds of oil and various combinations. The most common is boiled linseed oil in a mix of turpentine. You use it as follows:

For an open-grain wood: 6 parts boiled linseed oil to 4 parts turpentine.

For a close-grain wood: 4 parts boiled linseed oil to 6 parts turpentine.

Wipe it on and let it soak into the wood. Put as much into the wood as it will take. After a while, wipe it down with a dry rag. The rule for oiling is: *Once a day for a week; then once a week for a month; then once a month for a year; then once a year for the rest of your life — or the life of the wood.* Oil darkens and richens wood and gives it a very subtle glow. Like penetrating resin sealer, it is an in-the-wood finish.

Wood-finishing oils are petroleum derivatives mixed with other things. There are a lot of wood-finishing oils around: lemon oil, Danish oil, butternut oil, teak oil. Lemon oil tends to dry out on surfaces very rapidly, so it's a particularly good thing for furniture and things you are in contact with all the time.

Q. What about salad oil?
A. Sure. Good stuff. It makes the wood edible.

On-the-Surface Finishes

*Waxes:* Wax is the second most natural finish, for our money. Wax is an on-the-wood finish. Because it is an on-the-wood finish, the wood has to be sealed before it can be waxed. Our preference for penetrating resin sealer has already been expressed. Paste wax is the best wax. You spread it on, then buff it either by hand or with a machine. A buffer on the end of a drill is just fine and gives you the most clean finish. It won't yellow the wood very much at all, unless you put on layer after layer. But, of course, you won't do that — you'll take it off periodically and then apply new wax.

There is a kind of wax that comes in a spray can. What word can we use to describe it? Blasphemy? Ultraban? Abplanalp? The old ways of doing things seem, in this instance at least, to work a little better. And remember the adage: Pride goeth before a fall.

Shellac, varnish, polyurethane, and lacquer are other on-the-surface finishes. (And so wood must be sealed before you use them.) They all have their drawbacks. Shellac is very easy to put on, and it's relatively clean and unyellowing, and it can be patched. But it's not very durable. For example, it suffers from water stains. Varnish is harder to put on, but that doesn't mean it's substantially more durable. It isn't. And it's not patchable. Polyurethane is a kind of varnish that is very durable — and also very, very hard to put on. And it looks like plastic, not wood. And it's not patchable, either. If anything goes wrong with one piece of polyurethane, if it blisters or burns or gets scratched, the whole piece must be taken down to the bare wood to be refinished. So what you do, in order to avoid

*Table 11. The Wood Finishes*

| Name | Type | Ease of Application | Method | Dura-bility | Patch-ability | Suitability | Remarks |
|------|------|---------------------|--------|-------------|---------------|-------------|---------|
| Oil<br>*teak oil,*<br>*walnut oil,*<br>*boiled*<br>*linseed oil*<br>*(inorganic)* | In | Very easy | Once a day for a week, once a week for a month, once a month for a year, once a year forever. Pour on, wipe around; let stand, wipe off excess. Buff with lambs wool or soft lintfree cloth for a soft luster after oil is dry (24–48 hours). | Fair | Excellent | Sculpture, furniture that is not subject to abuse or people | Looks terrific, feels good. Best for dark woods. Prevents wood from drying out; darkens wood. Mixing boiled linseed oil with turpentine helps it penetrate the close-grained denser woods. |
| Oil<br>*lemon*<br>*(inorganic)* | In | Very easy | Same as oil | Same as oil | | Tabletops, furniture | Lemon oil comes from petroleum and is given a lemon scent. Mostly used as a polishing agent. Also prevents wood from drying out. |
| Oil<br>*olive,*<br>*salad*<br>*(organic)* | In | Very easy | Once in a while | Same as oil | | Chopping blocks, butcher blocks, salad bowls | Organic oil turns rancid after a time. Wood should be washed down (not soaked) with boiling water from time to time and immediately re-oiled. Prevents wood from drying out and cracking. |
| Penetrating Resin Sealer (look for the words penetrating and resin) | In | Very easy | Do not use filler. Brush, wipe, pour on, let stand 15 minutes to 1 hour depending on manufacturer and wipe off excess. Two coats best. | Excellent | Excellent | Floors, furniture, tabletops | This stuff is terrific. Pigments last as long as the wood, actually hardens wood fibers (from sanding across the grain). Best for use on soft woods and open-grain woods. Buff with lamb's wool for low luster finish. |
| Shellac<br>*white for*<br>*light woods,*<br>*amber for*<br>*dark woods* | On | Easy | Brush several thin coats, sand lightly between coats; flows on easily, hardly ever shows lap marks. | Fair | Good | Furniture, paneling, floors | Gives good clear color. Shellac is made of the natural resin of the lac bug dissolved in alcohol. Produces a medium gloss. Floors should be waxed (paste) after shellac has dried for 24 hours to provide additional wear and water resistance. |
| Varnish<br>*glossy* | On | Difficult | Brush or spray two or three coats — sand between coats. | Excellent | No | Floors, furniture | Dust is the problem. As varnish takes a long time to dry, all the dust that was in the room waits for you to leave before settling on the surface. Varnish is subject to scratching; best to wax (paste) over it. Darkens wood somewhat. |
| Varnish<br>*semi-gloss* | On | Difficult | Brush or spray one or two coats; sand between coats. Start with gloss. | Good | No | Floors, furniture | |
| Varnish<br>*satin* | On | Difficult | | Good | No | Floors, furniture | |
| Varnish<br>*flat* | On | Difficult | | Fair | No | Furniture | |

*(continued)*

| Name | Type | Ease of Application | Method | Dura-bility | Patch-ability | Suitability | Remarks |
|---|---|---|---|---|---|---|---|
| Varnish *Polyurethane* (available in gloss, semi-gloss, satin, and flat) | On | Difficult | Same as varnish | Superior in gloss, excellent in semi-gloss, satin, and flat. | No | Floors, furniture | The same as for varnish, but much better dura-bility. Some urethanes produce nausea and cramps in some people. Use in good ventilation, thereby putting out the welcome mat for visiting dust that stays. Urethane finishes do not adhere to shellac. |
| Lacquer | On | Very difficult | Spray or brush, dries very quickly. Do not overbrush; apply to small areas at a time. | Fair | No | Pianos, guitars | Builds rapidly to a very high gloss; whitest and least darkening of all the clear finishes. In any but the best conditions there is often difficulty with adhesion. Many fillers are softened by lacquer. Use *only* fillers and stains, etc., com-patible with lacquer. Lacquer is incompatible with rosewood and mahogany, as it bleeds with the natural pig-ments in the wood. Suitable for industrial application. |

*Table 11. The Wood Finishes (continued)*

such an awful thing, is cover the polyurethane with a couple of coats of wax. Why not just put down the wax and forget all about the polyurethane? Lacquer is probably a waste of time — it's fiend-ishly difficult to put down, not that durable, and certainly not patchable.

There are many books on finishing wood that cover the subject in great detail. Our own book on the subject has but a single page. It says: Oil furniture! Seal and wax floors! But, if you want to finish your wood off, here are some recipes:

### Recipe for Any In-the-Surface Finish
*(same for open-, medium-, and closed-grained wood)*

1. Make certain wood is thoroughly sanded and dusted (a tack rag will pick up all the dust).
2. For the finest finish, sponge wood with water, let dry, then remove raised and swollen wood fiber with light sanding of 280 grit (8/0 or extra fine) for hardwood or hardwood ply-wood. Use 220 grit (6/0 or very fine) for softwood or soft-wood plywood.
3. You're ready for your in-the-surface finish. See Table 11, "The Wood Finishes," for application.

After wood has been planed, rasped, sanded, Brilloed, and carborunded, it is ready for finishing. *Do not sand plywood, except as below,* as sanding with any sandpaper rougher than 240 or 280 will only roughen the wood.

---

### Recipe for Any On-the-Surface Finish

1. Assume wood is thoroughly sanded and dusted (a tack rag will pick up all the dust).

2. For the finest finish, sponge wood with water, let dry, then remove raised and swollen wood fiber with light sanding of 280 grit (8/0 or extra fine) for hardwood or hardwood plywood. Use 220 grit (6/0 or very fine) for softwood or softwood plywood. Step 2 is too much work for anything but a finish that is smooth as a baby's bottom (when a baby's bottom is smooth). It is, however, necessary if you are using water-based stains.

3. Stain (if you must) choices in order of preference:

   *Open Grain:*

   Pigmented wiping stain; non-grain-raising stain; water-base stain.

   *Medium grain:*

   Water-base stain; non-grain-raising stain; pigmented wiping stain.

   *Close Grain:*

   Omit filler; non-grain-raising stain; water-base stain; pigmented wiping stain.

4. Wood filler:

   *Open Grain:*

   Paste — tint to color of stain or natural wood (filler can be left out if rough wood is OK with you).

   *Medium Grain:*

   Liquid — tint to color of stain or natural wood (filler can be left out unless you desire a really smooth finish).

5. Sealer:
   Thin coat of shellac for shellac or wax finish.
   Thin coat of 1 part varnish to 2 parts thinner for varnish finish.
   Lacquer sealer for lacquer finish.

6. See Table 11, "The Wood Finishes," pages 57–58, for particulars about surface finishes and their application.

The universal what? We think it's kind of a funny name too, but as it happens most of the things around us are boxes. We live in boxes. We sit on boxes. We sleep on boxes. Our clothes, our cars, our food, our dishes all live in boxes. Different size boxes, different shape boxes, to be sure, but boxes all the same. It's hard to be sure where this habit of boxes began, but it feels like the right thing to do after all these centuries.

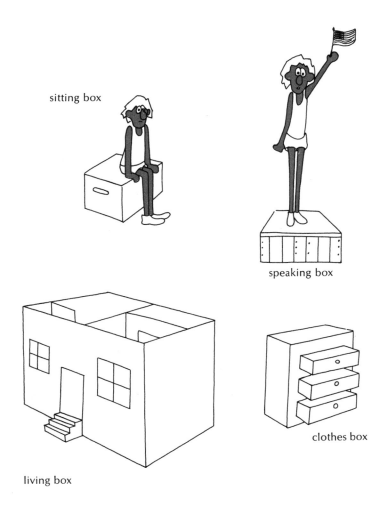

sitting box

speaking box

clothes box

living box

Probably the reason for choosing boxes to begin with was that they stack, which means that when you put boxes together there are no leftover spaces. Most other shapes are not so efficient. Hexagons work very well but only bees seem to be able to build them very efficiently.

Boxes have one thing in common: right angles. As nature would have it, right angles are the problem with building boxes. Right angles don't like to stay together too well. The joint between the two pieces tends to loosen up. At the top of the next page is a right-angle joint between two pieces of wood. It is the most com-

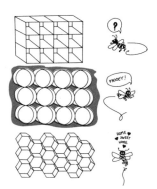

mon type of right-angle joint and it has a name. It is called a butt joint.

Butt joints are the most common because they are the easiest to make. As with many things that are the easiest of a type, they are also the least durable of all the types of joints. Butt joints loosen up quicker than other types of joints. A box made of butt joints will rack more easily than one made of other types of joints, although all rectangles rack. Racking is what your table does when it spills your coffee while you're buttering your toast.

Q. What can we do now, Tonto?

A. Several things.

The strength of a joint is determined mostly by the amount of surface area in contact. In a butt joint the surface area in contact is the end of the piece of wood being butted — the butter. It butts against an equivalent area on the piece being butted against — the buttee. If we can increase this area of butt the joint will be stronger.

One way to increase the area of butt (AoB) is to increase the size of the pieces of wood we're butting. This method works but is a dreadful waste of material.

Another way to increase the AoB is to be clever. We could cut both pieces at a 45-degree angle and increase the area by about 40 percent. This would certainly help. In fact, it would help more than you think as the strength varies as the square of the increased area.

Q. HUH?

A. Sorry. What that means is that if the area you now have is *twice* as big as it was before, the joint would be *four* times as strong, not just twice as strong. If the area got *three* times as big the joint would be *nine* times as strong. Three squared is nine. Strength varies as the square of the increased area.

It's not too important to remember formulas but it is good to understand principles.

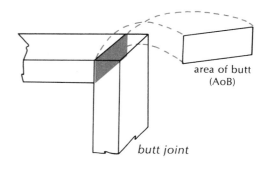

area of butt (AoB)

*butt joint*

*racking*

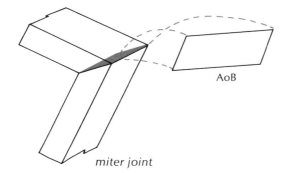

*miter joint*

AoB

The kind of joint we made by cutting the wood at a 45-degree angle is called a miter joint. This is the type of joint used in picture frames. Its principal advantage is not the increase in strength but that it allows one to put two pieces of wood together without ever showing the end grain of the wood. (See the earlier part of this chapter for the problems of end grain.)

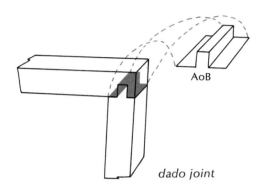

*dado joint*

Another way to increase the AoB is to make one of many types of dado joints. In the first one of these we have illustrated the AoB becomes *twice* as big as the plain butt joint. Therefore this dado joint is four times as strong as the butt joint. (Two squared is four.)

A better type of joint to make if strength is the crucial factor is a lap joint. Lap joints require some chiseling, as did the dado joints, but they can increase the AoB substantially. The one illustrated gives an AoB three times larger than the butt joint and is therefore nine times as strong. (Three squared is nine.)

*relative sizes of AoBs*

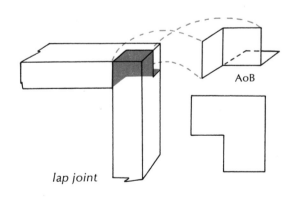

*lap joint*

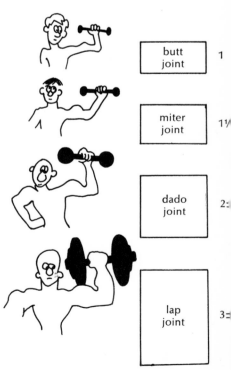

| | |
|---|---|
| butt joint | 1 |
| miter joint | 1½ |
| dado joint | 2: |
| lap joint | 3= |

Q. So why don't we ever see any of these fancy joints?
A. Because they are hard to make.

In all of the joints shown other than the butt joint, substantial effort and skill are required. One has to measure the cuts carefully, then execute them with precision in order for the joints to fit together properly (and thus take full advantage of the increase in AoB) and look good.

Q. What do we do now, Tonto?
A. We get even more clever.

As nature would have it (it seems we've heard this before), size is not the only thing that determines strength. Shape is also important, very important. Of all the shapes around the only one that is truly rigid all by itself is the triangle. What we will do now is turn all our rectangles into triangles. Listen carefully. At no time will the fingers leave the hands.

plus

The illustration shows a triangular plate attached to the corner. When this sort of magic is applied to the corner the joint suddenly becomes *rigid* — just what the joint doctor ordered. If we extended the *triangulation* as far as we could across the rectangle we would have put a back on our rectangle and created . . .

THE UNIVERSAL BOX

Q. What's so great about that?
A. It's everything you ever wanted to build, out of wood. It

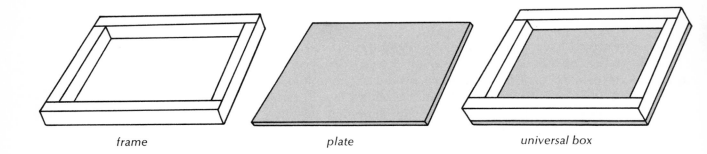

*frame*                    *plate*                    *universal box*

efficiently uses materials, it is easy to build, and it is strong. What more can you ask for?

Q. An explanation?

A. The universal box is strong because it is triangulated. It is easy to build because it uses the simplest of the joints, the butt joint. It is an efficient use of materials because the triangulation permits use of smaller pieces of lumber for an equivalent strength. Finally, it is everything you ever wanted to build because it comes in any size, and adapts to any orientation. For example it can be a drawer . . .

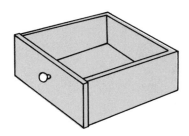

or, with some intermediate pieces, a bookshelf . . .

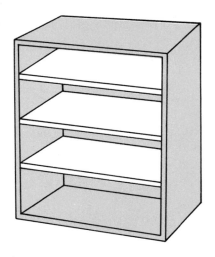

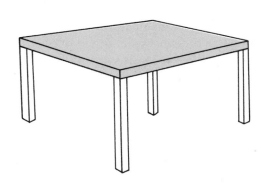

or, with legs, a table . . .

or, with other universal boxes for legs, a sturdier table . . .

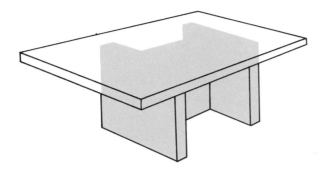

or, with shorter universal boxes for legs, a bed  . . .

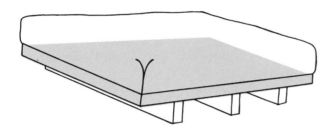

or, with some imagination, a chair  . . .

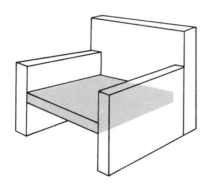

or, somewhat wider than above, a sofa  . . .

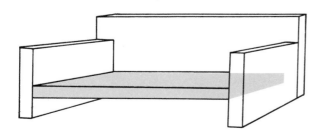

or, with many placed side by side, a wall (see also Chapter Three) . . .

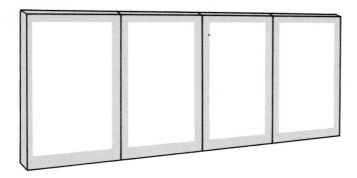

or, with walls as the sides of a huge universal box, a house . . .

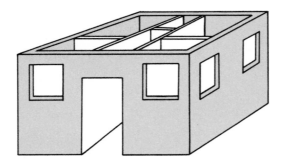

The limit is your imagination. Remember that universal boxes can be any size, so long as they are triangulated rectangles. Also four universal boxes can be the sides of a much larger universal box, and openings can be cut into the plate for doors, peepholes, etc. You should now be convinced of the merits of the universal box.

The universal what? We think it's kind of a funny name too, but as it happens most of the things around us are boxes. We live in boxes. We sit on boxes. We  . . .

---

Recipe for Building Any Universal Box

*Ingredients:*   4 pieces of lumber cut to desired size
1 triangulating plate (usually ¼-inch plywood)
2 corner clamps
1 hammer
some nails or screws
some glue

1. Put buttee into corner clamp and tighten.

2. Put butter into corner clamp and butt tight against buttee.

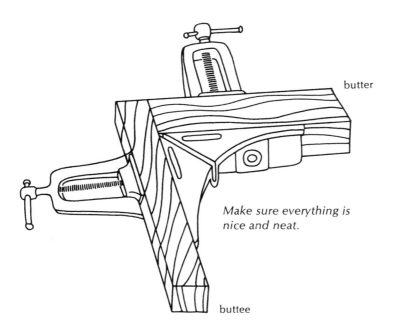

butter

*Make sure everything is nice and neat.*

buttee

3. Remove buttee from corner clamp; spread glue on both areas of butt; replace buttee into corner clamp and adjust so that corner is *flush* from all views.

4. Fasten corner with nails or screws to taste. The nails or screws are there to hold joint until glue dries. After that the glue will do most of the holding.

   Hint one: Always use more than one fastener or joint will *pivot*.

   Hint two: Loosen clamp on butter just before driving nail tight or screwing screw tight as this will assure a tighter joint.

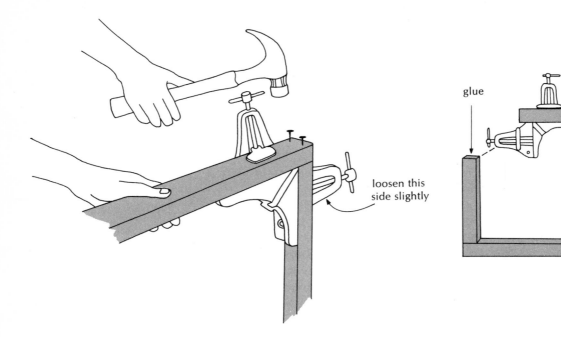

loosen this side slightly

glue

glue

5. Repeat process on other two pieces of wood.
6. Repeat process to join the two Ls together.
7. Place triangulating plate on completed rectangle. Mark and cut to size.

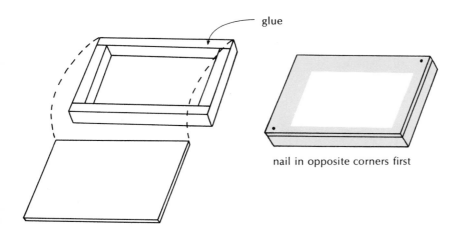

glue

nail in opposite corners first

8. Spread glue on surfaces and screw or glue to taste.
9. Mix and match completed boxes to make anything.

Three

Buildings

$\text{B}$uildings are imitation caves. They were developed because all the caves are up in the mountains. And then the words "building" and "house" were developed so that nobody would have to be an imitation–cave dweller.

In order to build a house you need a piece of land and three people: an architect, an engineer, and a contractor. The architect and the engineer draw up a plan for the house.

Plans are pictures of buildings or other things. But to make things very clear, plan drawers (called draftsmen) allow themselves to look at things only in very special ways. The full-frontal picture of the house is actually a very special way of looking at things. It is called a perspective.

*perspective*

All other views of this house depend on how you slice it. If you slice in front of the house, and make a picture of the slice, what you will see is a front elevation.

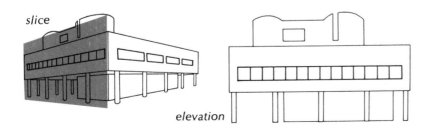

*slice*

*elevation*

You can slice in front of any of the other three sides of the house and get a left elevation or a right elevation or a rear elevation.

If you sliced above the house and looked down you would get a roof plan.

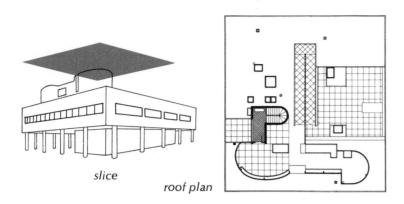

*slice*

*roof plan*

If you slice a little lower than before you will slice through the house. Remove the top, which you just sliced off, and you will be looking at a plan. Depending on which floor you sliced through it will be a first floor plan or second floor plan or basement plan or whatever.

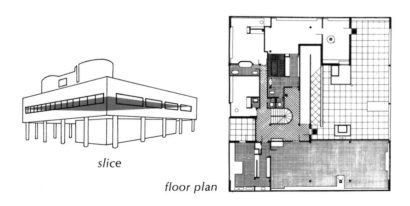

*slice*

*floor plan*

If you cut an elevation-type slice, but slice through the house instead of in front of it, you will get a slice called a section. Actually, the plan is a type of section, too, but it is such an important drawing that it gets a special name all its own.

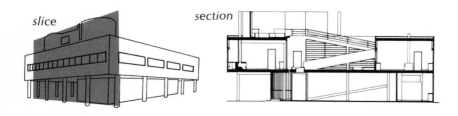

*slice*

*section*

There are some very specialized combinations of the basic drawings, too. In part of this chapter we will be using one of them. It is made by taking a section and then drawing whatever was not cut away by the sectioning as a perspective. This type of drawing is called a section perspective and is a very handy drawing as it is particularly easy to understand for nonprofessional draftsmen and can contain a great deal of information.

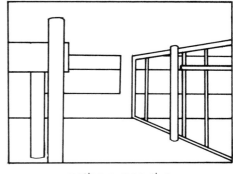

*section perspective*

That's all there is to it. You draw the type of drawing you need to show what you have to show. It all depends on how you slice it.

The architect prepares a design. The engineer checks the design for posture. He makes sure that everything in the design is balanced so that the house won't fall down. Then the architect signs a contract with the contractor and gives him the plan. The contractor builds the house. There's an old story in the building business about the difference between architects, engineers, and contractors. It goes like this:

An architect is a person who starts off in life knowing a little bit about a lot of things. An engineer, at the beginning, knows a great deal about a few things. And a contractor sets off knowing an awful lot about an awful lot. As these three people go through life together building houses, the engineer learns more and more about less and less, until he knows everything there is to know about nothing at all. The architect, meanwhile, is learning less and less about more and more. He winds up knowing nothing whatever about everything. At the same time, the contractor, through his association with the other two, goes around learning less and less about less and less until finally he knows nothing about nothing.

MORAL: And these are the people who build your house.

People in the building business really like this story a lot.

The contractor's first act after receiving the plans is to dig a hole, which he calls an excavation, in the piece of land. He digs this hole so that he can lay a strong foundation for the house. *"House built on a weak foundation will not stand. No, no, no."* — old Harry Belafonte calypso song. The contractor smoothes off the bottom of the hole, and gets ready to build the feet and legs of the house.

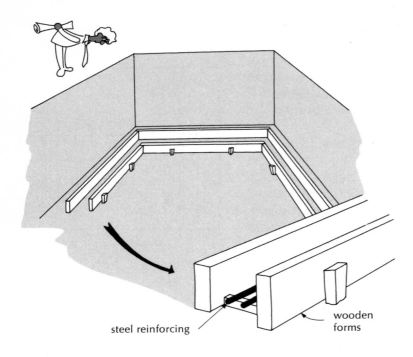

steel reinforcing wooden forms

Legs need feet for balance, so the very first thing the contractor builds is strips of concrete on the bottom of the hole. The foundation walls stand on these strips, which are known as footings.

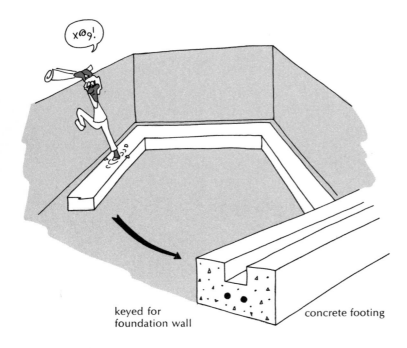

keyed for foundation wall concrete footing

Footings are always wider than foundation walls, so that the house can stand on snowshoes instead of on stiletto heels. The weight of the house gets spread around a bit, and that makes the house more secure, and the ground more secure. Footings are generally about 18 inches wide and about 8 to 12 inches deep.

The foundation walls themselves come next. Foundation walls are the legs of the house and will hold up the rest of the construction. They are built out of masonry, because all walls built below grade are built out of masonry. Grade means the level of the ground. Most other materials rot belowground. Masonry is stone or any combination of stone, clay, sand, cement, and water. Some of these combinations are:

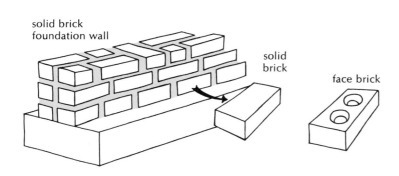

solid brick foundation wall

solid brick

face brick

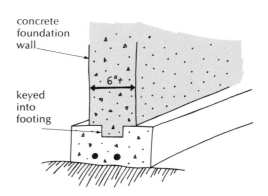

concrete foundation wall

6"†

keyed into footing

Bricks, made out of baked clay and water. ("Clay" is a polite word for "mud." If you live in a brick house, meditate upon the contention: "I live in a mud house.")

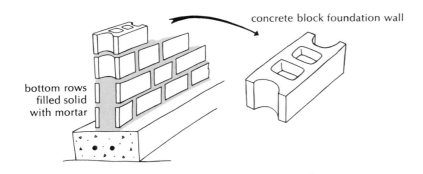

concrete block foundation wall

bottom rows filled solid with mortar

Mortar, plaster, grout, stucco, and spackling compound are different combinations of cement, sand, and water.

Concrete is cement, sand, and water with some gravel stirred in. Concrete can be formed into blocks called concrete blocks.

Cinder block is concrete block mixed up with cinders. Cinder blocks are lighter than concrete blocks, because cinders are lighter than gravel, and cheaper than concrete blocks, because cinders are cheaper than gravel.

While the contractor is putting up the foundation walls he is also bringing in all the services the house will need: running water, sewage (or running-out water) pipes, gas pipes, electric lines, and telephone lines.

We see the water supply lines coming into the house and

branching off into a Y. Part of the water will go directly to cold water pipes. Another part will go into the hot water heater. In cities and suburbs, water pipes come in underground, and sewage pipes go out underground. In a rural area you may have to dig your own well and/or find your own means of getting rid of sewage. Like water, electricity arrives underground in cities. In the suburbs and out in the country it comes to houses aboveground on wires that are quite high up so you won't bump into them. (Shocking!) In these places, the electrical wires have to run down the side of a house so they can then enter through the basement like city electricity. Once inside a house, electrical wires run through a meter and then through something called the main switch. You can keep all this information in the back of your head until you get to Chapter Five, Plumbing, and Chapter Six, Electricity.

Telephone lines usually travel along the same path as electric lines — in suburban areas they are even on the same poles. This makes sense, because the telephone system in your house is just another electrical system. The telephone system survives on very little electricity — and that's all you're going to hear about it from us. Telephones belong to the phone company — not to you, not to us. Don't mess with them. Ma Bell ain't gonna slap no accessory-before-the-fact charges on *us*.

The tops of all the foundation walls have big bolts stuck into them. The rest of this house will be made of wood, and if it weren't bolted to the foundations, a hurricane or a tornado could decide to put it somewhere else. It's like putting a strap around your chin so your bowler hat won't fly off.

The first part of the rest of the house is the sill, a piece of wood that sits on top of the foundation walls and runs all around the house like a sort of shelf. It's the sill that gets bolted down. The bolts are usually placed 4 feet on center. On center is a precise term of distance and it means, in this case, that it is exactly 4 feet from the center of one bolt to the center of the next bolt. It doesn't mean that the bolts are 4 feet apart — that would mean 4 feet from the edge of a bolt to the edge of another bolt — something only slightly different in this case, but quite a bit different in other cases, as we shall see. We've put up this wood sill so that we can build the rest of the house with wood and nails. It is very hard to drive nails into masonry, as we will learn later on in this chapter.

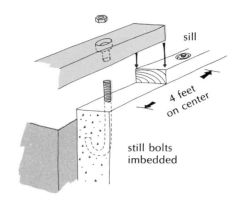

sill

4 feet on center

still bolts imbedded

"Well," the contractor says to himself, "I think it's time for the first floor."

Being the person he is, he does what he says and puts in the first floor. A floor is built by placing wooden joists onto the sill.

Joists are *always* horizontal and are *usually* 2 × 8 or 2 × 10 lumber. Joists live to hold up the floors and ceilings, and so are called *ceiling joists* or *floor joists* depending on whether you're looking up at them or down at them. "One man's ceiling is another man's floor."

Floors are put down on top of joists. Ceilings are placed beneath them. Generally speaking, every floor is two floors: a subflooring right on top of the joists, and then a finished wood floor on top of the subflooring. The contractor puts down the subflooring right after he lays the joists. It ties the joists together, and it forms a good working surface for the contractor himself. He can drop hammers on it, and step through it, and nobody will get upset because nobody will ever see it once it's covered up by finished floor. These days some houses come with wall-to-wall carpeting. These houses are not as much of a bargain as you might think. Because underneath the carpeting there's nothing but a subflooring.

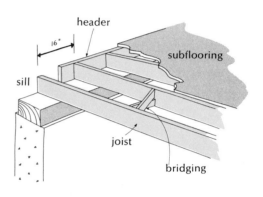

header

subflooring

16"

sill

joist

bridging

Joists are placed 16 inches on center. Here is a case where on center means something rather different from apart — every 2 × 8 is *almost* 2 inches wide.

Q. What you mean, *almost* 2 inches?
A. See Chapter Two.

To keep the joists steady at the ends, a sort of vertical sill called a band is nailed to the end of each joist and to the sill and to the plate. A plate is just another sill nailed over the subflooring. But we're not through yet. Joists have to be kept steady in the middle, too, or else they begin to do the *center joist shuffle* — they bend, bow, twist, and move back and forth to the rhythm of people, furniture, heat, or anything that gets to them.

The steadying influence in the case of joists is called bridging. Bridging can be made of wood, as in the good old days, or it can be made of metal, which is used more commonly today. In either case, bridging is shaped like an X that creates triangles between the joists. Triangles are wonderful for construction because they are rigid, as we learned earlier. Rectangles are not very stable at all,

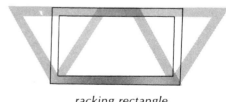

*racking rectangle*

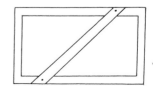

*diagonal bracing*

and a house made entirely of rectangles would rock back and forth — the way tables do as soon as they are used for a little while. Be honest now; don't you put rectangular tables against walls? You do this to stop them from rocking.

The longest joist is 24 feet long, so if a floor is more than 24 feet long, the contractor will have to put in a beam at the 24-foot mark and run some more joists the rest of the way. A beam is a big, thick, heavy joist capable of supporting joists (or even a wall), and it is itself supported by columns that rest on footings. Columns are made of either wood, metal, or concrete. The famous Lally column is a hollow metal tube used as a column and sometimes filled with concrete. A beam is two, three, or four times the thickness of a joist, and it may even be made of two, three, or four joists nailed together.

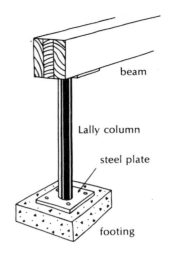

beam

Lally column

steel plate

footing

Now that we have our first floor down it strikes us that something is missing — the walls. We build our walls flat on the existing subfloor and then tilt them up into place.

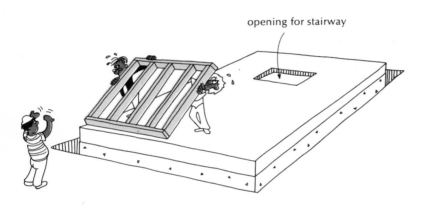

opening for stairway

Q. Why?

A. Because it is hard to swing a hammer over your head while holding up three pieces of wood unless you're Kali, the multiarmed Indian goddess.

The walls built on top of the sill start out looking like the contractor had changed his mind and decided to build a fence instead. Wooden 2 × 4s, 16 inches on center, are nailed vertically to the plate. (Here is another case where on center means something rather different from apart.) These vertical 2 × 4s are called studs. Studs can be thought of as vertical joists, only smaller. So invariable is the 16-inch spacing of studs that we can say this: If you can ever find a stud inside a wall, you will know just where the next stud is — precisely sixteen inches away. If you know one stud, you know 'em all. (Well, *almost* all. You know how contractors are.) The only place studs are other than 16 inches apart is if we are putting an opening in the wall other than the natural space between two studs (14½ inches), or three studs (30½ inches), or four studs (46½ inches) and we need to *frame out* for this opening.

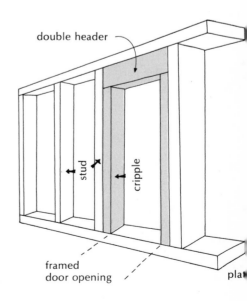

double header

stud

cripple

framed door opening

pla

But even this occurrence is not so common, as windows seem to be made at the factory to fit into 14½-inch or 30½-inch spaces. You see, there are *some* clever people in the building industry.

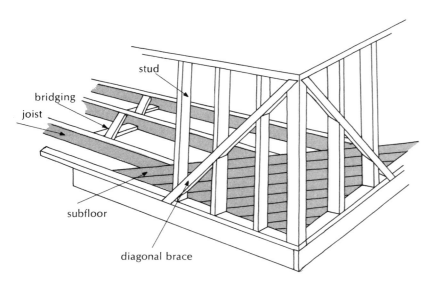

In the old days, the contractor would put in some other 2 × 4s between the studs that run, on a diagonal, from the top to the bottom of the wall. These connecting 2 × 4s are a species of *crossbracing*. Rectangular stud walls are the second act (after the center joist shuffle) and they do the *stud wall rack-rock*. Again, we are creating triangles to stabilize — in this case, the stud wall.

These days we let the *sheathing* do the stabilizing work; but you'll have to wait for sheathing. It's coming up in the fourth act.

The top horizontal 2 × 4 in this wall is again called a plate and so we can start again, if we like. On top of the plate the contractor puts either a second story (remembering to put in the floor/ceiling) or a roof. The second story — and the third, if there is one — gets built just like the first story. Studs, bracing, plate.

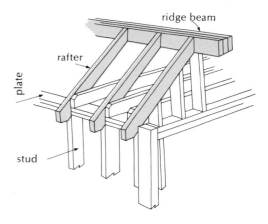

Roofs are made of sloping studs, and when a piece of lumber gets nailed onto a plate at a slope, it assumes yet another name: rafter. Rafters are just sloping studs or joists, only bigger (usually 2 × 8 or larger). The rafters lean up against a piece of wood at the very top of the house called a ridge beam. The ridge beam links up all the triangles formed up there by the rafters and makes the roof into a strong shape. As you might just expect, rafters occur on 16-inch centers.

The frame of the house is now complete. So the contractor starts to close the house in. First he covers the outsides of all the stud walls with sheathing — sheathing is big sheets of plywood ⅜ to ¾ inch thick. Boards used to be used for sheathing instead of plywood, but plywood is cheaper, faster, easier to erect, and just generally better. Better because it can also act as crossbracing because of its larger size. Then the contractor covers the sheathing with a layer of tar paper. The tar paper is a water vapor barrier. Then he nails shingles on top of the tar paper. He could put up any of the other common sidings — tongue-and-groove siding, for instance, or clapboard. Or he could put up a layer of bricks in front of the sheathing — we'd call such a wall a curtain wall, because the bricks would work only as a curtain, and wouldn't be doing any work to help hold up the house. A curtain wall, therefore, is a lazy wall that acts just like a curtain. Curtains hide the house from predators such as wind and rain. But the architect wants shingles on this house, so he puts up shingles.

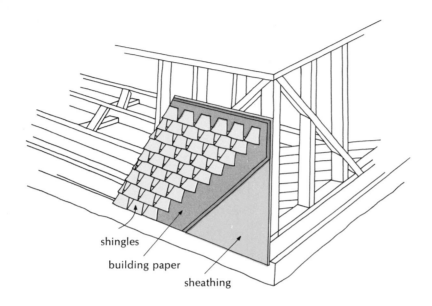

shingles

building paper

sheathing

He also puts sheathing, tar paper, and shingles on top of the roof, and this makes the roof water resistant. No building is ever watertight — it's got to leak somewhere. The question is making it leak where you want it to. The last watertight house was Noah's Ark. Sloped roofs do a pretty good job of keeping out the rain — the water runs down off them before it can soak through into the attic.

Under the roof and above the top floor lies the *attic*. This triangular nostalgic storage space has a purpose in the overall scheme of house building. It keeps your house cooler in the summer and warmer in the winter, but mostly cooler in the summer. Did you ever go up into an attic on a 90-degree day? If you did, you probably turned around and walked right out. The attic is a steam bath with your body producing the steam. (Better there than in your bedroom.) Attics should be ventilated. This usually consists of a window at both ends of the attic or it can be an opening under the *eaves* of the roof if it has an overhang.

Flat roofs are also pretty good for keeping out the rain. Water can't run off them quite so easily, but they are protected by a membrane made out of many layers of tar paper and hot tar. And they generally have a slight slope and plenty of drains. The membrane can be punctured, so keep women with spike heels off flat roofs. (Did you know that the spike heel exerts something like a thousand pounds of pressure per square inch? You should also keep spike heels off your big toe.)

The contractor also waterproofs the foundation walls before filling in what's left of the hole he dug. He coats the outside of the foundation walls either with tar or with something called iron coat, which is a sort of paint that's full of iron chips. The iron chips oxidize after the iron coat goes on. (Oxidation is fancy chemistry and mostly means rusting.) They turn into rust and get much bigger and fill up all the holes, and then the water can't get in. The contractor should also run a drainpipe around the house at the base of the foundation to pick up any loose water that may be trying to get into the cellar. This pipe is called a footing drain.

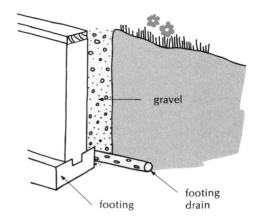

Now the services for the house are brought upstairs. Hot water pipes, cold water pipes, sewage pipes, electrical wires, telephone lines. They run through the hollow places between the studs in the walls and between the joists in the floor. The pipes are attached to faucets and toilets, the wires are attached to switches and outlets and overhead lights, and the lines get hooked up to phones, wall phones, and Princess phones. The switches and outlets are usually attached to studs. The tops of the sewage pipes stick out of the roof.

The contractor also puts a heating system into the house. In this case, being old-fashioned, he puts an oil-burning furnace in the cellar. The furnace heats up air and sends it upstairs through hot air ducts in the walls and floors. Cold air ducts at the tops of rooms return air to the furnace. This heating system is called *oil-fired hot air*. Instead of heating air the furnace might heat water. This is called *oil-fired hot water*. Or it might really heat water all the way to steam and use coal instead of oil — *coal-fired steam*. You probably get the picture. There are many possibilities for heating systems. Smoke and exhaust go out a chimney through the roof. So every house has a chimney, even if it hasn't got a fireplace.

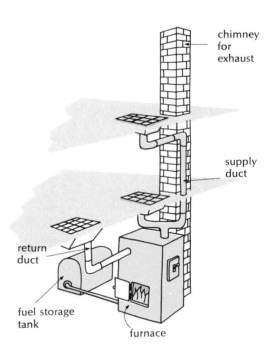

All heating systems work basically the same way. The trick is to heat up the air around you and make you feel better. If you don't heat up the air with something else, your body will try to do it and that makes you feel overworked, cranky, and cold.

The oldest heating system is a fire in the middle of your cave. Unfortunately, this leads to smoky caves, smoky saber-toothed tiger wraps, smoky clothes, smoky lungs. (Caution: The Surgeon General has determined that smoking is hazardous to your health.) Anyway, an open fire in the middle of your house is even more hazardous to your health, so that possibility is out. We could put the fire in a safe place like a fireplace, and that sure is romantic. *Unfortunately,* while fireplaces heat up passions very well, we were looking for a warm room. Most of the heat produced by a fireplace goes straight out the chimney.

Q. This is getting me cranky and cold and unloved. What should I do?

A. Be efficient in your heating and you'll have lots of time and money for better things. Here's how.

First, let's get a nice efficient ugly place to burn something. We can burn wood, coal, oil, natural gas, atoms, whatever. This efficient place we will give the efficient name of furnace.

Second, we'll need a place to store some of the fuel we will burn. We can call it a woodshed or a coal bin or an oil tank (the most common) or a gas pipe (the smallest) or a nuclear fuel chamber (so rare we had to make up the name).

Third, we'll need a place to keep all this ugly stuff. Luckily, the first thing we built was our basement and we can keep all the stuff there. This is the best use for basements.

Fourth, we have to get the fuel into the furnace and light it. Having done all this we are producing heat, and all we have to do is get this heat up to our room. And so . . .

Fifth, we set up a circulation system for the heat-exchanging medium of our choice. (It's the medium that conveys the message.) We can heat anything we want in our furnace — molasses, Pepsi-Cola, gin, anything. The easiest thing to heat up is air, and many systems use air as their medium. Big air pipes called ducts carry warm air up to the room. Hot things rise all by themselves, which is nice and which tells us why we don't put the furnace in the attic. Cold things fall all by themselves, and that's nice, too, because we get back the cold air from the room so that the furnace can heat it up. The ducts that take the hot air up are called hot air supply ducts and those that bring the cold air down to the furnace to be heated are called cold air return ducts. The principal disadvantage of this seemingly efficient system is that it makes for very dry and dusty rooms. Chap Stick and Endust love hot air systems.

We could have chosen to heat water instead of air and sent hot water around in pipes and through radiators. The air in the room sets up its own circulation system around the warm radiators. This is a very nice system: It is relatively clean and it does *not* make a room dry and dusty. Moreover, since we can heat water to whatever temperature we want, we can accurately control the temperature of a water-heated room. In fact, if we were to put a thermometer in such a room and set up some method to turn on the furnace automatically when it got too cold and then shut it off when it got too warm, we would have invented the thermostat and we would have a thermostatically controlled heating system.

Hot water is one of our favorite heating systems, and it is probably the one most commonly installed these days. Its older brother steam heat gets your room hot faster but it cannot be thermostatically controlled and also brings about very dry air in the room.

Helpful Hint: Steam radiators must be kept all the way on or all the way off. The little valve at the bottom of the radiator must be all the way clockwise or all the way counterclockwise or the valve will soon leak and the system will knock and bang in protest disturbing your happy reading of this book.

There's one more heating system that we're going to mention. We could either put wires in boxes and place them around the room or put wires in the floors (if they are not made out of wood) and then send too much electricity through the wires causing them to heat up (see Chapter Six). This system can heat up a room very nicely, and it leaves more room in the basement for a Ping-Pong table since no furnace is required. But it is a relatively rare system, requiring, as it does, fancy *insulation* (a term coming up soon) and fancy construction. It's known around town as radiant electric heat and it's probably the best system going. It is also the most expensive.

That's all there is to that, gentle reader. Pick a fuel, use it to heat up a medium of your choice, and ship it from your furnace up to your room.

Q. Wait a minute! Suppose it's summer and I'm hot.
A. Get an air conditioner.

An *air conditioner* is a machine that conditions the air. This is not double-talk. Most people think an air conditioner is an air cooler. That is only one of its functions. An air conditioner can also heat air (although the ones that sit in windows generally do not), humidify air, and filter air. There is a motor inside them that cools a gas (usually Freon) and thus allows the gas to suck up the heat from your room. Here's how it works: A fan pulls the air from your room into the A.C. (code for air conditioner). The cold gas inside sucks the heat from the air. (The heat is then squirted out the window. That's one of the reasons why it gets so hot in cities when all the air conditioners are on.) A filter removes dust and other impurities from the air. A humidifying unit adds the correct amount of water (usually water must be removed, which is why window A.C. units always drip on your head). This *conditioned* air is then pushed out into your room, and you feel good.

There are unit air conditioners (the type that blot out windows), and there is also something called central air conditioning. If you can afford it, *central air conditioning* is best. Central air conditioning has a centrally located unit that does all the cooling, humidifying, and purifying. In large buildings this unit is usually found on the roof. (Cold air falls.)

Hot, humid, dusty air is taken out of a room by a fan and is sent to the central conditioning unit in warm air return ducts. The unit conditions the air for us to just the way we like it, and then sends it through cold air supply ducts to the various rooms of the house. When your activities, or the sun, or something heats this air up again, the process is repeated.

Giving credit where credit is due, we must tell you that if you have a hot air heating system it is relatively easy to convert this system to a central air conditioning system. To do so you install a central conditioner (not cheap) and then you use the same ducts you were using to supply and return air — to supply and return air. If your house now has another type of heating system, it's hard to find enough room for all the air conditioning ducts of a central air conditioning system, and so most people plug up their windows with unit air conditioners and let them drip on the flower beds around their house.

Now that we've gotten the cold out of winter and the hot out of summer you can lean back and read this book in conditioned comfort — just as soon as we finish building the rest of your house.

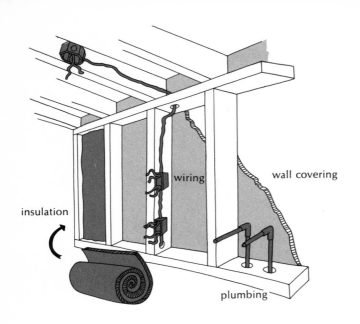

insulation

wiring

wall covering

plumbing

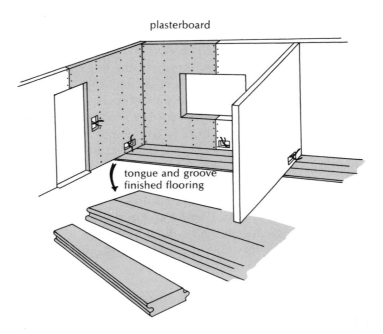

plasterboard

tongue and groove
finished flooring

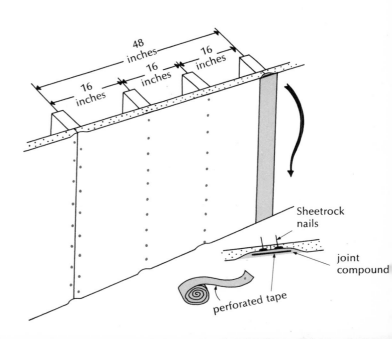

48 inches

16 inches

16 inches

16 inches

Sheetrock nails

joint compound

perforated tape

If there are any hollow places left in the walls and floors after the services have been installed, they get filled up with insulation. Insulation keeps the outside air from affecting the inside air by not allowing heat in or out of your house (depending on where the heat is). Insulation is usually put into only the outside walls and inside the roof. However, the more places you put insulation, the warmer (or cooler) you'll feel and the quieter the argument in the next room will sound. In the case of a house, the insulation is fiberglass between two pieces of paper. Insulation like this comes in rolls just wide enough to fit between two studs (14½ inches). Quick, what is the center-to-center spacing of studs? Correct! Sixteen inches on center is now permanently programmed into your brain.

Now all the contractor has to do is finish up the inside of the house. He puts the finished wood floor on top of the subflooring. He covers the walls with sheets of Sheetrock. Sheetrock is a plaster sandwich with paper or cardboard for bread. The contractor nails it to the studs. The nails are set in, or dimpled. The nail holes are covered with taping compound. Taping compound is a type of very-easy-to-use plaster. The seams between the sheets of Sheetrock are *taped* and *spackled* (that is, the cracks are filled in with compound). Sheetrock comes in 4-foot-by-8-foot sheets with the edges tapered.

The joints between sheets must be filled and the sheets tied together. Taping compound and tape do this. Tape is just perforated paper which goes over and under layers of taping compound. The tapered edge of Sheetrock is there so that you won't have a bulge every 4 feet along your wall.

Now windows and doors are fitted into the holes left over in the walls, and window trim is added to hold the windows inside the window holes. Then the walls get painted . . .

and the house is complete.

Doors let you get in or out. They have three positions — closed, open, and neither. When is a door not a door? When it is ajar. It is this last position that we will worry about. We will make the assumption that the contractor has done a reasonable job of framing out for and installing the door and now something has happened and the door closes only by means of a swift knee to the midsection.

So what's happened? Any one of several things. The most likely thing is that the screws holding the hinges have come loose. Wood screws hold because they have spread the fibers of the wood apart and the wood is trying to squeeze itself back together again. This is called friction, or grip. Wood screws do not hold by their threads. (There's more about the habits of wood screws later on in this chapter). Anyway, after several months or years of trying to re-squeeze, the wood fibers finally give up. The screw comes out. The door hangs improperly and jams. Incidentally, the side of a door frame (or window frame) is called a jamb (pronounced *jam*), perhaps for just this reason.

---

### Recipe for Loose Hinge Screws
#### (Applicable to all loose wood screws)

*Ingredients:*  1 screwdriver
1 drill and appropriate high-speed steel bit (see bit chart, page 99)
several toothpicks
glue

1. Remove hinge pins and door. If this is an exterior door, hope for a warm sunny day.
2. Remove all screws.
3. Stuff vacant screw holes with as many glue-coated toothpicks as you can get in. Pedants can cut a wood dowel or plug to fit.
4. Go have lunch. This allows the glue to dry.
5. Redrill pilot holes for screws.
6. Screw on hinges.
7. Install hinge pins, and thereby rehang door.
8. Clean up.

---

Another thing which may have happened is that the building may have settled or the door may have swelled from heat or humidity or too many milkshakes — whatever. This will also cause the door to stick.

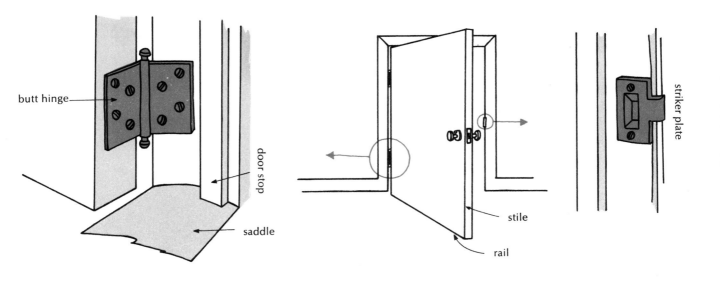

---

Recipe for Swollen or Settled Doors

*Ingredients:*  1 piece of chalk
1 block plane or 1 saw
1 screwdriver

1. Open door and spread chalk on the four door edges. The top and bottom edges of a door are called rails. The two vertical edges are called stiles.

2. Close door and reopen.

3. The part of the door which sticks is now clearly visible. Chalk rubs off the bulges. Remove pins and take door down.

4. Plane or saw off the offending material from the door rails and/or stiles.

5. Rehang door.

6. Clean up.

---

The other thing which may have happened is that all this settling, swelling, and shaving may have misaligned the door striker and the striker plate. The door may not close, or it may be loose when closed.

---

Recipe for Realigning Striker Plate

*Ingredients:*  1 file
1 screwdriver
l drill and appropriate bit (see bit chart, page 99)
several toothpicks

glue
chalk

1. If door does not close, spread chalk on striker plate and close door as far as it goes.

2. Reopen door. This will tell you just how close the striker comes to entering the slot in the striker plate.

3. If the error is small, file off that part of the striker plate still covered with chalk, then put the rest of the tools away. If the error is more than $\frac{1}{16}$ inch, or if the door is loose (the closing device jiggles) when it closes, the striker plate will have to be relocated.

4. Stand on the side of the door stops. These are the pieces of wood running around the inside of the door frame which keep the door from opening in both directions. Close the door.

5. Push the door as far as it will go. This will place the striker firmly against the striker plate.

6. Measure the space between the door and the door stop. This is the amount the striker plate will have to be moved toward the door stop.

7. Open door. Remove striker plate.

8. Stuff vacant screw holes with as many glue-coated toothpicks as you can get in. Pedants will cut a new door frame.

9. Watch the "Game of the Week." This allows the glue to dry.

10. Relocate holes for screws the measured distance (from step 6) closer to the door stop. If this is a substantial distance, you may have to get a chisel and chisel a larger slot for the striker.

11. Redrill pilot holes for screws.

12. Reinstall striker plate.

13. You just missed this unlucky step by finishing on 12. Pat yourself on the back as you have just done yourself a great service. Carpenters hate to do this kind of work and will make you pay for their displeasure.

## Windows

Windows were invented to let in air and light, both nice things. Some windows can do both of these things. They are called movable sash windows. Some let in only light, called fixed-glass windows. Some let in only air, called vents (or dirty windows). Four things can go wrong with a window. In order of difficulty to fix, they are: not enough light, too much light, not enough air, too much air.

## Recipe for Not Enough Light

1. Wash window.

2. Open drape.

3. Scrape away unwanted paint from glass with a razor blade. Watch it!

## Recipe for Too Much Light

1. Hang drape or shade. (See Fasteners later in this chapter.)

## Recipe for Not Enough Air

1. Cut away paint holding window shut.

2. Have someone else install movable sash.

## Recipe for Replacing Broken Glass (Too Much Air)

*A preliminary note:* Glass is held in by molding or by glazing putty. This acts to cover the otherwise messy joint and to cut down on drafts. Steps marked ''a'' are for molding-type installation. Steps marked ''b'' are for glazing putty installation.

*Ingredients:*  1 hammer
2 chisels (one wood and one cold chisel)
1 sheet of glass (see steps 5 & 6)
1 putty knife
1 can glazing putty (optional)
    or
wire brads (optional) (these are *very* thin nails)

1. *Very carefully,* remove any broken glass which pulls out easily. Wear heavy gloves to be safe.

2a. Slip a wood chisel between the molding which holds the glass in and the windowframe. This will lift the molding up slightly. Pry the molding up and off using a cold chisel or crowbar.

2b. Chisel away the hardened glazing putty along the windowframe with a cold chisel.

3. Remove little nails called glazier's points which are hold-

ing glass in. Remove all broken pieces from the bottom.

4. Repeat steps 2a or 2b and step 3 for the sides and then the top.

5. Measure the now exposed glass opening. Subtract ⅛ inch from each dimension.

6. Have a glass supplier cut a piece of window glass to this size.

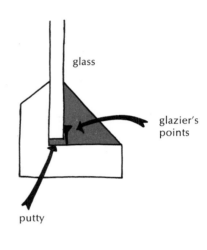

7a. Place glass into opening. Reuse existing glazier's points or drive little brads next to the glass to keep it from falling out. These should occur every 6 inches.

8a. After removing existing nails in molding, replace and nail new nails in new spots.

7b. After thoroughly cleaning all around the frame, apply a little bed of glazing compound to all four sides. Press glass against this bed and drive in those little nails to keep it in place.

8b. Roll the putty in your hands into a rope shape and press all around the glass. Use the putty knife to form the glazing putty into a nice, neat, triangular shape like the rest of the windows. Wait at least a week before painting.

## Walls

So now we talk about walls. We have to talk about walls in some detail because we want to talk about fastening things to walls. There are two types of walls: load-bearing walls and non-load-

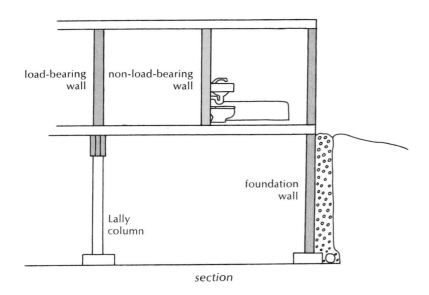

load-bearing
wall

non-load-bearing
wall

foundation
wall

Lally
column

*section*

bearing walls. Load-bearing walls help to support part of the weight
of the house — a floor, say, or a roof. Non-load-bearing walls only
support themselves and are held up by floors. A curtain wall is a
non-load-bearing wall, and so is a partition put into a room after a
house has been built to divide up space. How can you tell if a wall
is load-bearing or non-load-bearing? Two ways. One way — not
recommended — is to knock the wall down. If the house falls down
the wall was load-bearing. The other way is to trace the wall down
the building. All load-bearing walls are either sitting directly on the
foundation walls and the footing of a house, or they are sitting
directly on top of other walls that are sitting on foundation walls
and footings, or they are sitting on a beam.

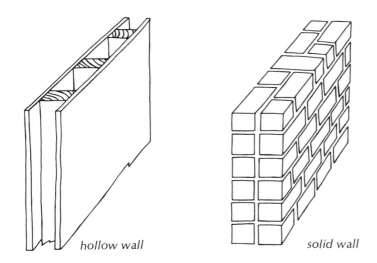

*hollow wall*

*solid wall*

There are also two different ways of making a wall. A wall can be
either a hollow wall or a solid wall. The wood stud walls in the new

house the contractor has just built for us are hollow walls — fences with surfacing nailed on top. In some older apartment houses in cities there are hollow walls made of thin hollow clay bricks. These walls are called hollow tile walls.

Hollow walls can be made with metal studs instead of wood studs. The foundation walls in our new house are solid walls — they are walls all the way through and contain no void space. Some solid walls: concrete walls, brick walls, concrete block walls, cinder block walls, gypsum block walls. A gypsum block is just a concrete block made out of *gypsum*. Gypsum is plaster. Concrete blocks, cinder blocks, and gypsum blocks have holes in the middle. These holes are sometimes filled up with cement, sometimes not. Whether they are or they aren't, walls made out of these blocks are called solid walls, and the possible void spaces inside them don't count. They are consigned to the void. Any wall made of masonry units, like bricks or blocks, is put together with layers of mortar. These layers are called mortar joints. Bricks and mortar go together like bread and butter. As a matter of fact, the process of mortaring a brick is called buttering. A wall made of solid plaster would also be a solid wall.

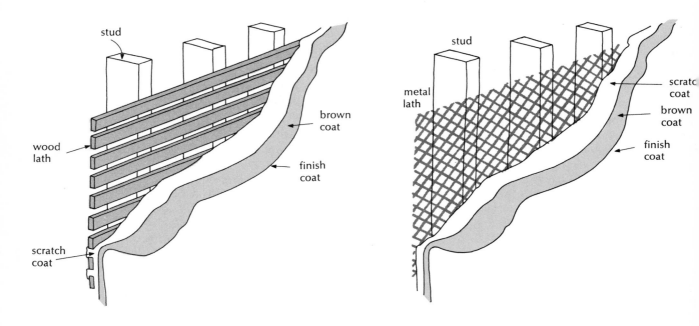

In some older houses built before plasterboard (another name for Sheetrock) was invented, walls are finished off with several layers of plaster fastened either to a latticework of wood slats called wood lath or to a metal mesh screen called metal lath. The nice thing about plastered walls is that they are often thicker than walls that have plasterboard on top, thus keeping out the sounds of "The New Price Is Right" and "Hollywood Squares" going on next door.

Both hollow walls and solid walls can be either load-bearing or non-load-bearing. In general, in all smaller residential construction, non-load-bearing walls are rarely, if ever, solid. There are literally dozens of possibilities for types and combinations of walls. We are going to illustrate the most common types. Your wall may be a combination of some of them. For example, you may have a solid block with plaster over it, or brick over it; or with small studs nailed to it and Sheetrock over that or whatever. Try to be a freethinker about this and be delighted with whatever is *your* wall.

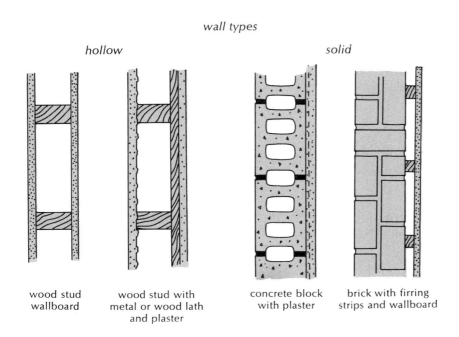

*wall types*

*hollow*                                        *solid*

wood stud          wood stud with          concrete block      brick with firring
wallboard          metal or wood lath       with plaster        strips and wallboard
                   and plaster

The drawing may look a little confusing to you at first. Never fear, here's how it's done. We took a big saw and cut through the wall about 4 feet above the floor. We then removed the top of the wall and are looking down into the wall.

## Fasteners

There are eleven different devices used to fasten things to hollow, solid, load-bearing, and non-load-bearing walls. The most common fastener is the common nail, and the chart on page 96 pairs off the nail and all its colleagues with their various possible uses. Dr. Henry Korman, a noted wall fastener — he began his career as a wallflower — has collected for us the General Principles of Wall Fastening. They are:

1. Whenever you can, fasten something to the structure of a wall — a wood stud, a metal stud, masonry — instead of to the surface of the wall. (The chart distinguishes between structure and surfaces. "Wood Stud" means fastening directly to a wood stud. "Wall-board" is a fastening to a surface — either plasterboard or some

Put a small bit on your electric drill, remove your Auntie Kate's picture, and go to it.

| *If you get:* | *It's probably:* |
|---|---|
| 1. White dust then light brown dust then nothing. | Plaster over empty space. |
| 2. White dust then light brown dust then wood shavings. | Plaster over wood studs. (You have been very lucky, advance to GO and collect $200.) |
| 3. White dust then light brown dust then metal shavings. | Plaster over metal studs. |
| 4. White dust forever. | Solid plaster or plaster block (gypsum block). |
| 5. White dust over red dust. | Plaster over hollow tile or brick. (You probably live on Park Place.) |
| 6. White dust over gray dust and it's not too hard to drill. | Plaster over cinder block or concrete block. |
| 7. Gray dust then nothing and it's not too hard to drill. | Concrete block or cinder block. |
| 8. White dust then nothing. | Sheetrock (plasterboard, gyp board) over empty space. Too bad! Do not pass GO, do not collect $200. |
| 9. White dust then wood shavings. | Sheetrock (plasterboard, gyp board) over wood studs. Advance token to Boardwalk. |
| 10. White dust then metal shavings. | Sheetrock (plasterboard, gyp board) over metal studs. |
| 11. Gray dust and no matter how hard you lean on the drill it doesn't seem to go anywhere. | Solid concrete. You really didn't want to hang it there anyway. Go directly to jail. |

Table 12. Know-Your-Wall Chart

other thin material: plywood, let's say, or homosote, a kind of cardboard. "Plaster" is fastening to a lath-and-plaster surface.)

2. Always be appropriate. Choose a fastener appropriate to the wall in front of you and to the weight of whatever it is you're hoisting up off the floor. Put Xmas cards up with Scotch tape (not on chart).

3. The more dense and more solid a wall is, the more problems you'll have fastening things to it.

4. There are two ways of finding out what kind of wall you're up against. You can knock and you can drill. You can knock on a wall, and if it goes "ock, ock" or "uck, uck," it's some kind of hollow wall. If it goes "rap, rap," it's some kind of knuckle-busting solid wall. You can drill and get very specific information, because a drill actually takes you inside a wall so that you can see what's there. Drill a small hole in the wall. Almost always the first thing that comes out is some white dust. This is either plasterboard or the first layer of a plastered surface. If the next stuff that comes out is a brownish dust, that will be from an undercoat of plaster and indicate that the wall has been finished with several layers of plaster. If wood comes out of the hole, then the wall is a stud wall. If metal shavings come out, the wall is a metal stud wall. A little bit of red dust or dark gray dust is a sign of a hollow tile. If the drill encounters hard going, it's some kind of solid wall. A lot of red dust would mean a brick wall. A sort of beige gray dust would mean a concrete wall. If the drill has a hard time and then breaks through into nothing, you can assume you have some kind of a block wall. If it's a cinder block wall the dust will be deep gray.

Table 12 is a guide to help you determine the type of wall you have.

*Rules of thumb:* In large buildings, exterior walls are likely to be solid walls and interior walls are likely to be hollow.

In small buildings like houses, all the walls (except foundation walls) are likely to be hollow.

5. A drill is also the only reliable way of locating a wood stud in a wood stud wall. Drive a small hole in the middle of the wall. (It's no good starting in the corner, because walls are usually built from the middle to the edges, so the studs on the ends may be irregularly placed.) If the first hole you drill goes *wirrrr* and you just encounter nothing, you haven't found the stud. Move the drill over about 2 inches and drill again. *Wirrrr.* More nothing. No luck. Move the drill. *Wirrrrrrrrrrrrrr.* Luck! You've hit wood. Mark the spot. You've found every stud in the wall. Because, of course, all the other studs in the wall are 16 inches and multiples of 16 inches away from the one the drill just found. By the way, little holes can be taped and filled very easily, and you can make them in inconspicuous places, like behind the couch or behind your grandma's picture.

6. A lot of a little is better than a little of a lot. About seven out of every ten fasteners you put in a wall will hold, so a lot of little fasteners will probably do more for you than a few big fasteners.

7. Don't kid yourself about the weights of the things you want to fasten to walls. Big mirrors weigh a lot more than small mirrors. Encyclopedias and records weigh a lot more than paperbacks. (On the chart, "Light" is only for pictures or small mirrors. Something that weighs less than 5 pounds. "Medium" is for big mirrors and for shelves for paperbacks and a little bric-a-brac. "Heavy" is for shelves for encyclopedias and records.)

Tables 13 and 14 are printed on the next two pages to give you a quick guide to the types of fasteners and their correct use. Use depends on type of wall, weight of fastenee, and properties of the fastener (pun intended).

Here's how to use the fasteners tables.

First. Decide what the weight category the something you're going to put up fits in.

Second. Determine what kind of wall you have at the point the something is going up.

Third. Find where the first two pieces of data intersect on the chart, and use the fastener indicated there. If more than one fastener is listed, they are listed with the preferred one first.

Now to specifics. First, nails. There are three kinds of nails, common nails, finish nails, and cut nails.

The common nail is the big fat nail with a head on it. It's used for attaching medium- and heavyweight things to wood studs. It's by far the easiest fastener around to use. Simply take the nail, point it at the wall, and strike it with a hammer.

Important tip: Always hammer nails into walls at a 45-degree angle. If you hammer them in horizontally they won't hold for long. Why? Because the weight hanging on the nail will tend to pull the nail down, and when that happens the nail will start pulling at the nail hole, and then the nail hole will get big, and by and by the nail

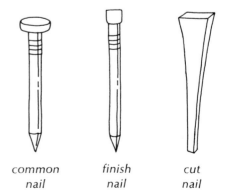

common      finish      cut
nail        nail        nail

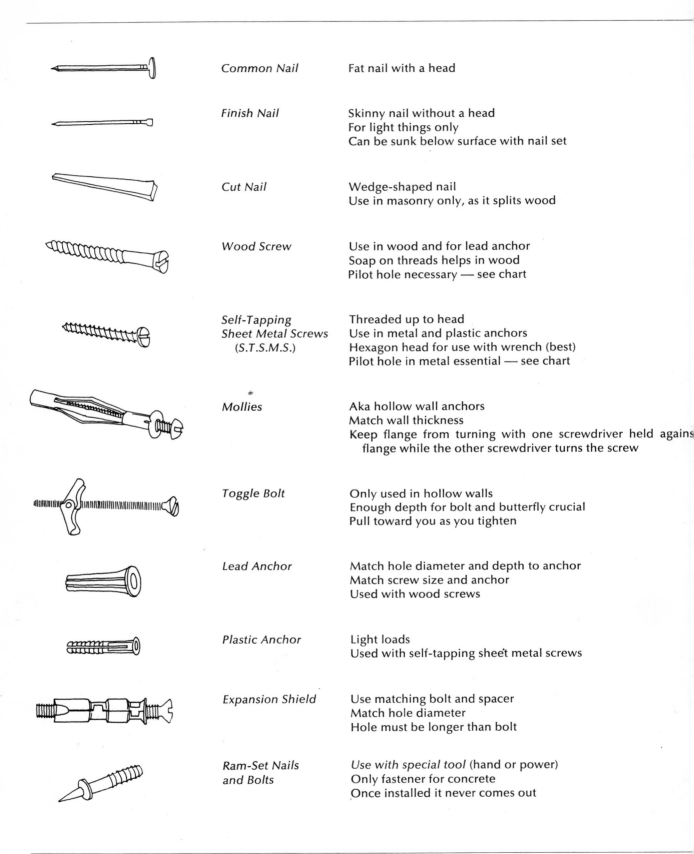

| | | |
|---|---|---|
| | *Common Nail* | Fat nail with a head |
| | *Finish Nail* | Skinny nail without a head<br>For light things only<br>Can be sunk below surface with nail set |
| | *Cut Nail* | Wedge-shaped nail<br>Use in masonry only, as it splits wood |
| | *Wood Screw* | Use in wood and for lead anchor<br>Soap on threads helps in wood<br>Pilot hole necessary — see chart |
| | *Self-Tapping*<br>*Sheet Metal Screws*<br>*(S.T.S.M.S.)* | Threaded up to head<br>Use in metal and plastic anchors<br>Hexagon head for use with wrench (best)<br>Pilot hole in metal essential — see chart |
| | *Mollies* | Aka hollow wall anchors<br>Match wall thickness<br>Keep flange from turning with one screwdriver held agains<br>flange while the other screwdriver turns the screw |
| | *Toggle Bolt* | Only used in hollow walls<br>Enough depth for bolt and butterfly crucial<br>Pull toward you as you tighten |
| | *Lead Anchor* | Match hole diameter and depth to anchor<br>Match screw size and anchor<br>Used with wood screws |
| | *Plastic Anchor* | Light loads<br>Used with self-tapping sheet metal screws |
| | *Expansion Shield* | Use matching bolt and spacer<br>Match hole diameter<br>Hole must be longer than bolt |
| | *Ram-Set Nails*<br>*and Bolts* | *Use with special tool* (hand or power)<br>Only fastener for concrete<br>Once installed it never comes out |

*Table 13. Types of Fasteners*

| Hollow Walls | Light (to 5 lbs.) | Medium | Heavy |
|---|---|---|---|
| Wood Stud | Finish nail<br>Common nail<br>Wood screw | Finish nail<br>Common nail<br>Wood screw | Wood screw<br>Common nail |
| Metal Stud | S.T.S.M.S. | S.T.S.M.S. | S.T.S.M.S. |
| Wallboard | Common nail<br>Finish nail<br>Plastic anchor | Molly<br>Toggle | Not recommended |
| Plaster | Finish nail<br>Plastic anchor | Expansion shield<br>Lead anchor | Expansion shield<br>Lead anchor |
| Hollow Tile | Finish nail | Lead anchor<br>Expansion shield<br>Toggle | Expansion shield<br>Toggle |
| Gypsum Block | Finish nail | Lead anchor<br>Expansion shield | Expansion shield<br>Caution |
| Cinder and Concrete Block | Common nail<br>Finish nail<br>Cut nail | Lead anchor<br>Expansion shield<br>Toggle | Expansion shield<br>Toggle |
| **Solid Walls** | **Light (to 5 lbs.)** | **Medium** | **Heavy** |
| Concrete | Ram-set | Ram-set | Ram-set |
| Filled Block<br>Concrete<br>and Cinder | Cut nail<br>Plastic anchor | Cut nail<br>Lead anchor<br>Expansion shield | Cut nail<br>Ram-set<br>Expansion shield |
| Brick | Finish nail<br>Plastic anchor | Cut nail<br>Lead anchor<br>Expansion shield | Expansion shield |
| Mortar Joints | Finish nail | Cut nail<br>Caution | Not recommended |

Table 14. Choosing the Correct Fastener

will fall out of the wall. Hammering a nail in a wall at a 45-degree angle requires the presence of an anchored thumb. Merely wanting a nail to go into a wall at a 45-degree angle is not enough. It will go in all right, and at the correct angle, but not at the spot you want it to go in, because nails hammered at angles have a tendency to *creep*. Creep is a very technical term meaning: slide slowly down the wall while you're hitting them. So squeeze the nail firmly to the chosen spot by putting the thumb of the hand holding the nail directly under the nail, and then hang on tight.

While hammering, look at the exact center of the nail. If you do this, the hammer will always hit the nail accurately and not hit it a glancing blow, or hit the wall, or hit the anchored thumb. How do we know this is so? There is an old story about an archery contest in India. The greatest archers of the country all aimed their arrows at a flying eagle. Only one man, the great hero Arjuna, hit the mark. All the archers were questioned afterward about their aim. The

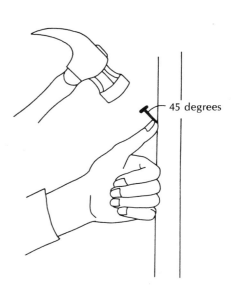

45 degrees

archers who had failed all said, "I aimed at the head of the eagle."
Arjuna said, "I aimed at the eye of the eagle."

Important tip no. 2: Make a mark on the wall where you want to put a nail. Take a finger and wet it and make a small smudge. (Fingers are always dirty.) Put two strips of adhesive tape in an X over the mark. Then hammer in the nail. The tape will hold the paint together and the plaster under the paint together. It will keep the nail hole small.

Don't hammer a nail all the way into a wall — for obvious reasons. Leave just enough nail outside to hang your hammer on.

A finish nail is a skinny nail with no head. It was developed to be an invisible thing. In woodwork, common nails are used for rough structure and for places where you don't mind looking at nails. Finish nails are for places where you wish to see only wood. They can be countersunk a little bit below the surface of a piece of wood with a nail set. The tiny hole is then filled with plastic wood. Common nails flaunt their presence. Finish nails have discretion. For fastening, finish nails are used for attaching lightweight things to gypsum block walls, cinder block walls, concrete block walls, brick walls, and to the mortar joints in masonry walls, and for attaching medium-weight things to wood studs. You will find that you can nurse a finish nail into a very hard wall if you are careful enough. Tap the nail. Apply very light blows. It ain't easy, but it's a technique you can develop.

Finish nails come in five sizes. Two of these five sizes — 4d and 6d — are used for fastening. "4d" and "6d" are pronounced "four-penny" and "sixpenny," because once upon a time, in England, people used to write "d" for penny — it has something to do with the Romans — and you could buy a pound of nails for four or six pennies, or whatever.

Picture hooks are just finish nails with hooks on them. Their only real advantages are that they are more elaborate and more expensive. Advantages?

A cut nail is a very hard wedge of a nail that has been cut or stamped out of a piece of metal. Common nails and finish nails are drawn out, or pulled out, of metal the way wire is. Cut nails split wood to pieces, but they can go into masonry without bending. So they are used to attach lightweight things to cinder block walls and to concrete block walls; and for attaching light- and medium-weight things to solid concrete walls; and for attaching medium-weight things to brick walls and to the mortar joints in masonry unit walls; and for attaching things of any weight to walls made of filled concrete blocks or of filled cinder blocks.

Now, two kinds of screws. The wood screw — next most easiest fastener to use after the nail — has a tapered head, a short shank with no threads on it, and then threads. The threads taper to a point. The wood screw is used to attach medium- and heavyweight things to wood studs. The way it works is: You drill a hole, called a starter hole, into the stud. The starter hole is a little longer than the screw; its width is approximately half the diameter of the shank of the screw, and Table 15, "Know-Your-Screw-and-Hole Chart," tells how to approximate drill bits to screw sizes.

*wood screw*

*self-tapping sheet metal screw*

| Screw size | Hardwoods (wood screws) | | Softwoods (wood screws) | | Metal (self-tapping sheet metal screws) coarse & fine threads | |
|---|---|---|---|---|---|---|
| Number | Drill bit size for threaded portion | Fit of screw in hole | Drill bit size for threaded portion | Fit of screw in hole | Drill bit size for threaded portion | Fit of screw in hole |
| 0 | $3/64$ | Loose | $1/32$ | Just right | $1/16$ | Hope for the best |
| 1 | $3/64$ | Just right | $3/64$ | Loose | $1/16$ | |
| 2 | $1/16$ | Loose | $3/64$ | Just right | $5/64$ | |
| 3 | $1/16$ | Snug | $1/16$ | Loose | $5/64$ | |
| 4 | $5/64$ | Loose | $1/16$ | Just right | $3/32$ | |
| 5 | $5/64$ | Snug | $5/64$ | Loose | $3/32$ | |
| 6 | $3/32$ | Just right | $3/32$ | Loose | $7/64$ | |
| 7 | $7/64$ | Loose | $3/32$ | Just right | $1/8$ | |
| 8 | $7/64$ | Snug | $7/64$ | Loose | $1/8$ | |
| 9 | $1/8$ | Loose | $7/64$ | Just right | $9/64$ | |
| 10 | $1/8$ | Snug | $1/8$ | Loose | $9/64$ | |
| 11 | $9/64$ | Loose | $1/8$ | Just right | $5/32$ | |
| 12 | $9/64$ | Snug | $9/64$ | Loose | $5/32$ | |

*Table 15. Know-Your-Screw-and-Hole Chart*

Then you screw the screw into the starter hole. As the fatter part of the screw gets deeper and deeper into the hole, the screw fits more and more tightly. As with a nail, it is friction that holds a wood screw in wood. The threads on the screw give the screw only a little bit of its grip — and, of course, they don't cut the hole at all — the drill does that. *Important wood screw tip:* Rub some soap on the threads of a screw before screwing it into a stud, and the screw will then enter the stud without protest.

The self-tapping sheet metal screw has threads from head to foot and not much of a taper anywhere. It's used for attaching medium- and heavyweight things to metal studs. Drill a hole into the metal stud about half the diameter of the self-tapping sheet metal screw (see Table 15), and then screw in the screw. "Self-tapping" refers to what happens when the screw is screwed into the hole: The male threads on the screw cut matching female threads in the metal. (The threads on the screw are male threads because male threads are threads on the outside of anything, and threads on the inside of something are called female threads, natcho.) By the time the screw is all the way inside the hole, it has cut a slot for itself that is its exact mate, and it sits in the hole just like a bolt inside a nut. *Important self-tapping sheet metal screw tips:* Before drilling, make a starting point for the drill bit with a hardened punch called a center punch. Put the center punch where the hole will be, and hit it with a hammer. It will make a little indentation, and this indentation will keep the bit from wandering while you drill. Put a little cutting oil on the tip of the drill bit before you start drilling.

Drill slowly, and pull the drill out before you're finished and put another couple of drops of cutting oil in the hole. The oil will keep the temperature in the hole down and will prevent the bit from burning out. L. S./M. F. T.

The First General Principle of Wall Fastening was "Attach things to studs whenever possible, and not to a wallboard or a lath-and-plaster surface." Mollies, or hollow wall anchors, as they are also known now that the original Molly patent has expired, exist for those occasions where you do have to attach something to the surface of a hollow wall. One such occasion: A poor designer has designed some shelf supports to be 24 inches instead of 32 inches apart. You can only attach one of the supports to a stud, so you have to use a Molly to put up the other one. Mollies are used for attaching medium-weight things (like light shelves) to hollow wall surfaces, for instance, a Sheetrock wall or a lath-and-plaster wall. Like toggle bolts, the fasteners we'll get to next, Mollies are things that flip out. They are a screw in a sheath, and they go into a hole in a hollow wall. When you tighten the screw, this pulls the back part of the sheath, which is behind the wall, closer to the wall. The main part of the sheath, also behind the wall, is made of metal strips, and when the back part of the sheath starts getting pulled toward the wall, the strips buckle outward and grip the wall like fingers.

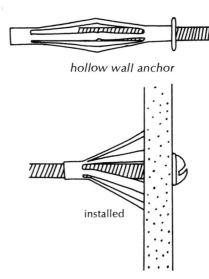

*hollow wall anchor*

*installed*

Hollow wall anchors are sized — they say on their sides things like "for hollow walls up to ¼ inch thick." So how do you know whether a hollow wall is ¼ inch thick? With a magic measuring device, of course. First drill a small hole through the hollow wall with a carbide tip masonry bit. That's a bit that's got a little wedge-shaped tip of carbide to do its work, and it goes right through any kind of masonry or stone with no trouble at all. A high-speed steel bit, on the other hand, which plows through steel and wood, goes all to pieces when faced with masonry. Even carbide tip bits, you will find, wear out rapidly, so it helps to have plenty of them around. The best ones say somewhere on them "masonry drill for rotary or percussion drilling." They're best because there's a specialized tool for getting through concrete and stone called a *percussion drill* that slams a bit against a wall, grinds it around a little, then pulls back and slams again. There's no need to buy such an instrument, but you might as well buy bits made to take that kind of slamming. Carbide bits have another problem — while we're on the subject. They're brittle, and if you drop one on a stone it will probably break in two. And we might as well say right here that drilling speed is important. You have to drill very slowly through metal (the drill going "gragglegragglegraggle" or "whorrrr") or you'll kill the drill. You can use a medium speed going through masonry ("warrrrrrrrrr") and a high speed on wood ("WREEEEEEEEEEEEE").

But we were talking about the magic measuring tool. It is made out of a piece of old coat hanger.

You stick the hooked end of it into the wall. Having inserted the hook, you pull straight back, and put a little mark on the straight part that is now just emerging from the hole. Then you take the magical thing out of the wall, and the distance between the end of the hook, which was resting against the far side of the wall when you pulled straight back, and the mark you made showing where this side of the wall is, is the exact thickness of the wall. Niftiness.

bent coat hanger

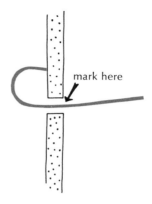

mark here

To insert a hollow wall anchor, drill a hole twice the size of the diameter of the screw that came with the hollow wall anchor. A 1/8-inch screw therefore requires a 1/4-inch hole. Put the hollow wall anchor into the hole and tamp it down nice and solid with a hammer. The two little spikes on the part of the sheath that sits on the surface of the wall should be grabbing wall. Now this is very important — important enough that if your wall is a wall of bad character and has lumps or unevenness you should put some tape over the place where you're going to drill the hollow wall anchor hole to help the spikes get their grip. The reason it's so important for the spikes to hold is that they are the only things that keep the sheath from rotating with the screw as you screw it into the wall. If the sheath rotates with the screw, the screw can't pull the sheath toward the wall and expand the metal strips that hold the anchor in place. One thing you can do to prevent the sheath from rotating — these things work only about 70 percent anyway, so don't worry — is brace the sheath with another screwdriver while you're screwing in the screw.

It takes quite a while to screw the screw in. At a certain point you can't turn the screw any more, it just won't go any farther. That means the strips are in place and the anchor is secured. Turn the screw in an anticlockwise direction and take it out. Screws generally tighten clockwise and loosen anti- or counterclockwise — except for the rarely encountered left-hand screws. Hang whatever you want on the screw and put it back in. You now have a permanent threaded hole in the wall for this purpose. You could bolt on a shelf standard (one of the upright supports for a shelf attached to a wall) or a piece of metal or a piece of wood or anything.

Now, we've said that Mollies don't always go in just right, so there are times when you get a wall with a half-inserted, nonfunctioning Mollie or two sticking out. Mollies are not removable (now you tell us!) but there are a couple of things you can do. If the wall is a plaster wall, you can take a punch and a hammer, and tap those no-good Mollies in until they're just below the surface of the wall. Then you can fill up the indentation with taping compound. If the wall is a Sheetrock wall, all you'll need is a hammer, and the only thing you can do is drive the Mollies all the way through the Sheetrock until they fall down behind the wall. That will leave you with some genuine holes to fill up with taping compound.

By the way, the meaning of the cryptic phrase "A lot of a little is better than a little of a lot," mentioned by Dr. Korman in the General Principles of Wall Fastening, is: If Mollies only work 70 percent of the time, then if you put up ten Mollies, seven of them will work, but if you only put up two Mollies, those two may be two of the three out of every ten that don't work. So it's better to use a lot of small Mollies than a few big ones.

*Toggle bolts* are the other hollow wall fastener. They can sustain a slightly heavier load than Mollies, so, in addition to being used for fastening medium-weight things to wallboard walls, toggles are used for attaching medium- and heavyweight things to cinder block, concrete block, and hollow tile walls. A toggle bolt is nothing but a bolt with a special kind of nut on it — a toggle. And a toggle is nothing but a nut with two little wings on it that can expand. This is why a toggle is also referred to as a butterfly. The terms may be confusing, but don't let them get you down — they're supposed to be confusing so exploiters can charge lay-people large sums. The principles are simple enough. Just remember the famous old tabloid headline: NUT BOLTS AND SCREWS.

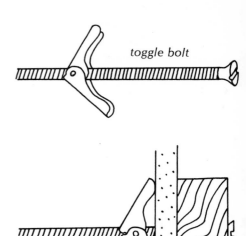

toggle bolt

installed

A toggle bolt works like a Mollie: It grips a wall from behind. You drill a hole and put the bolt through the hole with the toggle squeezed up. The toggle expands when it gets behind the wall, and you then begin a rather lengthy procedure that consists of pulling on the bolt to keep the toggle tight against the backside of the wall and simultaneously screwing the bolt into the wall. Push, pull, click, click.

The hole you drill should be twice the width of the bolt — so that the toggle can squeeze through. You may have to nudge the toggle through with a hammer, even so. The one thing you should make sure of is that there is enough room behind the wall for the toggle to open up. This is easy enough to make sure of — if you can get the drill into the wall as far as the bolt is long, then the toggle ought to be able to function. Whatever you're fastening — let's say a shelf standard — should be hooked up to the bolt the first time you put it into the wall, because you don't want to put it in another time. If you take the bolt out, the toggle will fall down and go boom. Which is horrible, because toggle bolts do not come with two pairs of pants. So the length of bolt you will want to use will be just a little longer than the width of the shelf standard plus the width of the wall (determined by magic measuring device) plus the width of the toggle.

Use a carbide tip masonry bit when you drill the hole. Which reminds us: The harder the masonry in the wall you're drilling, the more you'll have to lean on the drill. That's because regular bits cut their way through wood and metal, but carbide tip bits scrape away at masonry, and *you* do the cutting by pushing.

Toggle bolts are at their best when holding things tight against a wall — things like shelf standards. A toggle bolt is not so good if you want to hang something from it. Since the hole has to be bigger than the bolt, the bolt may wobble when there's a weight hanging down.

Next, three related kinds of fasteners:

A *lead anchor* is a way of screwing a wood screw into a concrete block. It's a little bit of lead arranged in cylindrical strips, and you put it into a hole you've bored in a concrete block, and you screw a wood screw into it, and the screwing pushes the lead of the anchor out to the sides of the hole it's sitting in, and then friction holds everything in place.

A *plastic anchor* is just like a lead anchor, except that you screw a self-tapping sheet metal screw into it instead of a wood screw,

*lead anchor*

*plastic anchor*

*expansion shield*

installed

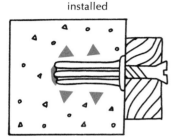

installed

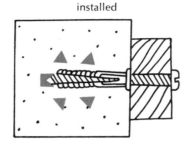

installed

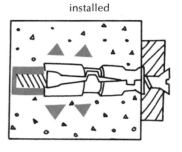

and it's only a little slip of a fellow and can't sustain much in the way of weight.

An *expansion shield*, the other relative, takes a bolt instead of any kind of screw. It's a little more complicated than its kin: There's a threaded wedge-shaped piece on the far end of an expansion shield that the bolt, during its passage through the shield, pulls forward toward the middle of the shield, and underneath the middle of the shield. The middle then expands outward to the sides of the hole the shield is sitting in, and friction keeps everything solid. An expansion shield is a heavier-duty item than either of the two anchors and can support a lot more weight.

So use plastic anchors for attaching lightweight things to wallboard walls and plaster walls, and to filled concrete block walls, filled cinder block walls, and brick walls.

Use lead anchors to attach medium-weight things to hollow tile walls, gypsum block walls, cinder block walls, concrete block walls, filled cinder block walls, filled concrete block walls, and brick walls — and to attach medium- and heavyweight things to plaster walls.

And use expansion shields to attach medium- and heavyweight things to plaster walls, hollow tile walls, gypsum block walls, cinder block walls, concrete block walls, filled cinder block walls, filled concrete block walls, and brick walls. And use tables 12, 13, 14, and 15.

The one condition required by all these three fasteners is a relatively solid wall. If a wall is very crumbly, very powdery, very dusty, friction won't have much of a chance, and as the anchors/shields expand, the holes you've drilled for them will just get bigger, and the fasteners will fall out.

It's important to drill the right size holes for these fasteners. Fortunately, lead anchors and expansion shields are labeled, so that takes care of that. It's also important with lead anchors and plastic anchors to drill a hole the right length — that is, just the length of the fastener. If the hole is too short, part of the anchor will stick out, and it won't work. If the hole is too long, when we thread a screw into the anchor and try to expand it, the screw will just go straight through the anchor instead of spreading it out and locking it into place. It will go straight through, because that's so much easier for it. In general, things do the easy thing, given a choice — just like people.

What you can do is put a piece of tape around your drill bit at the length of the anchor. When you've drilled into the tape, you've come to exactly the right point.

One more important thing — you have to use the right size and right length screw with these contraptions. You can either buy anchors with the right size screw, in pairs, or you can buy a box of anchors. The box will say something like, "Use either No. 6 or No. 8 screws, 1¼ inch long." You can use the smaller size screw (the No. 6) if you're drilling through a hard material — because then the anchor won't need to be spread out so much to hold. If you're drilling through a fairly soft material, like plaster or gypsum block, you'll need a thicker, heavier screw (No. 8, in this case). The larger diameter of the heavier screw will give you more force inside the hole. *If* you were to put a No. 4 screw into an anchor that required a No. 6 or a No. 8, it would very likely pull right out of the wall and dump books on you when you were sleeping in your bed, something that actually happened a few years back to one of the authors of this book. He doesn't read books anymore; just writes 'em.

As for length of screw, keep in mind whatever it is you're attaching to the wall with the anchor — a shelf standard or a piece of wood. So, if the box says you need a screw 1¼ inches long to fit your anchor, and the piece of wood you're fastening is an inch wide, then you'll be wanting a 2¼-inch-long screw.

Lead anchors will work pretty well on a ceiling, too, if it's a plaster ceiling in solid condition or a light density concrete ceiling. If it's a plaster ceiling that has seen better days, a Molly or a toggle would be a better bet. Your *best* bet, however, if the ceiling has wood joists, is to find one of the joists and hang something directly from it with a wood screw. Or find two wood joists and string a wood plate between them and then hang plants, or whatever they are, from the plate with wood eye screws. Joists are, like studs, generally 16 inches on center, although in some places where roofs never have to hold much snow the joists on the ceiling under the roof may be as much as 2 feet on center.

Expansion shields are much bigger than any of the anchors, and hence require much bigger holes. You can't get a big enough hole from a regular masonry bit, and what you usually have to do is rent a percussion drill for the job.

And now for the last fastener of our bunch, the *ram-set nail*, called also the *drive pin*. This is an expensive device that is plenty difficult to apply, but it is absolutely the only thing that will penetrate solid concrete. The ram-set nail is used to attach heavyweight things to filled concrete block walls and filled cinder block walls — and things of *any* weight to concrete walls.

A ram-set nail generally has a washer on it that rides up the shaft as the nail enters the wall. The washer, like any washer, spreads the load of the head of the nail so that the nail won't crack the wall. There are two ways of persuading a ram-set nail to enter a concrete

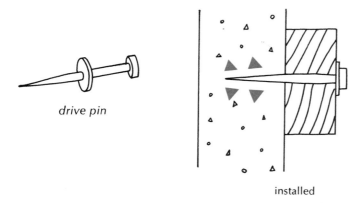

*drive pin*                installed

wall. One is hammering, and you should live so long. You should use at least a 2-pound sledgehammer to pound at the nail — and you should put the nail inside a special tool called a drive tool before hammering, or, hard as it is, the pounding will bend the nail. The washer on a ram-set nail fits into a slot in the drive tool, and the nail itself sits in an even smaller slot inside this slot. Then the metal pin of the tool comes down and touches the head of the nail. Hitting the pin will drive the drive pin into the wall.

You don't have to try to get one of these nails all the way into a wall — rest assured, once it goes in at all, it's in to stay.

The other thing to do with ram-set nails is shoot them. There's a fine thing called the *stud gun,* which fires .22 caliber blanks and shoots ram-set nails into walls instantly. It's a .22 caliber hammer, and it rents for about $5 a day, and it's very safe. It only goes off when you lean it against something very, very hard and put all your weight on it before pulling the trigger. There are four different sizes of shot for the stud gun — 1 through 4 — and the higher the number, the harder the shot. Different concrete walls have different densities, so you'll have to experiment to find out which shot you need to make the nail go in as far as you want it to. If you use a No. 1 shot and the nail rebounds off the wall, you need a harder shot; if you use a No. 4 shot, and the nail disappears into the wall, you need a softer shot.

Since ram-set nails are a permanent addition to any wall they enter, we recommend that you begin by fastening a wood plate to a concrete wall, and then fasten whatever you're hanging to a wood plate. That makes the hung thing removable. Some ram-set nails have threaded connections on the ends that protrude from the wall so that you can bolt things to them.

Final fact about these things: Ram-set nails go straight into a wall, not at an angle like other nails. It's the only way you can get the miserable things in.

Also a final note of caution about fastening: Brick is untrustworthy, and it's best to try to avoid fastening things to it. Holes, for instance, tend to change in size from brick to brick; they are also apt to powder. Furthermore, bricks are brittle. Pretty, though. You could ease a cut nail into the mortar between some bricks for a very light load.

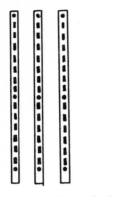

1. match standards

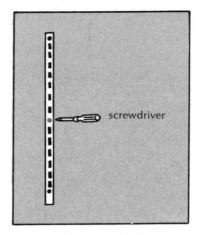

screwdriver

2. locate standard
on wall

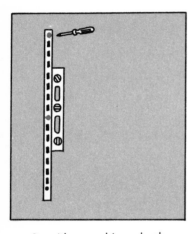

3. with screwdriver plumb
standard and put in
second screw

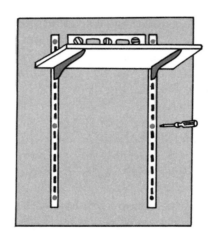

4. put brackets in
same slot

Recipe for Erecting Shelves

*(Applicable, fortunately, to just about whatever
you want to put up)*

This recipe assumes that you will be screwing the shelves into wood studs with wood screws, but you can follow the very same steps if you have a hollow wall or a block wall and toggle bolts or lead anchors or expansion shields. The point about fasteners is that you use whatever fasteners you have to use wherever you have to use them.

*Ingredients:*   3 shelf standards (arbitrary number)
18 wood screws
1 electric drill
1 bit brace screwdriver
1 scratch awl
1 level

brackets
shelves

1. Match up the shelf standards. Shelf standards are the long vertical parts of shelves with slots in them for the brackets that support the shelves and with holes in them so they can be screwed into the wall. They have to be matched up because they have a top and a bottom, which means that if you put up a tête-bêche pair, the holes and slots won't match up unless you put one standard a couple of inches higher on the wall than the other one, which would look funny.

2. Decide how high you want the shelves to be, remembering that if the top shelf is any higher than you yourself can reach, you'll have to climb up a ladder to get to it.

3. Time to put up the first standard. We're assuming you've already found a stud to attach it to — using the technique presented in the first part of this chapter, which consists of drilling holes 2 inches apart until you hit pay dirt. Put the standard against the wall, top up, with the top where you want the top shelf to be, and mark the first hole, through the standard, with your scratch awl. The first hole wants to go in someplace that is a comfortable working height for you — and a comfortable working height is defined as anywhere from your waist to your shoulder, or thereabouts. Now take the standard down and drill the first hole. Put the standard back up and screw in the first screw, but don't tighten it down all the way. We want the standard to be able to swing free.

   Why? Well, no reason, really — in the present instance. The drill bit you're using for the wood screws will fit through the holes in the standard. But if the wall was a masonry wall or a hollow wall — that is, if you·were using Mollies or toggle bolts or lead anchors or expansion shields or such like — you'd be using a carbide-tip masonry drill bit which is too big to go through the screw holes in a standard. So you would mark the other holes with the scratch awl, swing the standard out of the way to drill them, put the fasteners in the drilled holes, and then swing the standard back and screw the bolts or screws through the standard and into the fasteners. OK?

4. Before marking the second hole, plumb the standard with your level. That means put the level lengthwise against the standard and line it up so that the bubbles at the top and the bottom of the level are both centered between their respective two black lines. Now mark the second hole — anywhere above the first hole — and drill it and then screw the second screw in fairly tightly. Make the first screw fairly tight now, too.

5. Plumb the standard again. If the level says you're not in bubble trouble, you're ready for the third screw — and all

the other screws. But if, after tightening the second screw, the standard is for some reason now not level, then you have to curse and remove the second screw, and, after re-plumbing, put a new second screw where you would otherwise have put a third screw. And then see whether *that* is plumb, and if it is proceed with further screws. If the standard is plumb, mark all the other screw holes and then drill them. (If you're putting in fasteners that aren't wood screws, you just remove the second screw prior to drilling so that the standard swings free again. Exception: If you're putting in toggle bolts you can't take the second screw all the way out because the toggle will fall off behind the wall. The only thing to do is loosen both the first and the second screw somewhat and then sort of shove the standard out of the way to drill the other screw holes.)

6. Put the other screws in, but before tightening them, tighten screws number one and two first — because they're the ones you know are plumb. (If the second screw you put in wasn't plumb, and you had to put a new second screw somewhere else, put a screw in the old number two hole last. When everything else has been secured, this screw will now be forced to enter the wrong hole at the right angle.)

7. Do everything again with the second standard — starting with putting the top of the standard at the top. The ideal distance between standards is probably 32 inches. When you're fastening to wood studs, 32 inches is, of course, the precise distance between three studs. When you're not fastening to wood studs, 32 inches still happens to be just about the right span for holding up heavy books on a shelf made of ¾-inch-thick plank. Three feet is the maximum except if you're not going to put anything on the shelf heavier than a single, perfect rose. In that case, you can allow yourself a span of up to 48 inches. You need to make sure that the shelves are level, and the way to do this is to put a bracket on the first standard, and put a bracket on the exact same slots of the second standard. Then you put your level between the two brackets before you put any screws into the second standard.

8. Third standard — same procedure as second standard. And the same goes for any other standards.

9. Brackets.

10. Shelves.

# Four

# Painting and Other Surfacing

The origin of painting was fear. People painted their bodies so that they could go around frightening other people. The Ancient Britons painted themselves bright blue and succeeded in terrifying the Romans for some time. The origin of house painting was snobbishness. Calvin Caveman moved out of his cave into an artificial cave, and changed his name to Condominium. The artificial cave was a wooden shelter that leaked when it rained. It also wore out quickly, because the rain rotted the wood. This was distressing, and Mrs. Condominium talked about returning to the cave, so Calvin went down to the local tar pit and picked himself up some tar and spread it all over the outside of his house. Well, the tar stopped the leaks, and it preserved the wood, and it lasted about twenty years, until Calvin's son, Cranbert Condominium, went off to school to Cave City and learned how to be a decorator. Cranbert came home for Christmas, took one look at the tar house, and said, "Oh, *Ghod*, how embarrassing!" So, being an inventive youth, he looked around and found some powdery red dust, mixed it up with some mastodon fat, and shmeered it on the house, thus repainting the house. So Cranbert became the first shmeerer, which is what house painters are called even today. Modern shmeerers paint houses for the same reasons Cranbert did: (1) Paint protects houses, (2) paint makes houses pretty.

Paint is pigment suspended in a vehicle. "Pigment" means little flakes of color. The pigment Cranbert used was iron oxide — the same pigment still used to make red paints red. It's an expensive pigment — Cranbert had expensive tastes — and that's one of the reasons why red paints are more expensive than other paints. A "vehicle" is any liquid that can carry paint flecks. Mastodon fat, Cranbert's vehicle, was made of oil — and oil is a very good vehicle for pigments and still the most common one around. Any liquid that will carry pigment will do — we actually know a guy who used to use chicken fat as a vehicle. Many modern paints use water as a vehicle.

"Suspended" means that the little bits of pigment are hanging around in the vehicle like bits of apple, pear, and banana in fruit

Jell-O. They are not all at the top or all at the bottom. The vehicle in paint is somewhat gooier than Jell-O, so the pigment does eventually settle to the bottom, which is why you have to stir paint before you use it. If you dissolve something in a liquid instead of suspending it — think of stirring sugar into tea — it disappears. One of the reasons water has only recently been widely used as a paint vehicle is that water tends to dissolve pigments, and the problem of how to suspend pigments in water has only recently been solved. The solution hit upon was adding a rubberized compound to the pigments and the water, and it's for this reason that paints that use water for a vehicle, or base, are called latex paints. Oil-based paints are called either oil paints or enamel paints or alkyd paints.

Another problem with using water as a vehicle is that water dries too fast. When paint is dry, it isn't good anymore, because when it's completely dry it has lost its elasticity. When you put a coat of paint on a wall, you are coating the wall with about three mils of paint — a mil being 1/1000 inch. (Three mils is thinner than a sheet of newspaper.) The surface of that coat of paint only stays wet for a little while — the time it takes to put up and take down all the Wet Paint signs. The mils underneath the surface stay wet — remain a liquid — for quite some time: a year in the case of latex paints, three years in the case of enamel paints. Now, this is important because the wall is getting bigger and smaller all the time, thanks to the seasons of the year. It gets bigger in the heat of the summer, smaller in the cool of the fall, bigger again in the fierce steam heat of winter, smaller again in the gently wafting zephyrs of spring. The Empire State Building grows several inches every summer.

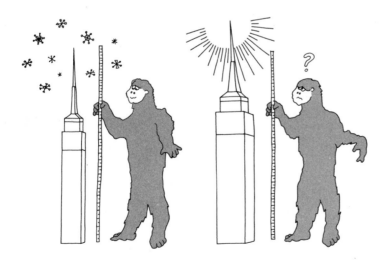

A wall in your house will expand and contract only a fraction of an inch, but unless the paint on it can move as it does, the paint will crack. In technical terms, the paint has to have the same coefficient of thermal expansion as the wall in order to be able to stretch as the wall stretches. The paint will only retain this ability as long as it's wet underneath. As soon as it dries out it develops hairline cracks. If paint develops cracks on the outside of a house, water sneaks in behind the cracks, and then the paint starts to flake off. Whenever you see paint flaking, that's what's happening.

So, oil paints are far better than latex paints. Oil paints dry so much more slowly. In addition, it takes only a thin coat of oil paint to cover a wall and a far thicker coat of latex paint. This brings up another thing. As you paint and repaint and rerepaint with any paints, oil or latex, the paint will eventually crack anyway. The paint will be so thick that it won't be able to have any elasticity. If you pull on a thin sheet of Saran Wrap it will stretch. If you tried to pull on a sheet of Saran Wrap ¼ inch thick it just wouldn't budge.

When paint gets too thick it cracks in a pattern of little squares called an alligator, after the handbags of the same name. There's no way to cover up an alligator. If you add another coat of paint, you are just making the paint thicker. So the only solution to alligatoring is to remove the paint.

Paint buildup also causes paint to crack away from a wall. The only thing that holds paint to a wall is the surface tension between the wall and the first layer of paint, and if you put on five or six coats, you're asking a hell of a lot of that surface tension. That means you should paint as infrequently as possible. Too many layers of paint is a real bad idea. Now, this only applies to paint indoors. Outdoor paint wears itself away — but we will get to that in a minute.

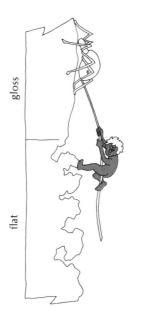

There's another difference between oil and latex paints. Latex paints are made with very large pigments — relatively speaking, very large. All pigments are pretty tiny, but the pigments in latex paints have to be bigger than the pigments in oil paints so that they won't dissolve. The pigments in oil-based paints can be almost as small as you like because the oil doesn't want to swallow them up. If you were small enough, you could see what we mean. Here, thanks to the miracle of subminiaturization, you have become ⅛ mil tall and are skimming over the surface of the wall you just painted. We will say that you painted the top half of that wall with an enamel paint, the bottom half with a latex paint. As you can see, the top half of the wall is a bright rolling plain, full of waves and bumps, not flat at all; but look at the bottom half: a desolate, mountainous, big-pigment region of crags and dark pits and peaks and lightless hidden valleys.

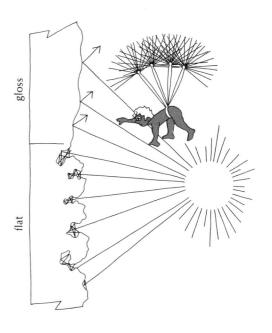

The top half of the wall is bright because, being relatively smooth, it reflects most of the light that hits it. The bottom half can only reflect some light — the rest is trapped in all the holes and ledges. This is the difference between shiny paint and not-so-shiny paint. One has quite a smooth surface, the other one doesn't.

Paints are available in a number of degrees of shininess. The four basic ones are: high gloss, semi-gloss, satin, and flat. Flat isn't shiny at all. Because of their pigments, latex paints only come in semigloss and flat. You can get enamel paints in the whole range. Flat enamel paint has a rougher surface than glossy enamel paint, but enamel surfaces are never as rough as latex surfaces, so a flat enamel surface always has a bit of gloss to it.

There's a difficulty with flat paints. The holes in a flat paint surface don't look very big once you've returned to normal size —

in fact, you can't see them — but they're just the right size for dust particles. The old dust particles drift in the window and see the holes and say, "Oh, here's a place to sit, and here's *another* place to sit, and here's ANOTHER place to sit. Glory in the morning." And they move in and live very happily in the holes, and they are very hard to dislodge, whereas on a glossy surface they have no place to adhere. And if they *do* try to settle down on a glossy surface, you can wash them right off.

This means:

We will use high gloss paints on all walls that we want to stay clean — like bathroom walls and kitchen walls.

We will also use high gloss paint on all places that are likely to get dirty — like windowsills, and doors, and door frames — because then we can scrub these places.

Three more points about flat paint:

1. The unevenness of flat paint surfaces means that the paint is three mils thick in some places but only a mil and a half thick in others. It will dry quicker in the low places and, hence, tend to crack quicker in such spots.

2. When you wash flat enamel paint, you will wear down the tops of the ridges in the surface, thus making the whole surface smoother — and glossier.

3. When you wash flat enamel paint, you will also take off chunks of pigment from the low places, leaving a very thin covering. Sometimes you can start to see through the thinnesses.

One more point about latex paint:

1. You can't scrub latex paint, period. Some of the pigments, no matter how big they are, will dissolve in the water you slosh on. *Doucement.*

There are two different categories of oil and water paints: exterior paint and interior paint. Exterior paints are more elastic than interior paints. They have to be; the outside of your home expands and contracts a lot more than the inside does. Exterior paints have more permanent pigments than interior paints. They have to; the sun bleaches pigments, and it can do a better job of bleaching outdoors. Exterior paints, curiously enough, are more expensive than interior paints. They also have more odor than interior paints.

The best kind of exterior paint is something called self-cleaning, or chalking, paint. You put on three layers of paint. The first layer goes on raw wood, that is to say, unfinished wood, and is known as a prime coat. It's about a mil thick. Then, when the primer is completely dry, you put on a second and a third coat. Each coat will be three mils thick. The months pass. The paint dries at about the rate of half a mil a year. When it dries, it turns back into the powder it was before it got mixed up with a vehicle. Now, this is OK, because while the top half-mil of paint has been drying, dust has been collecting on it. And when the top half-mil of paint turns to powder, the rain comes along and washes it and the dust away, leaving a clean surface underneath, which itself is just waiting to dry, collect dust, turn to powder, and get washed away.

In about three or four years, all the paint has been washed away.

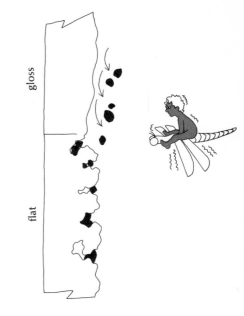

gloss

flat

That's good, too, because by then it would have been time to re-paint the outside of the house anyway, no matter what kind of paint you put on in the first place. Any other paint would still be there, of course, but it would be all dirty. Self-chalking paint is strictly an exterior paint. You really couldn't even think of using it indoors, because you just wouldn't want to brush up against it. Self-chalking paint comes in both latex and enamel, but remember that exterior wood trim should be painted with glossy paint, and glossy paint ain't available in latex nohow.

For reliable national brands see publications such as *Consumer Reports*.

Nearly every paint store also stocks its own brand of paint — Joe's Paint or Señor Paint or something like that. The house brand is invariably much cheaper than the national brands — it goes for maybe $2 a gallon. Sometimes (meaning 25 percent of the time), the house brand is good paint. Sometimes (meaning the other 75 percent of the time), the house brand is just junk. The difference between good and bad paint is: Bad paint has a kind of transparency to it when you use it and requires a lot of coats. Good paint is like butter. Bad paint is like margarine. Good paint is yummy, and just a pleasure to slap on. It goes into corners perfectly, and it adheres to surfaces immediately. This may sound mystical, but when you paint you'll know what we mean.

Now, as we'll soon see, the way to paint inside is to put two coats of paint on a wall, an undercoat, called a prime coat, and a finish coat. The prime coat can be of any kind of paint as long as it's flat. What you might do is buy enough house brand paint for the prime coat and see what it's like. If it's OK, then use it for the finish coat, too. If it's not OK, buy some good paint.

A precautionary measure: If you're going to use more than a single gallon of paint for any painting job, get the store to mix all the paint together. No two containers of paint contain the same color paint. The paint in them may come from the same batch of paint, and the two cans may even have the same batch number, as it's called, printed on them. The colors will be different, anyway. One can may have come from the top of the batch, the other can from the bottom.

When you get paint, you also need to get a solvent — something that can dissolve paint. You'll need it for thinning the paint, for washing off your hands, for cleaning off the brushes. Solvents are things akin to the vehicles in paints. The solvent for latex paint is water — no purchase necessary. The solvents for enamel paint are any of the refined oil products, namely, gasoline, kerosene, turpentine, and subturpentine. Of these four, gasoline gets the nod. It's the most effective, it's the cheapest (well, it was when we wrote these words), and it's also quite safe to have around the house.

*Note:* Gasoline is quite safe to have around the house *if* it's kept in a tightly closed metal container, and *if* the container is kept away from *heat*, and *if* the can is vented. Room temperature heats up gasoline so that it makes fumes. The fumes need to be let out so they won't blow up things.

The second cheapest solvent is subturpentine, which is just like

| Type of Paint Vehicle | Surface | Application | Drying Time | Thinner | Weather Resistance |
|---|---|---|---|---|---|
| Oil (generally linseed oil) | Wood, masonry | Brush, spray, roller | 48–72 hrs. | Turpentine | Good |
| Alkyd resin *Synthetic oil vehicles* | Wood (flat), masonry | Brush, spray, roller | 24 hrs. | Mineral spirits Naphtha | Good |
| Vinyl (*polyvinyl acetate emulsion paints*) | New masonry | Brush, spray, roller | 1 hr. | Special | Excellent |
| Rubber | Masonry | Brush, spray | 1 hr. | Special | Excellent |
| Enamel (*varnish vehicle*) | Wood | Brush, spray, roller | 6–24 hrs. | Turpentine or mineral spirits | Good |
| Latex | Wood | Brush, roller | 1 hr. | None | Very good |

Table 16. General Paint Types

turpentine except for its color. Turpentine is clear and subturpentine is sort of an off-yellow color. Calling it subturpentine is like calling wholewheat bread subbread. Clear turpentine is very expensive, and you should probably avoid it unless you are painting a car or a fine old lacquered cabinet. The difference is that *subturp* can discolor the paint slightly. Kerosene has a little bit of oil in it, and this makes it less effective as a solvent than gas.

Certain paints require a thing called odorless paint thinner. And that's nothing but a special kind of refined oil or hydrocarbon distillate, as they say, that doesn't stink.

A solvent is the kind of commodity that costs as much to package as it does to make. So the way to buy solvent is to take your own container to the hardware store and say, "Fill 'er up." You can get your own gallon can filled with subturpentine for about 35 cents. The alternative is to buy a half-pint of turpentine in the manufacturer's can for 80 cents. Table 16 is a synopsis of paint types and properties.

# Tools

The key to good painting is good tools — and that means quality tools. There is only one thing more important than a good tool, and that is the person using it. Recently, we were able to obtain an exclusive interview on the subject of purchasing quality painting tools with Mr. O. Paik Lacker, a distinguished paint contractor who has in his possession a brush and a roller with which he has painted 103 gas stations in the last six years. (He is now trying to line up some jobs painting train stations.)

Q. Mr. Lacker, how do you buy quality painting tools?

A. You're asking me? I haven't bought painting tools in years. I got one brush and one roller that're going to last me a lifetime. But if you want to know, the difference between good tools and bad tools is the difference between the front of the paint store and the back of the paint store.

Q. What do you mean?

A. Wait. First I'll tell you how to buy bad tools. Go to the front of the store. They have there a display counter with a painting kit for $1.98, maybe $2.98, and it's got a roller and a handle for the roller and a little tray for the roller, my goodness everything you need, all in one package, and all covered with plastic. And so cheap! And right next to the kit is a brush, only 79 cents. It's so easy to buy crummy tools; and then you get them home and go to work; and the roller from the kit is so narrow, you're painting everything over and over again; and the handle is very thin, and it keeps bending; and the roller fits onto the handle with a wing nut that gets all full of paint, so you can't unscrew it, or you can unscrew it and then you can't screw it on again; and there's no support in the middle of the roller, so it starts to sag; and then you're only painting two stripes of paint, like the lady on TV who thinks she's testing a new type of mop; and you can't push down too hard on the roller to make the middle paint again, because then the thin little handle is going to bend some more. Also the roller itself is very thin and made out of some funny material that doesn't carry much paint so you have to go back to the paint tray after every swipe. And then you try to clean the roller, and the nap on the roller just peels away like cellophane. So you throw the whole kit away and take up your brush, and the brush doesn't carry paint well, either, and it paints all unevenly, and it keeps shedding little hairs all over the wall, which you spear out with your fingernail, and then it won't clean, and you throw it away. And you either never paint again or you buy good tools.

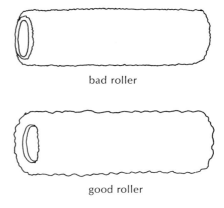

bad roller

good roller

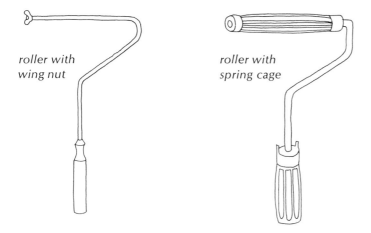

*roller with wing nut*

*roller with spring cage*

Q. And you go to the back of the store?

A. Right, you go to the counter that doesn't have the kits and the bargains. Now, I'll start with brushes, because I like brushes particularly much. There are two kinds of good brushes, one for each kind of paint: nylon brushes for latex paint, natural bristles brushes for enamel paint. You can't use a natural bristle brush for latex paint, because the bristles will get all soft and no good. Now, the best bristles in the whole world are Chinese hog hairs. And they're available, like pandas, because ex-King Richard got relations with China going again. And these Chinese hogs have got very long hairs — 8 inches long — that come to a very nice, sharp point up at the end away from the hog. Now, that's very good, because if you have got one of the bristles on the end of a brush, the little point is going to hold the paint until the brush meets the painting surface, and then the paint is going to flow right off onto the surface. So *look for pointed bristles.* Because what happens, see, is those bristles are so long, the brush manufacturers chop them in half and they put the natural pointed ends in the best brushes, and the blunt chopped ends into not-so-good brushes.

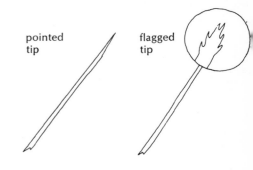

pointed tip

flagged tip

Another characteristic of these remarkable Chinese hogs is that their bristles have tiny little flags near the end — that's tiny little split ends — and they are just great, because they give you a whole lot more little surfaces to carry paint on. So *look for flags.*

*tapered brush*

Now, the next thing that should happen is that the bristles in a good brush should naturally curve and taper up to a point. This means the bristles are shorter at the edges and longer toward the middle. This makes painting a whole lot easier, so *look for tapering bristles.* A good brush should be 3 inches wide, with the bristles about 1½ times as long as the brush is wide, so *look for a brush that's 3 inches wide with bristles 4½ inches* long. This will be the only size brush you need for everything you're going to do, short of painting oil paintings. The next characteristic of a good brush is that *you should be able to take the bristles apart and not see the bottom.* That's a measure of how dense the bristles are. The more bristles there are, the happier you are, because that way you can carry the maximum amount of paint on your brush, and the thing that takes a long time in painting is going back to get more paint. *So look for a brush where you can't see the bottom of the bristles.*

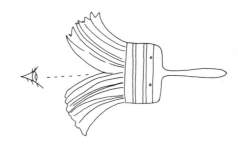

Can you see bottom when bristles are spread apart? No? Good.

The next thing you should do, if you've found a brush that has passed all these tests, is *beat the brush up and down a few times on a table to see if any bristles come out.* They shouldn't. Because if they come out now, then they are going to come out when you are painting, which means fingernail time.

Finally, *the handle should have a hole in it,* so you can hang up the brush. You have to be able to hang up the brush, because the only professional way to store brushes is to hang them in motor oil. Don't be squeamish. You don't want the bristles to dry up, do you? Put a stick or a piece of coat hanger through the hole, suspend the brush in a jar, DON'T let the bristles touch bottom or they're going to bend out of shape, and insert into the jar just enough oil to cover all the bristle area. *Voilà!* You can leave it in there for a week, a year, and it will emerge fresh and supple, with its proper shape. Store it lying down, and it's going to forever assume the shape of whatever it's lying down on. So don't do that.

*Q.* Mr. Lacker, you have told us more than there is to know.

*A.* Wait, I'm not finished. What about the cost? This brush is going to cost you $7 to $12 to $15 and you're not interested? It's going to last you a lifetime, you know. Also, if you're buying nylon, a good nylon brush has artificially flagged and pointed bristles so it will behave just like real pigs. Look for these things.

*Q.* What about rollers?

*A.* Simple. The only kind of roller worth your attention is a *spring cage roller.* You can use it for either enamel or latex paint. It's got a real thick-gauge metal wire frame, and a thin metal cage set on ball bearings that spins around easily. The cage holds the roller on, and it also fights against the middle of the roller so it can't sag and so the paint can roll on easily. The handle has a threaded metal end, which is terrific, because it means you can screw an extension handle onto the handle, and that gives you a big lever advantage. You can paint without pushing like hell on the roller, and you can paint without constantly stretching up and bending down. Just stand a few steps farther away from the wall and let the lever action of the extension handle do all the pressing work for you. You can reach from ceiling to floor, and you can even paint a ceiling without climbing up on a ladder — if it's a reasonably low ceiling. Believe me, you don't want to climb up and down a ladder if you can help it. Very cumbersome occupation.

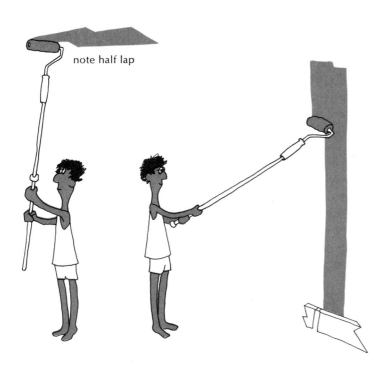

note half lap

You *will* need a ladder for corners, so here's some ladder advice. Ladders are either wood or aluminum. For painting outside, always use a wood ladder. An aluminum ladder will blow over in the wind with you on it. Inside, you can use aluminum. Get the strongest and most expensive aluminum ladder. A lightweight cheap one is going to self-destruct into component parts after you've climbed up and down it ten times.

What else? A roller for enamel paint should be made out of lamb's wool. Rollers for latex paint are made out of miracle fibers — Orlon and Dynel. Dynel is the miracle fiber that's just exactly like human hair, almost. They make wigs out of it. Any roller should have a nap of about ½ inch — meaning the lamb's wool should be about ½ inch thick. You'd need a longer nap for a rough surface. For instance, for a chain-link fence you'd use a 1¼-inch nap. For a very smooth surface — a very glossy finish — you can get a roller made of mohair. A good roller has a core that has been impregnated with plastic. Look for that. If the core is just paper, the paper is going to dissolve after a while. The roller should be tapered at one end, so that when you're painting in a corner, you can point the tapered end at the corner and squash down on the roller and not build up a little edge of paint that flips onto the other wall. The roller should be 9 inches long. The roller tray should be about 10 inches wide — so that the roller will fit into it — and that's the only thing you need to know about roller trays. Get as cheap a tray as they've got, they all work fine. Cost? Maybe $4 for the cage and handle, $2, $2.50 for the roller, another few dollars for the extension handle, a dollar for the tray. Like the good brush, the good roller is kept in the back of the store. You may even have to ask for it. Do so. It's worth it, and it's going to last you a lifetime. Good painting to you!

Q. Thank you, Mr. Lacker.

A. Listen, I just thought of something. There's a product called *Pro-tek*, a miracle, one of the great things of the twentieth century, like plastic garbage bags and Master Charge. Pro-tek is an invisible glove. You put it on your hands, and paint can't get through it, oil can't get through it. It's made of lanolin. The only thing that gets through it is water. You can put on some Pro-tek and dig your hand into a bucket of paint, take out your hand and wave it about and let the paint dry, walk over to the sink and run a little water on your hands, and ten seconds later they're clean like a baby — when a baby's clean. If your hands get a little dry after using it, rub in a little Vaseline. Pro-tek is good for working on your car, too. Isn't it delightful? It's expensive in small cans and cheap in big cans. You can buy a gallon for a dollar — and guess what? Now you don't have any more excuses for not using enamel paint. Hah, hah. Too bad.

Well, we're ready to paint. There are three parts to painting: surface preparation — which means getting a surface ready to receive paint — painting, and cleaning up. Surface preparation is the horrible part. It takes up 80 percent of the time you're going to spend on painting, and it's very tiresome work. (Painting itself will account for 10 percent of the painting time. Cleaning up ditto.) But you just have to prepare the surface properly, because if you don't, you'll have a tough time applying paint, and the paint you put on will peel off very quickly. And then you'll just have to reread this chapter and start all over again.

So here goes. Grrrrruff. You prepare a surface by making it clean and free from any loose anything — paint or plaster or dirt. The first thing you do is cover the floor and the furniture and anything you don't want to get dirty, plastery, or painty. And the second thing you do is take a scraper or a wire brush and scrape off all the loose paint you can find. A scraper looks just like a putty knife, but it has a blade you can't bend.

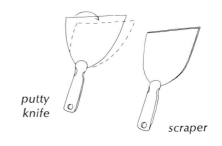

putty knife

scraper

Paint loosens around places where it has cracked, and it loosens and cracks because the person who painted before you didn't prepare the surface properly. If you want to remove all the paint from a surface, use heat. To do this you can either get an electric paint remover, an implement that looks like an iron, or you can put a flame spreader on a propane torch. The flame spreader keeps the flame from scorching the paint and cooks the paint under the surface into a blister. Then you scrape off the goo. If you're removing paint from a wood surface with heat, apply the heat and scrape in the direction of the grain. It's a very simple process, and the only time you have to be cautious is when you're taking paint off a wood surface with a thin veneer (or working next to glass or flammable — inflammable? — flammable liquids). If you aren't cautious you may take the veneer right off with the paint.

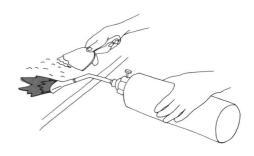

A torch, by the way, is a very useful little tool, and costs about $10. You can use it on a nut that's frozen onto something, and you can charm cranky plumbing fixtures into relaxing their grip. Wallpaper is removed with steam. And that means a steam jenny, a classic little machine whose picture appears in the 1904 Sears, Roebuck catalogue. It has a little boiler that you fill with kerosene. Connect it up with a hose and a water supply and it produces steam for you. The steam melts the glue on the wallpaper.

Next step. Wash the whole wall down. Dissolve a cup of trisodium phosphate in a gallon of lukewarm water. Trisodium phosphate is a fat. Fats are used as cleaning agents because fat molecules take one look at dirt and say, "I only have eyes for you." And they latch right on to the dirt, and the dirt is attached to the fat molecules instead of the wall molecules. Which is how soaps and detergents remove dirt. Trisodium phosphate used to be the business end of all detergents until people got upset about phosphates, but you should still be able to get it at any paint store if you ask for it quietly. It's what you need. After you wash, you rinse with clear water. A sponge mop — a floor mop — will do both jobs very well. It could be that when you've got the wall washed and rinsed you'll decide that it looks fine now and you don't want to paint after all. This has been known to happen.

Now, there's one thing you cannot do, and that is paint flat paint directly over glossy paint. You cannot because glossy paint is smooth and the flat paint can't adhere to it. So if you wish to cover an existing surface with paint that is to any degree less glossy, you have to roughen up that surface — or "cut a tooth" in it, as shmeerers say. You cut a tooth by washing the walls with a saturated solution of trisodium phosphate and water. A saturated solution is when, instead of putting a cup of trisodium phosphate in a gallon of water, you tilt the box into the bucket of water, turn your head, and keep dumping in the trisodium phosphate. When the water is carrying as much phosphate as it can, and you can't get another particle to dissolve, and the phosphate floats on the surface of the water, the solution is saturated. So if you want to paint semi-gloss on a glossy wall, or satin on a semi-gloss wall, or flat on a satin wall, you might as well start out by washing with a saturated solution. Rinse with clear water after you've finished the saturated wash, and then wash again with an ordinary mix of phosphate and water — a cup to a gallon. And then rinse again. Walls have to be rinsed thoroughly, because if there's any detergent residue at all, the paint will slide right off the fats.

When you've finished rinsing you'll notice that your wall looks a little lumpy in places — where you scraped off loose paint and where washing and rinsing took off some paint. Greatly exaggerating, as is our wont, these places on the wall look like this drawing.

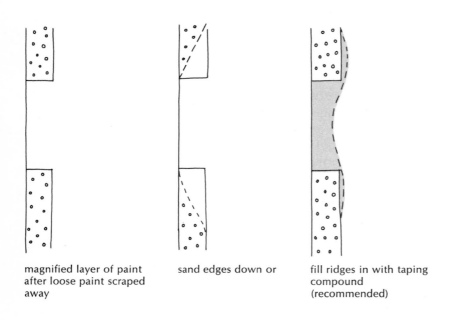

magnified layer of paint after loose paint scraped away

sand edges down or

fill ridges in with taping compound (recommended)

If you just ignore these places and paint away, you'll be sorry, because the light in the room will cast a shadow on the edges of these places, and then you'll see them, and be filled with guilt, remorse, and embarrassment (if you still feel these things). You can do one of two things. The hard thing you can do is sand the edges of the paint. This is hard because paint doesn't sand very well and because then you have dust all over the place that takes forever to clean up. The easy thing you can do is to fill the hole with a little *taping compound*. So what's a taping compound? It's a form of plaster that's better than plaster because it's ready-mixed, doesn't dry before you get it on the wall, and has a little oil in it, so that it spreads easily and forms a smooth surface. For $7.50 you can get a 5-gallon can that weighs almost 50 pounds. You spread on taping compound with a taping knife — that's a putty knife that's 6 inches wide or so with a bendable blade. You have plenty of time to spread it out, smooth it down, and feather the edges —

meaning breaking up the line of the edges by going back and forth over them so that the edges aren't ridges. Then let the taping compound dry and sand it just a bit. You have to sand it just a bit because, like any plaster product, it develops cracks when it drys. If you put the taping compound on thin, these cracks will only be hairline cracks. So then you put on another very thin layer of taping compound just to fill in those little cracks. And this time, when it dries, there won't be any cracks. So you just sand it a little bit more, and it sands very easily.

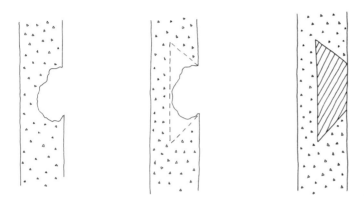

If you have a medium-size hole to fill, undercut it before filling it. This means take your scraper and rub it around the bottom of the inside of the hole to create a hole that's bigger at the bottom than at the top. This is what a dentist does when he is filling your teeth, and he does it — and you do it — because otherwise the plug that's inserted will fall out when it dries. Taping compound — and fillings — tend to shrink a little as they dry. When you have undercut the hole, fill it up to the top with taping compound and wait for it to dry. Being a big chunk of taping compound it will have big cracks in it when it drys. So you'll need two finishing coats. Sand the chunk, apply a thin coat, feather it, and wait for it to dry. Now it will only have hairline cracks, so put on a final thin coat of taping compound, let it dry, and sand once more. This all takes time, but it's the right way to do things.

If you have a really big hole to fill, you can either fill it after undercutting it by layering in taping compound about seven or eight times to build up to the proper thickness or you can cut out a piece of Sheetrock and nail it in the hole, and just go over the Sheetrock with taping compound until you have a smooth surface. Layering is probably your best bet.

The final part of surface preparation is *spot priming*. All this is is painting the places you have plastered with a thinned-down version of the paint you're about to use on the wall. The plastered places are much more porous than the rest of the wall, and they want to soak up a lot more paint. Spot priming gives them the paint they want, and then when you paint the wall, you get a uniform surface. Feather, with your brush, the edges of the spots you spot prime, so that the spot blends in with the rest of the surface. There is a special kind of priming paint, called *primer,* that you can use for priming. Primer has an alcohol base and dries very quickly. But a thinned-down version of your regular paint works just as well.

Before you paint, take off the rectangular plates around the electric light switches and outlets (see Chapter Six if you need help).

Now, how do you paint? Well, there are two parts to painting — brushwork and rollerwork. Windows, window frames, doors, moldings, baseboards, trim, and corners get painted with a brush. The big blank places in between them get painted with a roller. The brushwork is known as cutting in, a term that refers to painting edges and straight lines, and to using a brush like a knife. We'll get to that technique in a minute. OK, you have a choice of two approaches to these two parts. You can do either the brushwork or the rollerwork first. You can be a tortoise or a hare. Guess who wins? The hare gets out his roller, rolls the whole apartment, gets that finished in a couple of hours, steps back and says, "Look at all I've done! Think I'll step out for a cup of coffee." He comes back in another couple of hours; all that's left are those few little places that need to be painted with a brush. Picks up the brush, and he's still painting at two o'clock in the morning. Must be the wrong approach. Why? Part of his problem is the phenomenon known as drag. The paint from the places where the roller's previously been is drying; and when hare pulls his brush across these places, the drying paint, very noticeably, pulls back on the brush. Very tiring. There's an incredible difference between painting on an unpainted surface and painting on a just-painted-and-starting-to-dry surface. Another thing, it's very hard to get a smooth surface when you paint with a brush over a just-rolled surface.

So you have to be a tortoise, the guy who does all the brushwork first and who knows how to cut in properly. That way you start painting at noon, and by about four o'clock the brushwork is done, and you look up and say, "My God, I've worked all day, and I haven't done anything," because you've only painted the doors and the little windows and places like that, and there are all those acres of unpainted walls left over. All right, but then you take out your trusty roller, and half an hour later you're completely finished. For good.

So. The sequence for brushwork is this. Start with all the little guys. All the little moldings on the inside of the windowpanes. Work your way out to the outside of the window frame. Same with doors. If you have a door that has little panels in it, paint the little panels first. Then paint around the panels, and paint the edge of the door, the door frame, and around the outside of the door frame. Then paint all the trim in the room, all the corners (rollers can't get into corners), corners in the ceiling, the top edge of the walls just below the ceiling (if the ceiling is going to be a different color), and the baseboards of the room. Remember that at least the windows and door frames and baseboards should be painted with enamel paint, but we think it's best to paint everything with an oil-base paint.

Remember that a new, unpainted metal or wood door has to be primed before you paint.

Oh, yessss. One tip. Paint from the top down. Paint flows down, you know.

With this sequence in mind, you're ready to begin painting. The first thing you do is — open the paint. If you're using oil-base paints, cover your hands with Pro-tek (and if you're not, don't), and take an old screwdriver — the screwdriver with a little chip in it, you know, the screwdriver you had before you started reading this book — and pry off the lids of the paint cans. The next thing to do is take a nail and a hammer and punch some holes in the lips of the paint cans. By lips we mean the rims on which the lids sit. You do this unexpected thing because paint tends to accumulate in the lips, or rims, of paint cans, and if you put holes in a rim the paint can drip back down into the can. If there's no way for paint to drip, it just sits in the rim, and then there's no way for the can to seal properly when you come to put the lid back on after painting. An unsealed can can't preserve paint, and so if you don't knock holes in the rim the first time you open the can you'll find, when you go to open it up again a month later, nothing but crud inside — crud, with a big thick film on top. And you can't use that to paint.

Mixing comes next. It's always a good idea to mix your paint, even if you're only using a single gallon of paint. Because pigment, being heavier than paint, tends to settle to the bottom of a can. You mix paint by pouring, not by stirring. Pouring is quicker than stirring, and more positive. Buy yourself two plastic buckets. Plastic buckets cost 39 cents apiece. Paper buckets are only a quarter a throw, but you have to throw them away, as soon as you've used them once. The second bucket is for your solvent, whatever it is — water or kerosene or gasoline or whatever. The first bucket is for mixing and for painting. Pour the paint, back and forth, from can to bucket four or five times, until it's mixed.

Now pour the proper amount of paint into the paint bucket. The proper amount is just enough paint to cover half the length of the bristles of your brush when the brush touches bottom. You will be painting from the bucket, not from the can. Many painters paint from the can. They dip their brush into the can, and then they wipe their brush, very carefully, against the inner edge of the rim of the can. This is very bad, because it takes almost all of the paint that's just been put onto the brush off of the brush. It also builds up paint on the rim of the can. You do need to get some paint off the brush, of course, so the brush won't drip. Hence the bucket. Dip the brush into the bucket, pick it up above the paint, and then slap it back and forth once or twice against the side of the bucket. The slapping will remove the paint that wants to drip and leave on the brush all the paint it can hold. You can't slap in a can.

There's an amazing thing about painting with a brush. You can paint an exact straight line. You do it by means of the bead technique. Here's a description of how to perform the bead technique. When you've finished reading it, give up, and look at the pictures. You'll find that it's a little harder than it looks but a lot easier than it sounds. Pick up your brush as though you were wearing a *mitten* — a device which turns five fingers into two and keeps them warm. Grasp the handle of the brush with your thumb on one side and the tips of your other four fingers on the other side, and hold it so that the flat side of the brush is facing you. Your whole hand is at a 45-degree angle to the axis of the brush. The bristles of the brush point down.

To paint up to a horizontal straight line, hold the brush parallel to the line and below it. Press the brush against the wall and push it slightly so that the middles of the bristles on the top side of the brush bunch out upward toward the line. When you do this, a bead of paint will form at the top edge of the bunching bristles. Pull this bead of paint along with your brush (right to left, left to right, it doesn't matter) about 1/16 inch below the straight line you want to paint. Capillarity will push the bead up 1/16 inch — and you will then have painted an exact straight horizontal line. If your hand doesn't shake.

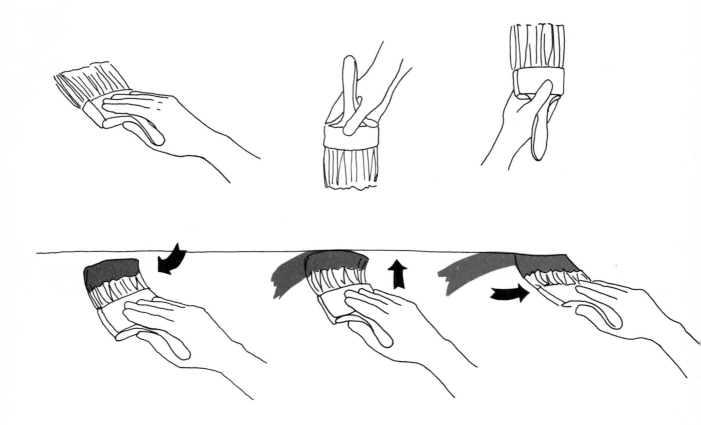

To paint down to a horizontal straight line, hold the brush above and parallel to the line, thumb pointing down, and press the brush against the wall pushing up slightly so that the middles of the bristles on the down side of the brush bulge downward and form a bead. Then follow your bead, and keep it 1/16 inch above the line. Don't let that bead get too big or it will dribble and make you look silly. But don't worry about looking silly. We used to double dribble all over the court. Just practice a few times and you'll get the hang of it.

Vertical straight lines are much easier — if you remember to paint them from the top down so that you can pick up any dribbles.

You can paint up to a vertical straight line either from the left or from the right. It's just like a horizontal line, only sideways.

The bead technique makes it remarkably easy to paint window frames. There's always a little space between the glass in a window and the mullions and muntins, the little strips that hold the glass in the window. You can run a bead up close to the edge of a mullion, and capillarity will pull the bead up to the edge and around the corner into the space between mullion and windowpane, thus making a dead smooth line and also sealing the joint as well.

The only alternative to the bead technique is covering up the places you don't want to paint with masking tape. Beware. Masking tape is wayward. Putting it on just right takes time. And then it picks up paint when you take it off and leaves a ragged edge. In fact, it has the horrible property of coming off when you don't want it to and not coming off when you do want it to. We used to use masking tape before we got tipped off to the bead technique, and we can show you a window we painted years ago that's still got masking tape on it. Just couldn't get it off. Not with a razor blade or anything.

There's one other thing you paint with your brush, and that's a little strip of wall. You have to paint a strip 1½ to 2 inches wide around every window and door and molding and baseboard with the brush because that's as close as the roller can get to all of these things. Feather the edge of the strips you paint with the brush so that the brush-roller interface doesn't have ridges.

Roller painting is all fun.

The way to paint with a roller is as follows: Fill up a roller tray with paint. The tray should be on the floor — because now you're of course always using a roller with an extension handle. Roll the roller around in the tray so that it's got as much paint on it as it can hold without dripping, and walk over to the wall. Put the roller on the wall about four roller widths away from one of the feathered strips of wall you painted with the brush. Run it up and down and get the great big gloopy globs of paint off the roller. Then go back to the edge of the brush-painted strip and roll either up or down — it doesn't matter which. When you get to the end of the roll, flip the roller over and half lap your way back (see page 119). Meaning: Instead of moving the roller over one complete lap, you move it over half a lap so that the next roll covers half the first roll. Then continue flipping the roller and half lapping. You should be just running out of paint when you reach the gloopy glob you first put on the wall. Use the roller to spread it out and smooth it out. And then go back and get some more paint, and continue as before. (You keep flipping the roller so it won't get bent out of shape.)

If you're painting the ceiling as well as the walls it makes sense to paint the ceiling first. What happens when you paint a ceiling is that you reach up very high and roll the roller nice and slow. But no matter how slow you go a little paint mist precipitates from the roller as you paint. This spritz winds up on the walls — which is why it makes sense to paint the ceiling first. It also makes sense to wear a hat, because the spritz also winds up on your head. It *also* makes sense to have a good long extension handle on your roller when you paint a ceiling so that you can reach all the way up without killing yourself.

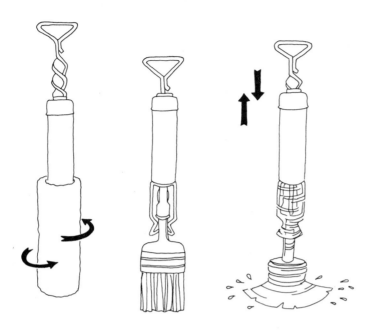

Cleanup time. And time to introduce the pièce de résistance of painting, the *brush and roller spin cleaner*, the gadget that paint stores hate to sell because it actually gets brushes and rollers so clean that you don't have to throw them away. If you don't have a brush and roller spin cleaner, you probably will have to throw them away, because, as everyone knows, you can wash and wash a brush and the paint still keeps oozing out. A spin cleaner is just like the fancy kind of spinning top that has a handle that you push up and down. The spin cleaner has a handle that you push up and down, and when you do the bottom part twirls — and spins off the paint. The thing costs about $7, and it saves you at least three hours of cleanup time.

First soak your brush and your roller in the second bucket you bought, the one that has the solvent in it. Make sure that the solvent gets in among the bristles of the brush. Then attach the brush to the twirling part of the spin cleaner, as shown above, and hold the whole business inside a bucket or a bag or a garbage can. Pull and push the handle of the spin cleaner, and watch the paint fly off. The roller fits right over the twirling part of the spin cleaner, and spins just as clean as the brush. But don't forget to hold the cleaner inside a bucket or a bag or a can.

You don't have to throw your solvent away after cleaning up. It won't work as a thinner anymore, but it's still plenty good for cleaning. When you do want to throw away any enamel paint solvent, get yourself a waste can of some sort and take the gunk to a gas station and ask them if you can pour it in their waste oil place. That way it all gets rerefined and reused and you don't have to be not nice and throw it down the drain into the rivers and lakes.

You don't need a store-bought solvent to clean yourself. If you're painting with latex paint the only solvent you'll need, bien sûr, is water. And if you're painting with enamel paint, you've got Pro-tek on your hands. Which washes off with water.

By the way, the best way to seal up a paint can good and tight is to stand on it. Try not to lose your balance, though, or you'll have to paint the floor — a subject not covered in this chapter.

To sum up, here are

### The Nine Steps of Painting
*(Scientifically arranged logically)*

1. Cover up floor and furniture and everything you don't want to have to paint.
2. Get rid of all loose paint with a scraper or a wire brush.
3. Wash the walls with trisodium phosphate and then rinse them. Use a saturated solution of tsp to cut the tooth *if* you're painting anything *below* over anything *above* on this list:

    Glossy

    Semi-gloss

    Satin

    Flat
4. Fill up all the cracks and holes with taping compound.
5. Spot prime.
6. Remove electrical switch plates and outlet plates.
7. Brushwork. Paint down, pliz. Pro-tek if enamel paint. Stand up on your legs.
8. Rollerwork. Ceiling first. Hat on. Be like two fried eggs.
9. Clean up with brush and roller spin cleaner. Keep your sunny side up.

## Wallpaper and Paneling

The easiest thing you can do to a wall to pretty it up is to paint it, and if you have a wall and you want to do something to it, our advice is: paint it. There *are* two other things you can do to walls, if you don't like advice. And some walls give paint a hard time. Bathroom walls, for instance, get wet. Kitchen walls get greasy. Badly alligatored walls and walls with plaster mumps need a tremendous amount of surface preparation before you can begin to paint.

The two other things you can do to a wall are wallpaper and paneling. They are both dry surfaces that are attached to a wall, unlike paint, which, as we all know, is a liquid that dries into a flexible film and takes the shape of the surface beneath it. Wallpaper, these days, is not just wallpaper. A lot of other materials are getting in on the act — like wallvinyl, wallfoil, wallburlap, wallcork, and wallwhateveryouallwant. Of them all, wallvinyl seems to make the most sense, because it is strong, flexible, very resistant to water, and available in plenty of fancy decorator colors and patterns and textures. A kitchen wall covered with wallvinyl is a pleasure to wash. (Wallvinyl is not such a joy in bathrooms, where water tends to seep behind it.)

*wallpapering tools*

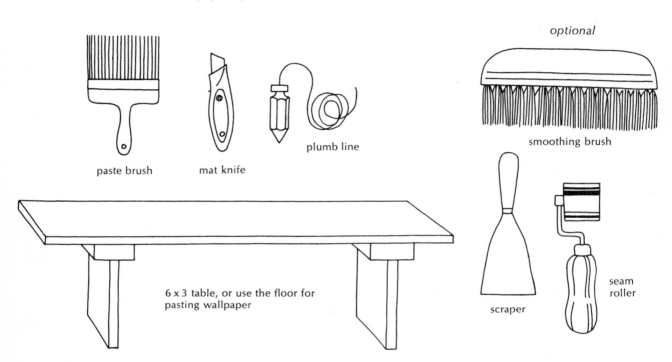

optional

paste brush          mat knife          plumb line

smoothing brush

6 x 3 table, or use the floor for pasting wallpaper

scraper          seam roller

Wallvinyl is subdivided into wallvinylpaperback and wallvinyl-clothback. Cloth backing is stronger and also easier to take off a wall, should you later decide to do something else to the wall. Wallvinyl and wallpaper come in rolls that are, invariably, 27 inches wide. A single roll has about 36 square feet of wallop in it. Then there are double rolls, with 72 square feet of material in them, and triple rolls, 108 square feet big. To know how much wallvinyl you need for a job, you have to know the area of the walls to be covered. You get that figure by multiplying the height (in feet) of each wall by its length (in feet). Don't bother to subtract anything for doors and windows. In fact, if there aren't any doors and windows at all in a wall, you have to increase the area figure by 20 percent — the amount of wallvinyl or wallpaper that always gets wasted through cutting and trimming and making mistakes.

*Suggestion:* Always buy pretrimmed wallpaper. Otherwise you will spend a perfectly good day cutting off unpatterned borders from both sides of various rolls of paper.

### Recipe for Wallpapering

*Ingredients:*   enough wallpaper or wallvinyl or wallsomething (do the arithmetic)

enough adhesive or paste (buy whatever the salesman suggests — it's cheap)

| | |
|---|---|
| 1 scraper | basic tool kit |
| 1 utility knife | ditto |
| 1 plumb bob | ditto |

1 sponge

1 paste brush (not your very good basic tool kit paintbrush)

1 smoothing brush (or a dust brush, or a whisk broom)

1 seam roller

1 pasting table (or pasting floor)

1. Remove loose anything and smooth and feather edges (see the surface preparation pages earlier in this chapter).

   *Note:* Old wallpaper should be removed unless it is very secure. The best way to remove wallpaper is with steam, which means: rent a steam jenny.

2. Plan your attack. Decide how you want the paper to join so that the pattern comes out pleasingly and is emphasized in the places you want. Plan to begin by a window or a door and proceed along the longest unbroken wall. But remember, somewhere there's going to be a seam that doesn't match, no matter what you do. So it's all right.

3. Use a plumb bob with chalk line to get a vertical line. Cherish this line. It is the *only* vertical line in your house (others only look vertical). Use this line as a guide to hang the first length of wallpaper vertically. Make additional vertical lines as required.

4. Cut as many lengths of wallstuff as you feel up to, making certain that the pattern will match on both sides.

5. Remove all switchplates, receptable plates, ceramic roosters, cat clocks, etc., from walls.

6. Turn the first length of wallstuff face down and spread paste over the entire surface. Take great pains to get paste everywhere on the wallstuff, particularly along all the edges.

7. Bring pasted length of wallstuff to wall and, beginning from the top, first align it vertically and then smooth it out, working simultaneously from the top down and from the center to the edges.

8. Trim off excess paper at top and bottom with utility knife. Add a little more paste if required.

9. With a wet sponge, clean off any paste that may have squeezed out the sides or got on the front of the paper.

10. Repeat steps 6 through 9 over, and over, and over.
11. And over.

*Three Helpful Hints*

1. Do as much trimming as possible before applying paste to the paper, but be careful not to overtrim.
2. Cut sheets so they will overlap at corners about ½ inch.
3. Don't worry about slight mismatches over doors and windows. They are unavoidable and people, in general, are quite unobservant.

---

Paneling is the other thing you can do to a wall. It differs from wallpaper by being rigid, and when you put up paneling what you are really doing is building a new wall on top of an old wall — which is why paneling is the quickest way of fixing up a really pathetic wall. There is cork paneling, and there is Formica paneling, and there are tin panels stamped to resemble fancy plasterwork, and there is Sheetrock, which is paneling actually made out of plaster.

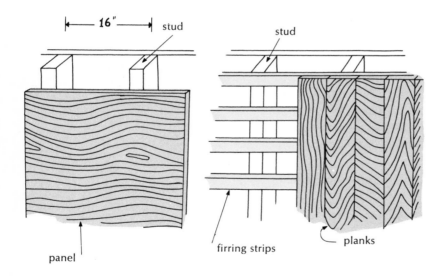

Most paneling resembles wood. Some of it is real wood planks. Most of it, these days, comes in sheets 4 feet by 8 feet. These sheets are made just like plywood. The more expensive sheets have a surface veneer that is scored so that it looks like real planks of wood. Less expensive sheets are made out of pressed sawdust, again with a scored wood veneer. The cheapest sheets of all are pressed sawdust with a photograph of wood pasted onto the surface. The cheap stuff turns out to be OK because it needs next to no upkeep. All paneling goes up vertically.

Recipe for Installing Sheet Paneling

*Ingredients:* enough paneling. Compute required sheets but don't subtract for anything. Sheets come in standard plywood thicknesses (⅜-inch thickness recommended).

enough nails — available in colors to match wood. (Paneling can also be glued but we don't like to.)

1 hammer

1 drill with high-speed steel bit

1 crosscut saw

1 keyhole saw

1 plumb bob

1 nail set

1 level

1 putty stick of appropriate color

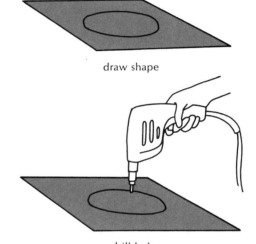

draw shape

drill hole

1. Locate studs. See Chapter Three if you've forgotten how.

1a. When you have no studs, as when covering a brick wall (tsk, tsk) or other masonry wall, firring strips will have to be applied. Firring strips are lengths of 1 × 2 or 1 × 3 lumber applied to the existing surface that will allow you to nail or glue the paneling neatly to them. Firring strips should be put up 16 inches on center vertically for sheet paneling and 16 inches on center horizontally for planking. Use your level and plumb bob liberally here.

2. Make a dry run with the panels to be sure you know what you're doing.

3. Remove all molding from the corner of the ceiling and wall and from the corner of the floor and wall.

4. Starting anywhere where no openings have to be cut, put the first sheet into place. Align it with the plumb bob and then nail it up. Nailing down opposite corners positively locates this sheet.

   *Caution:* Don't let the sides of a sheet hang free, or completely cover a firring strip or a stud. This should not happen if steps 1–1a were done correctly.

5. For all other sheets:

   a. Measure and cut out all openings required for switches, windows, doorways, etc. An inside hole is cut by first drilling a hole and then cutting out the proper opening with your keyhole saw.

   b. Check the panel for proper fit, adjust if necessary, and nail in place.

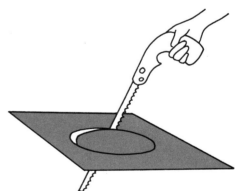

cut shape with compass saw

6. Set all nails, and cover holes with putty stick.

7. Replace ceiling molding and baseboard. This should cover

any discrepancies between your square piece of paneling and your not-so-square floors and ceilings.

8. Take a well-deserved vacation.

Floors are special. They have to be extradurable. This means you can't paint them, because paint can't hold up against feet. Wood is nice and hard and makes a fine floor. In fact, you can't beat it. But some people don't like their wood floors. Those people have these choices: 1) They can put up with the wood floors they've got and learn to love them. 2) They can buy area rugs that almost reach the walls. 3) They can get someone to come in and refinish their floors. 4) They can get someone to come in and install a new floor or cover an old floor with vinyl asbestos tiles or with sheet vinyl. 5) They can put down vinyl asbestos tiles by themselves. 6) They can install vinyl floors by themselves. 7) They can move.

Choice number 5 is the only choice other than 1 that doesn't involve a tremendous amount of hard work. Floor tiles were invented because, being small, they are easy to work with and harder to waste than big chunks. Also, you can replace damaged sections of a tile floor without tearing up the whole floor. Tiles are squares, either 9 or 12 inches on a side. You waste more material when you install 12-inch tiles, but you don't have to work so hard. So 12-inch tiles are becoming increasingly popular.

Tiles come in asphalt, vinyl asbestos, vinyl, cork, and wood. We choose vinyl asbestos, because it's pretty cheap, lasts almost as long as vinyl, and is available in hundreds of colors, patterns, textures. *Dirty trick:* Textured, multicolored tiles hide dirt and installation mistakes better than solid-color, smooth tiles.

Sheet vinyl is one of two kinds of sheet material used as a floor surface. A sheet material is like a floor tile, except you cover the whole floor with one big chunk. Linoleum is the second kind of sheet material. It is so cheap that if we told you the price, you'd want to buy it. So we'll just tell you that it's crummy stuff that breaks up and doesn't wear. Sheet vinyl is a composition material that has cushiony stuff on the bottom and a thin sheet of vinyl laminated to the top. It comes in 6-, 9-, and 12-foot widths and in plenty of colors and patterns. You want a vinylslate floor? It exists.

Now, sheet vinyl looks like less work than vinyl asbestos tiles. Big mistake. The whole sheet has to be cut before you put it down on a floor. So you're constantly moving it in and out of a room to make measurements. You can't make mistakes. And then, sooner or later, you do make a mistake. And when you goof you wind up with tile. Great big odd-shaped pieces, of course, but if you've got more than one piece of material on the floor — you've got tile.

*Surface preparation.* Tile and sheet vinyl must be put down on a smooth, dry, clean floor. Old floor coverings should be on good and tight. Peeling paint or tile will only cause peeling tile or bumpy sheet vinyl. Wooden floors must be leveled: loose boards nailed down, missing sections or badly damaged boards filled. All nails must be driven flush.

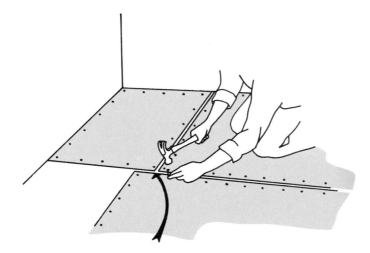

leave space between sheets

In most cases, a good tile installation begins with the installation of a new floor. This new floor is called an underlayment, hardboard or plywood sheets nailed to the existing floor. This levels the floor and assures a clean dry surface. The hardboard or (preferably) plywood should be at least ¼ inch thick, but ⅜ or ½ inch is an even better idea. The sheets should not be butted — shouldn't touch: a very small space (less than 1/16 inch) should be left between all sheets to allow for expansion. Also, stagger the sheets so that four corners never meet. Nails should be of the threaded type to prevent their pulling out, and all nails must be sunk flush.

*Caution:* An underlayment raises the height of your floor. You will certainly need new baseboard molding and you may have to undercut existing doors, and put in new door saddles. (Saddles are what you trip over when walking through a doorway.)

---

Recipe for Installing Tile Floors

*Ingredients:*   enough tile (see step one)

enough adhesive (buy latex adhesive and consult can)

1 notched trowel — a special tool

1 chalk line

1 utility knife

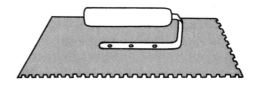

*notched trowel*

1. Measure floor in feet. Get area of floor in square feet. Add 10 percent for waste. If using 12-inch tiles buy that many (each tile is one square foot). If using 9-inch tiles, multiply

by 16 and divide by 9 to get the number you'll need.

*Example:* Floor measures 10 feet by 12 feet. Area is 120 square feet. Add 10 percent of 120, which is 12. Buy 132 tiles if they are 12-inch tiles. If they are 9-inch tiles, multiply by 16 and divide by 9 (16 × 132 = 2112, 2112/9 = 234.5). Buy 235 9-inch tiles.

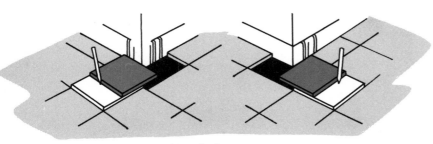

marking tile for a corner

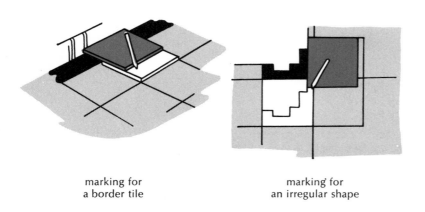

marking for
a border tile

marking for
an irregular shape

2. Remove existing baseboard. Be certain floor is level, clean, and dry. Install underlayment, if necessary.

3. Snap chalk line across the middle of floor in both directions. Lines to be perpendicular to one another and, if possible, parallel to walls.

4. Lay out perpendicular rows of tiles along chalk lines in a dry run. Adjust chalk line so that no row of tiles will be less than 3 inches wide against a wall.

5. Work out from the center spreading adhesive over about 10 square feet at a time. Use the notched side of the trowel to spread adhesive. This gets just enough adhesive on the floor.

6. *Lay* tiles into place. *Sliding* them in forces adhesive to goosh up at the joints and makes everything messy.

7. Repeat steps 5 and 6 until you reach the edges.

8. Measure and cut the tiles for the edges by placing a dry tile directly over an installed tile nearest the wall and use still another tile to mark the right amount to cut.

9. Install edge tiles.

10. Go away for a few days and let the floor and you rest.

---

### Recipe for Installing Sheet Vinyl

*Ingredients:*  enough sheet vinyl

enough metal thresholds (see step 10)

nails or screws for threshold (usually come together)

1 chalk line

1 utility knife

1 pair scissors

1. Lay out sheet vinyl in nearby room so that it may flatten and reach room temperature.

2. Remove baseboard. Be certain floor is level, clean, and dry. Install underlayment, if necessary.

3. When vinyl is good and warm, drag it into the room in which it will live and decide how the pattern will run.

4. Drag vinyl back to other room.

5. With chalk line snap line along the side of sheet vinyl which will be going along the longest wall. Cut this line nice and neat with a utility knife.

6. Measure and transfer location of pipes, bumps, doorways, etc., along first wall and make these cuts, *very carefully,* in sheet vinyl. Make hole ⅛ inch larger than pipes, bumps, doorways, etc.

7. Measure, transfer, and make any large cuts which will have to be made in the sheet — such as·for cabinets or other major projections into the space.
   *Caution:* Do not try to make these cuts precise. Leave yourself some material to trim off later.

8. Drag sheet vinyl into room and lay it down as best you can. Leave about ⅛ inch space along the one side already cut.

9. Material will be curving up at all walls other than first. Gently press down the material in these places forming a valley between wall and floor. Cut along this valley slowly and deliberately and the piece will fall into place as neat as pie. Retain the ⅛-inch gap between wall and sheet vinyl. This gap is to take care of expansion of the sheet vinyl.

10. Install metal thresholds at doorways. This keeps people from tripping over the curled-up sheet vinyl. Do not nail through vinyl.

11. Replace baseboard molding, leaving a little space between

cut to leave 1/8-inch space

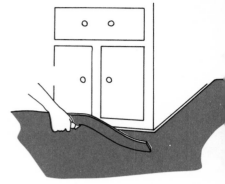

cut to leave 1/8-inch space

it and the top of the sheet vinyl so that the sheet vinyl can move around when it hears the beat.

12. There are metal trim pieces available to go around pipes that will cover up a less-than-perfect fitting job. (We only tell you this so that you can tell your friends how to make their work neater.) Any good hardware store carries them. Measure for the size your friend will need and then pick the style he would like and help him install them.

　　*Caution:* Do not glue any of the sheet vinyl. Just lying there it will level itself out and make itself fit. Glued sheet vinyl will turn into rolling plains.

13. Use tile.

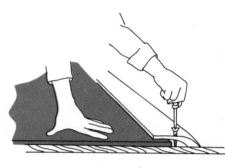

screws not in sheet vinyl

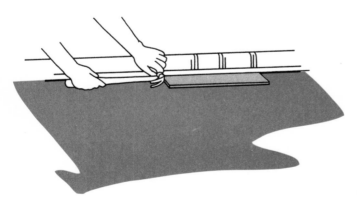

leave space above sheet vinyl

Five

Plumbing

What is plumbing? Plumbing is plumbing. You turn on the faucet and water comes out. You flush the toilet or pull the plug and water goes away. Simple stuff except when the water won't come out. Or when the water comes and won't go away.

Water coming and water going. These are two different systems. The water supply system and the septic system.

Let's get the water to us first and worry about getting rid of it later.

## Water Supply System

Calvin Caveman got his water over at the river, a very convenient place. The river had lots of fresh water. He could drink it, he could wash in it, it was free; and when he threw his garbage in it, the garbage went away. The habit of throwing garbage into the river is still with us today, and it's all because of Calvin, who thought it up ever so long ago. Doesn't that make your ecology conscience feel better? No? Good!

Anyway, it got very crowded at the river, after a while. Zero Population Growth was not yet right up front in the consciousness. Things being what they were, the tough guys got to hang around the river, and the more genteel folks had nowhere to go but inland to the suburbs.

"Just moving inland," one of these scrawny cavemen later noted in his memoirs, "didn't make me any less thirsty. So I decided to get intelligent. I found other ways. For example, I dug a well. Wells were fine, and the water they gave me was every bit as tasty and useful as river water. You had to get a bucket down and pull the water up, and you only got a little bit of water at a time, but I tried not to think about these things too much.

"Eventually, us ordinary guys multiplied, too, and then we needed more water than our wells had to offer. At that point we got cleverer — or, at any rate, ambitious. We went up to the mountains. Lots of snow melting, lots of streams. Clean, good water and only a few hermits and shepherds to drink it. We built dams and reservoirs and aqueducts and brought the water down to our town, a little place called Rome. When the water got to town, we found that it spurted up and looked very pretty and then ran away. This was an unexpected development and we had to invent fountains. We built pools around the water — simple idea once you've thought of it — and added some statues of horses and topless maidens. People came to the fountains to drink, wash clothes, chat and do other things, and they were a great community success.

"A financial success, too, as it turned out, because you had to pay for the water. Incidentally, the pipes inside the fountain were made of lead, and the Latin word for lead is *plumbum*. And that's how plumbing was born.

"About that spurting in the fountains. It was a great discovery. We'd thought, you know, we'd bring the water to town, and then it would just be there, but instead we discovered that water wants to get back to the level from whence it started. We had a natural law on our hands: Water seeks its own level."

The seeking is responsible for the phenomenon called head pressure, because water seeks to reach its own level by pushing. Pressure is great. If we didn't have it, we'd open the taps and nothing would happen. As for the aqueducts — why, we still have very much the same system in the USA. The water for New York City comes from the Catskill Mountains to the north of town. There are reservoirs in the Catskills, and pipes leading underground from the reservoirs down to the houses of the city. The water in the pipes from the Catskills has a head pressure of about thirty feet, which means that to bring water to a New York City faucet thirty feet off the ground, all you have to do is put in some pipes between the ground and the faucet. Thirty feet is about the height of a three-story building, so this faucet is presumably somewhere on the third floor. Now, the city mains in New York don't provide enough pressure to bring water above the third floor. If you happen to live on the fourth floor of an old four-story brownstone in New York, and you open your tap, and the water just goes ngynnnnnnnng, that's because it can't do any better, not having the pressure.

What we do to help that problem is build water tanks on top of all the taller buildings. We put little pumps in the cellars, and we pump the water up into these tanks above the houses and store it up there, and then we feed the building with water straight down. And the water has pressure and everything. Because the level it is now trying to seek is the level of the tank it just came from.

New York is full of cylindrical wooden water tanks with conical tin roofs, and if you do live in New York, or if you've visited the place, you've probably seen them. They're all over the top of the skyline. And, by the way, they are still made by hand, by coopers working in Brooklyn. Some of the big apartment buildings have big steel and concrete tanks instead of wooden ones, and sometimes they try to hide their tanks inside little Greek temples. In the case of an enormous building like the Empire State Building, which has sixty miles of water pipe, there may be five different floors with water tanks on them — every twenty stories or so. If the water tanks were any more than twenty floors apart, the pressure would be so great that if you opened the tap you'd get knocked right out of the Empire State Building and into New Jersey.

Another reason water tanks work is that there isn't a constant demand for water. You usually use a lot for a short period of time, and then you don't use it, and when you don't, the pump has a chance to catch up.

OK, we have water coming into a house and we have pressure. Let's run it through a house and see what happens. On the next page is a very good drawing of the plumbing system in a house with a good number of water fixtures. It is an urban, or shall we say "peri-urban," house, presumably, because the water comes in underground, as it does when it is municipally supplied. City water pipes are at least 3½ feet below the ground so they won't freeze in the winter. (Pipe depth varies with the latitude.)

The water comes into a cellar and goes through a valve. Valve is a crucial plumbing term. If you know about valves and you know about pipes, then you know about plumbing. Pipes carry water. Valves shut off water. Water come, water stop. From the valve the water goes through a water meter, and then through another valve. Shut off the two valves and you can take out the water meter and change it.

Now the water splits. Half of it goes up and half of it goes over. The half that goes straight up goes directly to the fixtures and becomes cold water (which, of course, it already is). The half that goes over winds up in a hot water heater, where it becomes hot water, and then it, too, is shipped up to the fixtures.

The pipes that ship the water up to the fixtures are smaller than the pipe that brought the water into the house. The pipe coming into the house will be, say, 2 inches in diameter. The pipes inside the house are generally ½ inch thick. Water supply pipes have to be stepped down like this. Otherwise, you literally could not turn on a tap without flooding the building.

As the two water pipes — hot and cold — go up they branch off to feed all the fixtures and pass through innumerable valves. There are valves in front of and after the heater. There are valves on the pressure side of every connection or fitting. The pressure side is the side the water is coming *from*. There are shut-off valves in front of

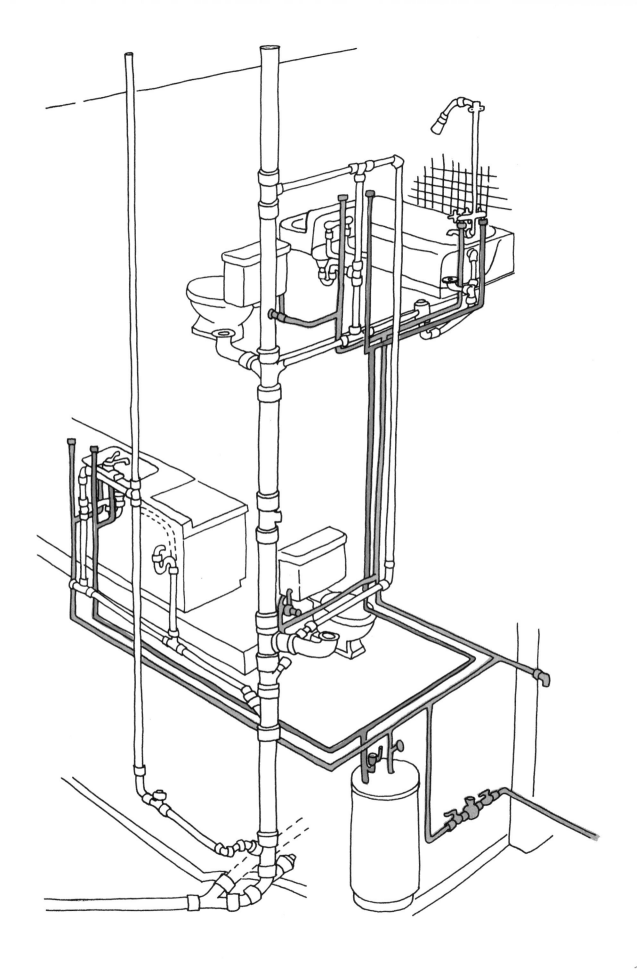

every sink, tub, toilet, and faucet. They're there so that you can shut off the water and work on the plumbing. If something went wrong at the sink, you'd be able to shut off the water before it laid eyes on the sink, on the pressure side of the sink. So you could work on it without getting squirted at.

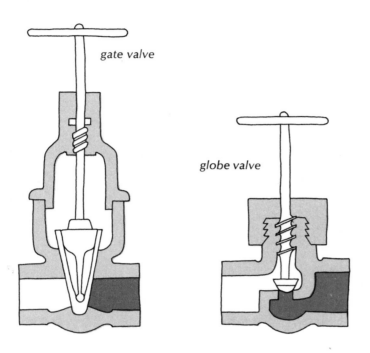

Now, a faucet on a sink is just another kind of valve. But since it's the kind of valve you may have to work on sometime, there are other valves on the pressure side before every faucet in the house.

Basically, there are two kinds of valves, globe valves and gate valves. The names refer to their methods of operation. Faucets and all other valves that are often opened and often closed are almost always globe valves. When a globe valve is closed, a little hemisphere is sitting in a hole preventing water from coming through. Turning the handle to open the valve removes the half-globe from the hole. We are mostly going to concern ourselves with globe valves because they are the kind you can repair. You really can't repair a gate valve; you have to replace it. Gate valves are used for main valves and for other valves that don't see much action and must have a strong connection. When a gate valve is closed a gate extends across the pipe, shutting out the water. When you open the valve the gate goes up into a slot, and water can flow through the pipe.

The only other thing that needs to be mentioned about water supply systems is the antiknock chamber. Look at the second floor sink on the plumbing diagram. Notice that the two pipes going to the two faucets extend a little way above the faucets and are then just capped and don't go anywhere? Those extensions are antiknock chambers. Antiknock chambers are optional — they are not required by code; they don't have to be there. The pipes could just go into the faucets. But they shouldn't; antiknock chambers are a good idea. If you have ever shut off the water and heard the pipes go "Bang, bang" (or "Knock, knock"), the answer to "Who's there?" is: There's some water rattling the pipes around. What has happened is like when you stop a car suddenly and the car rocks back and forth and you're jostled around. Well, you have stopped the water suddenly, it rocks back and forth, jostles the pipes, and the pipes bang against the hangers (that is, the straps that hold up pipes), the studs, anything that's in their way. The little antiknock chamber is nothing more than a column of air that just sits on top of a pipe. As you shut off the water, the water backs up the air column, and it pushes up on this column of air and compresses it. The air works exactly like a shock absorber, and by absorbing the shock of the shut-off pressure, it keeps the pipes quiet. A better view of this is shown at right.

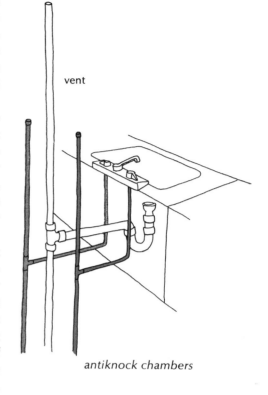

*antiknock chambers*

And that's all there is to a water supply system. If a house isn't in a city or town, if it's in what is known as a rural or an advanced rural situation, then it may have a direct water supply from a well, and it may, or may not, have a water pump, depending on the natural pressure of the spring feeding the well. Sometimes a spring has a hell of a lot of pressure in it — it might be pumping out something like 150 gallons of water per minute, which is a lot of pressure. If the stream is more of a trickler, then you use a pump and pump the water into an airtight storage tank in the cellar.

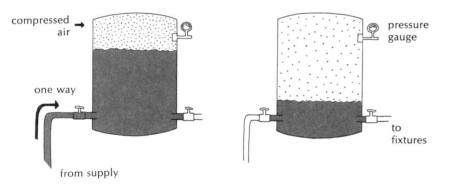

There's some air inside the tank, but it can't get out, and the water being pumped in compresses the air. And the compressed air, pushing against the water, gives the water enough head pressure to run up to the fixtures in the house. This is the system that puts the *OW* in suburban sh*OW*ers. You are taking a shower, and all of a sudden the water gets very cold, or very hot, or even colder, or even hotter. It's very difficult to maintain a constant pressure with this kind of system, and what is known as a differential flow of water develops.

The water supply system in the house sends the same water to every fixture. The water you drink is the same water that goes into the bathtub and into the toilet. Now, wait a minute. This information is supposed to make you feel good, not all squirmy. It means that when you work on your toilet everything's OK. Incidentally, and while we're on the subject, we have some good news and some bad news for you. First the good news. By the year 2000 we will all be drinking raw sewage. Now the bad news. There won't be enough to go around.

So the water's been distributed all over the house, and it isn't very long before we use it and put soap and grime and everything else into it. And then it's all used up and we want to get rid of it. Getting rid of water is called the sewer system or the septic system.

## Septic System

The easiest way of getting rid of anything in the house is to throw it out the window, and the early sewer system developed by man consisted largely of throwing sewerage out of windows. London started out with streets full of little one-story houses. There was a sidewalk, of sorts, and the street pitched to a little cavity in the middle, and when people (they were known as Cockneys) had accumulated some dirty water in the houses, they put the water in buckets and dumped it out the window. And it would roll along the street into the gutter in the middle. And then, presumably, it rained and all the stuff got washed away into the Thames.

Well, then London began to get more and more densely populated, and the Cockneys added on to the houses. They didn't build them straight up, they cantilevered the new stories out over the street, 'cause it gave them more room, and then they had fancy little Tudor houses. Now they had covered walkways, but there wasn't very much rain coming in to wash away the garbage. So London got ravaged with disease and rats and awful foul smells, and people hated to go into town. And the people who had to go into town — well, they didn't change the sewerage system, they changed the social code instead. They developed the whole idea of having the lady walk to the inside of the gentleman. Sewerage now descended from the second story windows, and less sewerage came down on the head of the person walking directly along the wall. There were other ramifications of the code. If one peer met another peer walking down the street, he would say, "Do you take the wall of me, sir?" And if the other peer said, "Yes, sir, I do, sir," then they had to take out their swords and have a fight over it, to find out which guy had to get the garbage. It was a big deal.

Eventually — and this was only within the last couple of hundred years or so — people decided to develop septic sewerage systems, and matters of social position had to be settled in other ways. How do we get dirty water out of a sink these days? There is usually a screen over the hole to catch toothpaste caps and aspirins. Underneath the hole is a pipe that goes through a funny bend and then over into the wall. There is another pipe inside the wall, and it goes straight down, and then bends inside the cellar and goes underground, and then goes into a river and out to sea. This is a septic line. It has no pressure; it's a pure gravity system. The dirty water wants to go down, so it just goes down the pipe. Maybe it will go into a fine sewerage treatment plant before it hits the river, but very likely not.

The septic pipe that goes straight down also goes straight up to the roof. The upper half of the pipe is called a vent, or a stack vent,

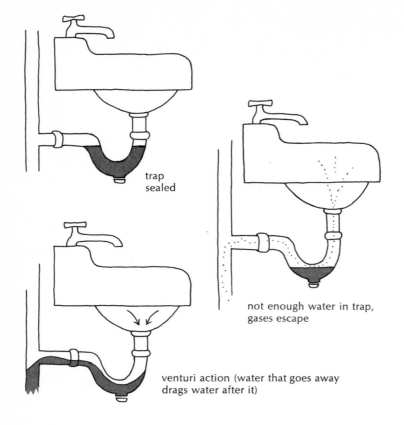

trap
sealed

not enough water in trap,
gases escape

venturi action (water that goes away
drags water after it)

and it vents the sewer system. It turns out that a lot of chemical
reactions go on in a sewer system that produce foul-smelling and
sometimes volatile gases. We don't want them in the house, and
we certainly don't want them to build up any pressure, so we have
a vent going up through the roof. So every house always has a pipe
sticking out of the roof, just a plain old pipe, to let the gases out.
It isn't covered because it doesn't matter if rain or snow goes down
the pipe — they'll just join the sewer system.

The funny bend in the pipe under the sink is called a trap. We
need it because we want to make sure that the sewer gases do go
up the vent and out of the house. Without the trap they might
come up through the hole in the bottom of the sink and percolate
around the house. The trap's funny U shape prevents that from
happening. What happens is that as the water runs out, most of it
runs out but some of it stays and sits right in the U. Sitting there
it's a gas-keeping-out seal, so the gases go up the vent. The trap
traps the gases, and it works very well.

Now, the trap works so well that it also traps oil, grease, paper,
hair, and a bunch of other things. Blockages are the single thing
that can go wrong with a sewer system. Wherever a pipe bends in a
sewer system is a place where waste tends to accumulate and cause
a clog. But it's the single thing that can go wrong, unless a bull-
dozer dozes through the yard and snaps the pipe. So every time a
pipe makes a turn of 90 degrees or so in a sewer system you'll find
a little funny-shaped thing called a clean out.

If the water backs up in your sink, there's a block in the sewer
system somewhere along the line. The most likely place for it to

150

be is in the trap under the sink, so that's what you'll try to clean out. But if it's not the trap, the clog may be at the next bend or, even more likely, at the next bend after that. And, fortunately enough, every clean out has a little plug on it that you can unscrew, and then you can put something into the pipe and break up the blockage. Fortunately again, clean outs and traps are generally accessible and are not hidden behind walls just when you need to get at them.

There is an exception to what we have just said: tub traps. Bathtub traps are almost always buried under the floor and are most difficult to reach. A tub trap will be under some tile. The plumber who put the tub in will know just where it is, but you may not know. Some tub traps are in walls. Well-designed houses have removable panels behind fixtures so you can get at the traps. Sometimes there's a little metal plate in the bathroom floor that you can lift up and so get at the tub trap. In old New York City apartment buildings there's often a little vertical cylinder next to the tub with a kind of lift-up thing in it that lifts up or pushes down and functions as a stopper for the tub. Such a cylinder is actually an extension of the tub drain trap, and all you have to do to get to the trap is unscrew the whole cylinder.

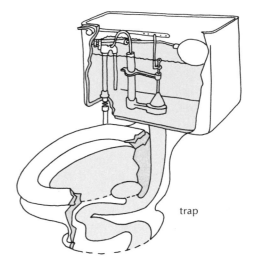

trap

As for toilets, a toilet is its own trap. Some modern houses have things called wall-hung toilets, and all the guts of a wall-hung toilet sit inside the wall. A well-designed wall-hung toilet system includes a removable wall panel to provide access to the pipes and systems. A badly designed one doesn't. Sometimes people just plain don't think of putting in a removable panel. And then they have to come in and rip up your wall to fix the toilet.

The main clean out is the final clean out in the house, and it's found in the cellar, where the sewer pipes bend to join the sewers of the city. A little vent called the fresh air intake extends from the main clean out up to the ground or sidewalk. It brings fresh air into the sewer system, and it helps prevent suction. A heavy wind across the top of the house could create a vacuum that would suck the water out of the traps of the house — if you didn't have a fresh air intake. A vacuum can't exist with a fresh air intake: When the wind pulls on the vent, fresh air just enters the fresh air intake and goes straight up the vent to the roof.

Also down here in the cellar is the house trap — a U-shaped pipe

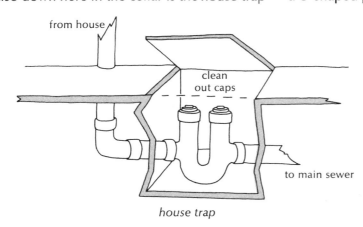

from house

clean out caps

to main sewer

*house trap*

at the last stop in your house. This trap tells all the sewer gases in the street to use someone else's house as a vent.

Q. How do you fix it when something goes wrong with a sewer system?

A. Well, we've said that the only thing that can go wrong with a sewer system is that it can develop a block someplace, and that the most common place for blocks is in the first trap dirty water runs through after you use it.

Q. OK, so how do you clean out a trap?

A. There are five ways to clean out a trap.

## Five Ways to Clean Out a Trap

Way Number One is the way we are all familiar with already. It's the Drāno way, the Sani-Flush way, the Liquid Plumber way, the Clobber way. You pour something down the drain. The something in question is basically lye or some kind of caustic soda or sulfuric acid. The something in question is supposed to eat up the blockage, whatever it is, and clear the path. The label on the can will say Don't get the something on the porcelain or Don't get the something on your hands. That's because the something will eat up the porcelain and eat up your hands. The label on the can will also say The something will not harm pipes. You can draw your own conclusions.

In spite of all the gobbling, Way Number One is not very effective, and it is more expensive than any of the other ways.

Way Number Two (the cheapest way of all) is the plunger, aka "The Plumber's Friend." It works very well, and we think it is always the first thing you should try. The one on the left costs a dollar. They come a little fancier for $2, and also in a special design (seen on the right) especially — but quite unnecessarily — made for toilets. The regular design works fine on toilets. Now, there's a three-step right way to use a plunger, which you may or may not know about. Say the sink is blocked up and not working and full of water. All you have to do is:

1. Bail out the sink so there is just enough water left to cover the top of the plunger. (The bottom of the plunger is sitting on the bottom of the sink over the drain.)

2. Plug up the overflow hole in the sink. Some sinks have some kind of overflow somewhere — back, side, or front. It's a little slot that drains water from the sink, when you leave the water running and forget to turn it off. You want to plug it up at this point because it is most likely to be directly facing you, and when you use the plunger to develop pressure in the pipe, the easiest place for the pressure to go is out the overflow — so it can hit you right in the nose. Plug up the overflow. Use a rag or a piece of tape or something.

*plumber's fancy friend*

*plumber's friend*

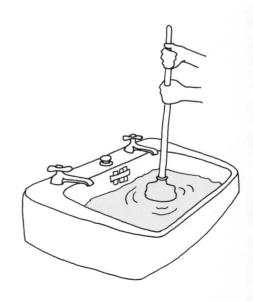

3. Put the plunger over the drain and push it up and down in short, quick, decisive-type motions. This sets up a rocking motion in the pipe and rocks the blockage back and forth until it breaks up and loosens and goes away.

Way Number Two works 950 times out of 1000. It is also a fine prophylactic technique. Use it once a week — excellent preventive maintenance.

Way Number Three is for the next 40 times out of 1000: a plumber's auger, aka snake. You'll only need to use a snake for a clog that's too much for a plunger. A snake is a coil of wire that gets a little bigger down at one end. It comes in various lengths. It is available with a fancy windup contraption. It is quite adequate without a fancy windup contraption. The snake pictured here is 8 feet long. It is a wire with an expanded coil at the end and a bent piece of pipe that can slide along the wire if you loosen a little thumbscrew. Take the screen off the drain first, of course — the screen will either twist or pry off. Push the snake into the drain, and keep pushing it until it won't go any farther. You have just hit the blockage. Now, slide the bent piece of pipe to a convenient spot and tighten the thumbscrew. You now have a convenient handle for pushing, pulling, and twisting.

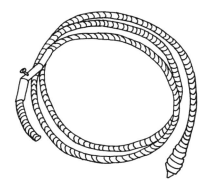

*snake, or auger*

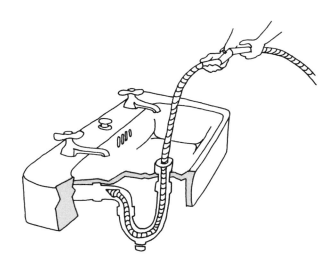

Turn on some James Brown records and go at it. Push, pull, twist, push, twist, pull, push. Any rhythm you like. Eventually the coil bites into the blockage, breaks up the clog into little chunks, and they get washed down the drain. Pull out the snake, replace the screen, pat yourself on the back, and buy another good tool with the money you've saved.

Way Number Four. Now we are down to 10 times out of 1000. These are the only times you really have to do some work. If the blockage is in the trap you will have to either remove the trap or remove the clean out plug.

About half the sink traps in the country have a little plug on the bottom called a clean out plug. You put a wrench on the plug, and you unscrew the plug, and you put a bucket underneath the plug — 'cause it gets messy if you don't. Let the water run out into the bucket, and then you can put your snake in the clean out plug hole and get right up next to the clog and break it out. Sink traps without clean out plugs have a union nut at each end. Remove the two union nuts on a sink trap, and the whole trap will come off. Then you just look at the trap and see what's in it and run the faucet over it or punch something into it and clean it out that way. Union nuts are removed with a wrench. Sometimes they are very big nuts and require a very big wrench called a spud wrench. Can you say "spud wrench" ten times very quickly?

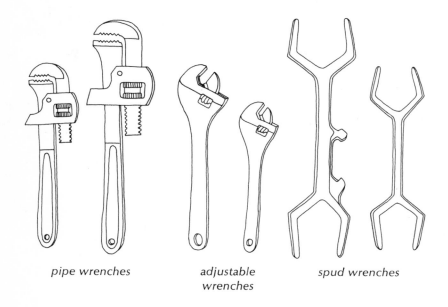

pipe wrenches        adjustable        spud wrenches
                     wrenches

It's not a good idea to use pliers on either union nuts or clean out plugs. It ruins them forever, and then you can't use them again.

Way Number Four will work the next 9 times out of 1000.

If the clog turns out not to be in the trap, look at the next bend of pipe. Just keep walking along and look for the spot. It may be behind a wall. If it is, you have reached the final time out of 1000, and it is time for Way Number Five. Way Number Five is: Call in outside assistance. If you live in an apartment, call up the owner of the building. He's going to have to search through the walls and find the clog. If the clog is farther down the line than your trap, it will be probably clogging up the sinks of other people in the building as well, so you won't have to feel bad just because the matter is now out of your hands.

Q. What about a clogged toilet?

A. A toilet is its own trap. The water sitting in the toilet bowl prevents sewer gases from reaching the bathroom. The three most likely spots for clogs in a toilet are into the tunnel, around the bend, and out of the tunnel. A plunger will

deal with almost all clogs in any spot. And if ever a plunger
can't, a snake can.

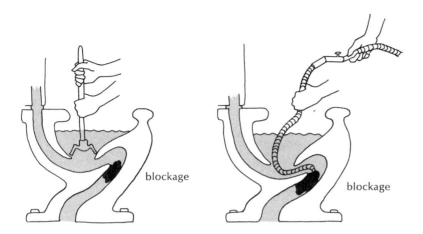

Q. What do you do if a toilet isn't clogged, but it's not flushing right? Can I fix that?

A. Of course you can.

What you do depends on what kind of toilet you have. There
are two kinds of toilet. There is the kind of toilet with a tank and
the kind of toilet without a tank.

The toilet without a tank has nothing but a little valve; actually
a very fancy, not so little, valve. You push the valve to flush the
toilet, and there's a lot of noise and the toilet is flushed. This valve
is called the Sloan flush valve, and it's a very nice little, or not so
little, invention. It's a simple contraption — it either has a piston
inside that pumps several times and then shuts off, or it has a
diaphragm that opens and closes several times and then stops and
flushes the toilet that way. It takes advantage of the principle that
makes the pipes shake. There's only one requirement for a Sloan
flush valve toilet: The water supply line to the toilet must be at
least 1½ inches in diameter. A half-inch pipe won't supply enough
pressure to the piston or the diaphragm in the Sloan flush valve to
flush the toilet. Big pipes cost big money, and as a result most
houses are built with tank toilets — which can operate with half-
inch water supply pipes.

Sloan flush valves can be repaired but they rarely go bad. The
only thing that usually goes wrong with them is that they don't
flush just the way you want them to; they will flush too long or not
long enough. The way to adjust the flushing is: Take the cover off
and underneath you'll find a screw. It'll be the only screw you can
find, and it'll be the adjusting screw. Turn it counterclockwise to
increase the length of flush, clockwise to decrease the length of
flush.

If something does go wrong with a Sloan flush valve itself, you
can buy a Sloan flush valve repair kit for about $1.50. There are four
or so rubber things inside a Sloan flush valve that could possibly

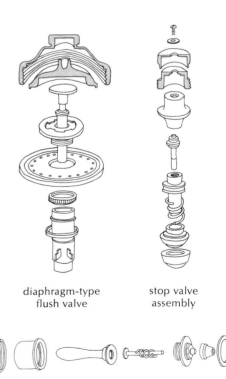

diaphragm-type          stop valve
flush valve             assembly

handle assembly

go wrong, and all you have to do to fix it is shut off the water at the nearest shut off valve (turn the valve clockwise as far as it will go), take the valve apart, replace all the rubber pieces in the valve, put it back together, and turn the water on again.

Let's give ourselves a commandment here: When working on the water supply system, shut off the water before doing any work. Then check by turning on a faucet or flushing a toilet to make sure the water has been shut off. Check never — flood once! Check once — flood never! Words to live by (no extra charge).

More than four things can go wrong with tank toilets. How do they work? Well, you have a toilet, and sitting on top of the toilet is a tank with a handle on it. There's a hole in the bottom of the tank connected to an opening in the toilet behind the toilet bowl. The tank has the same function all water tanks do: It provides pressure. One toilet tankful of water provides just enough pressure to flush one toilet. So a tank toilet is a toilet that can function on an ordinary half-inch house cold water supply pipe. And it is therefore the kind of toilet most commonly found in houses.

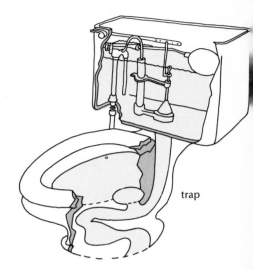
trap

When you want to flush the toilet you press down on the handle of the tank. The handle lifts up either a metal rod or a chain, and the metal rod or the chain lifts up a rubber flapper covering the hole at the bottom of the tank. The water in the tank rushes out the hole to flush the toilet, and when it's gone, the rubber flapper drops down into place again.

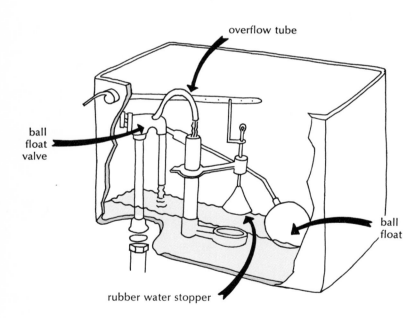

overflow tube

ball
float
valve

ball
float

rubber water stopper

While the water has been rushing away, something called the *float* has been sinking to the bottom of the tank. The float sits on top of the water in the tank. When the tank is full, the float sits up at the top of the tank. When the toilet is flushed the float sinks, and in sinking it removes pressure from a little pin. This pin turns out to be a valve, called the ball float valve. It's connected to the toilet's cold water supply, and when the sinking float removes pressure from it, the ball float valve opens and the tank starts to fill up again so that it will be ready for the next flush. As the tank fills, the float rises, and as the float rises, it puts pressure on the ball float valve controlling the water supply. And so the water shuts off when the tank is just exactly full. Neat, huh? A perfectly functioning system.

While the tank is refilling, a certain amount of the water coming in is diverted into a small tube that runs into a big vertical tube called the overflow tube. This diversion is necessary because of something known as venturi-type action. When the water from the tank rushes down into the toilet it pushes all the water in the toilet trap into the sewer, and venturi-type action sucks whatever water is sitting in the toilet bowl along behind it and pulls it down into the sewer. The toilet has been rinsed clean, but there isn't any water left in it, and it's now an unsealed trap. So, while the tank is refilling, water trickles down the overflow tube into the toilet to refill the toilet trap. A clever little system.

If you have a tank toilet, please go into the bathroom and take the cover off the toilet and flush it a couple of times and watch it work. Then you will know how it works when it's working right, and you'll be ready for the day when it isn't.

Welcome back! Things can go wrong with tank toilets, as we've said:

A lot of toilets are budding opera stars. They sing and go buzz in the night. That almost always means that the ball float valve hasn't shut off. The reason it hasn't, presuming it's a good valve, is that the float hasn't been lifted high enough by the water in the tank to apply enough pressure to shut it off. All you have to do is bend the float *down*. Now the water doesn't have to float the float so high for the float to do its job.

Or it may be that the ball float valve does shut itself off, but it seems to do so before the tank is full enough to flush the toilet quite enough. You can get better flushing action by bending the float *up*. The tank will then fill more before the inflow valve shuts off.

Or it may be that the float itself has a hole in it. This is very rare but possible. If it's leaking, it can be unscrewed, and you can go and buy another one for 39 cents. You may have a copper float now. If so, buy a plastic float. It's perfectly good, and cheaper. If the rod connecting the float to the ball float valve has broken after years of being bent up and down, it can likewise be unscrewed and replaced cheaply.

The next possibility is that the ball float valve won't turn off, not because there's anything wrong with it or the float mechanism, but because the water in the tank can never rise to the proper level because the hole in the bottom of the tank isn't properly sealed by the flapper. You can always tell if this is the case. If it is, water will always be running through your toilet. The flapper can't work properly if it's on a chain and the chain's too tight. The flapper can't work properly if it's on a rod and the rod is binding up on one of its guides. So check to see whether the flapper can move freely, and if it can't, loosen the chain or straighten the rod. A flapper also can't work properly if it has developed a lot of muck and corruption on its bottom. If this be the case, clean off the flapper, or buy a new one. Don't be afraid to work in the water. Remember, it's just delicious water.

Q. What if a lot of corrosion material and rust from the pipes has fouled the sides of the tank?

Answer #1. If there's stuff on the sides of the tank, it's stuff that is also inside of you, because it came from the water.

Answer #2. It's good for you.

Answer #3. It isn't rust from the pipes. They are all copper and brass and they don't rust. It's just iron from the water.

If the toilet won't shut off, and it isn't the float and it isn't the flapper — and you can make sure it isn't the float by picking it all the way up and seeing whether the water shuts off — then the ball float valve itself is dead. All right. Shut the water off first, please. There's usually a valve down below the tank that will take care of that. If you then flush the toilet, the tank will be empty and you can work in comfort. Then you take off three screws on the ball float valve, open it up, and you discover a little O ring inside that needs replacing. The little O ring has no name at all, except in the repair manual, put out by the company, and the repair manual name was only invented by the technical writer who did the book. But you don't have to be embarrassed about ordering it in the hardware store, because the man in the hardware store doesn't know what it's called, either. Just take the old one along and say, "May I have one of these, please?" You could invent a name for it, of course. How about "outnrat"?

The outnrat will be very cheap. And so will all the other parts. They're designed that way. A bunch of little stuff that costs just about what it should. Plumbing, you see, is basically free. Only plumbers cost bucks.

If you have the old type of brass float valve and it goes bad you should replace it with a new plastic type like the one illustrated.

Incidentally, there's a new guy on the block called Fluidmaster, which is a simpler device that works on water pressure and is designed to replace the ball float valve. If you're the gambling type or you would like to do some research on the longevity and reliability of the device, feel free to do so and let us know how it works out. We'd like to find out.

Q. What about a leaky faucet?

A. At the right is a cutaway drawing of every faucet in the world. A lot of faucets have fancy stuff on the outside so they look niftier and more modern, but inside every faucet is the same. There are three places where a faucet can leak, and they are all easy to fix.

First Place: A faucet can leak at the joint with the water supply

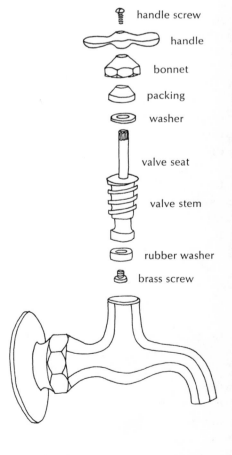

handle screw

handle

bonnet

packing

washer

valve seat

valve stem

rubber washer

brass screw

pipe. Turn off the water supply, remove the faucet, spread pipe joint compound on the male threads, and tighten it all back up again. Pipe joint compound is wonderful stuff. A lifetime supply costs about 40 cents. Whenever you take apart any plumbing joint at all, put pipe joint compound on it when you put it back together. The pipe joint compound is always spread on the male threads. (Remember, male threads screw into female threads; female threads accept — nice, polite, Victorian concept — male threads.)

If you don't have any pipe joint compound, you can use a small piece of old cotton string. It breaks after a while, but it works in an emergency. Some people use a new kind of silicone tape these days for pipe joints. It's neater than pipe joint compound, and it's not messy and gooey, and all you do is wrap it around the pipe joint, and it doesn't stick on your hands. But it's super expensive. The only time you really want to use it is on an old, corroded, rusted, eaten-up joint that always drips a little and has some play in it no matter how tight you tighten it. If you wrap silicone tape around the male threads of this joint, the tape will effectively increase the diameter of the male threads, and give you a tighter fit.

Second Place: A faucet can drip out the end, when the faucet is shut off.

Third Place: A faucet can leak out of the handle when the water is running.

To fix leaks in either of these two places, you have to take off the handle. Sometimes there's a screw sticking through the top of the handle, and sometimes you can't see anything at all, up top, that looks like a means of detaching a handle. In that case there will be a little thing on the top that says H (hot) or C (cold). And it either screws off or pries off. And underneath it you'll find a screw.

Before you unscrew the screw, turn off the water supply before the faucet. You might plug up the drain in case the screw drops into the sink and down the drain to screw you. Now, unscrew the screw. And take the handle off. What you're facing now is the valve stem, the square-shaped thing sticking up that the handle was screwed onto, and the bonnet, the piece of metal that the stem is sticking through. The bonnet is screwed onto the faucet. You are now going to want a 10-inch adjustable wrench (it's part of the basic tool kit) to take the bonnet off the faucet. You *aren't* about to use pliers to accomplish this purpose. Repeat: ix-nay on the iers-play. So you loosen up the bonnet with the wrench, and then you thread it off.

By the way, you keep all these parts that you've removing around. It's troublesome to keep running back and forth to the hardware store for little parts that got lost by mistake.

Underneath the bonnet you'll find some packing, packed into the bonnet. If it's old packing, it'll be a gasket, which is a little piece of waxed hemp rope, and if it is new packing, it's a kind of nice plastic string called mate-washer. If your problem is that the faucet's leaking out the handle when the water's on, this is the little guy that's at fault. So you replace the packing, with mate-washer, preferably, you tighten up the bonnet, you screw the handle back on, and you snap the Cold button back on. And you leave our story here.

If the problem is a dripping faucet, continue dismantling. Un-screw the valve stem itself — it's got some threads on the bottom, and it's screwed into the faucet. You can now see that there's a screw on the bottom of the valve stem. This screw holds a washer, called the stem washer, onto the valve stem, and it is this washer which is supposed to stop the water from flowing when the faucet is turned off. It sits down on top of something called the valve seat on the bottom of the faucet and seals the opening. If the faucet is leaking, the stem washer ain't doin' its job. So you replace it. Re-move the screw on the bottom of the valve stem, remove the stem washer, put in another one of the same kind. You can buy stem washers individually or in bulk — meaning a box of a hundred assorted sizes and shapes, cost: approximately $1. If you buy a box, then you have always plenty of washers around the house. (They will, however, never be the right size — well, hardly ever!)

And then you put the whole assembly back together again. Screw in the valve stem, replace the washer, insert the packing, spread pipe joint compound on all available male threads, and screw on the bonnet. Put the handle on, screw it down, and put the little Cold button back on top (after turning it around to face the right way). Everything works out just fine and — you've just fixed that faucet.

Alternate ending to story: So then you put everything back together — and you find that the faucet still drips. And you say, "Rats!"

If the faucet still drips, what's probably happened is this: For years the faucet has leaked off and on, and this has irritated you, quite rightly, so you've taken a pair of pliers to the top of the

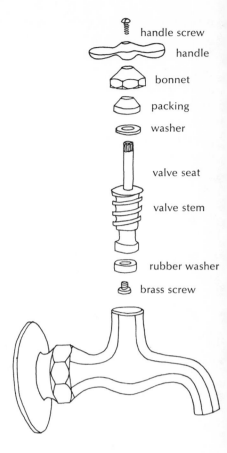

handle screw

handle

bonnet

packing

washer

valve seat

valve stem

rubber washer

brass screw

faucet and turned it and tightened it down harder, and the dripping has stopped for a while. And then you've turned on the water, and turned it off again, and there was the drip again. So out came the pliers, and in the process you wore down the stem washer, so that when you turned off the faucet, you were closing metal on metal — the metal of the valve stem on the metal of the valve seat. And this scored the valve seat.

Now, in this situation you might call in the plumber and have the following conversation.

Plumber. Sorry, folks, you have scored your valve seats, and you're going to have to get those valve seats reground, and that'll cost you $35.

You. Oh, no. What else can I do?

Plumber. Well, you can replace the faucets. That'll cost you $55 apiece.

You. Oh, regrind my valve seats.

Or, instead of this, you can let the plumber stay at his place and regrind your own valve seats for a dollar.

Q. You mean you can do it yourself?

A. Yes, you can do it yourself. (Sounds like a good motto, don't it?)

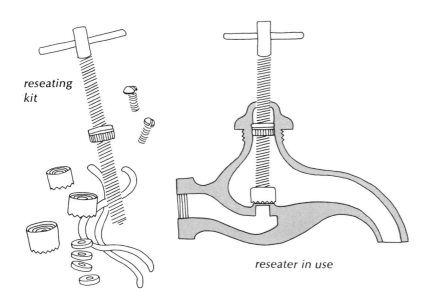

*reseating kit*

*reseater in use*

Buy a *valve reseating kit*. It costs about a dollar, and it contains a valve reseating tool, three cutting points of different sizes (for different-sized openings in faucets), several assorted washers, and packing, and string. The valve reseating tool does a fine job of smoothing out valve seats so that valve stem washers sit flush on top of them once more.

Then we have the mixing valve. One mixing valve replaces two faucets — one hot and one cold — and allows you to get warm water instead of skin scald or finger freeze. If you would like to replace two faucets with a mixing valve — you can do it yourself.

There is the real mixing valve and there is the lazy man's mixing valve. The lazy man's mixing valve is a device that clips onto the two existing faucets on a sink and sends out a stream of water in the middle. The left side of this stream burns your hand, and the right side of it cryonically ices your hand. After that the whole device falls off into the sink — but that's OK, because it's tricky, and you're glad it fell off.

A real mixing valve really blends the hot and cold water, and it replaces the faucets altogether. Turn off the hot and cold water supply, take the two faucets off, and then measure the center-to-center offset (center of cold water opening in the sink to center of hot water opening). If there is nothing in the way in the middle of the sink, you then get a mixing valve with that kind of center-to-center offset, and you put it in, and you have got a mixing valve. Sometimes you have a very old porcelain sink with a very fancy little gizmo in the middle. If you do, you have to chop the gizmo away before you put in the mixing valve.

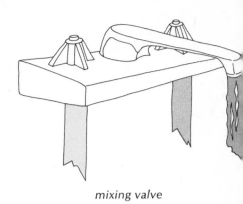
*mixing valve*

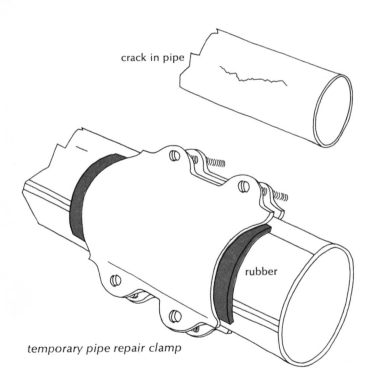
crack in pipe

rubber

*temporary pipe repair clamp*

The only other thing that needs to be said about plumbing is that sometimes the pipes can break. Most pipe breaks are little breaks. If a little break develops, and it happens to be Sunday night, and also snowing, and the plumber doesn't want to come, and you can see where the break is, you can put on something called a *pipe repair clamp*. Fifty-nine cents.

The clamp is two pieces of metal lined with rubber and fastened together with bolts. Put the two pieces of the clamp around the pipe where the break is and tighten up the bolts — very hard. The pipe repair clamp is called a temporary repair, and you should treat it as such, although, quite honestly, the pipe repair clamp often outlasts the pipe. But, officially, it's a temporary repair. Pipe repair clamps fit ⅜-, ½-, and ¾-inch pipes. They take about two minutes to apply.

More likely, pipes will leak at joints.

First: Shut off the water.

Second: Being *very* careful, put a pipe wrench on the pipe and turn the pipe a very little bit.

Bonus time! At last you're going to always know which way to turn your pipes. Hold the pipe in question and face the fitting which is, or will be, its mate. It's important that pipes and fittings face each other during mating. Now turn the pipe clockwise and it tightens. Nice technique, eh? It works in all cases. And it doesn't matter if you're holding the pipe, or a fitting, or a bolt, or a nut, or anything. Just face the anything's mate and remember to screw "as time goes by."

Back to our story. Having turned the pipe a *very* little bit, go and turn on the water and hope for the best. The reason you only turn it a little is that as you tighten one end of a pipe, you loosen the other end. If this doesn't work, remove the pipe, then put it back again, only this time put it back with a healthy dose of pipe joint compound.

A major caution point here. Don't force any plumbing connections; metal tends to be hard to move and easy to break. Some heat (as from your torch kit) applied to the female parts usually releases their grip and lets you do your work.

That's all there is to plumbing. Just remember that it's really incredibly simple. It's pipes and connections and threads and some valves, and it's very logical. Pressure moves water from somewhere through valves to you. Gravity takes it away again around turns and turns. The turns can get blocked, the joints can leak, the valves can leak, and the pipes can break. And you can fix them all.

# Six

# Electricity

E lectricity is scary or mysterious to most people. There is no cause for fear. Actually, it's the simplest, the most standardized, the best organized, and probably the most versatile of all the trade disciplines. The number of electrical things you have around bear witness to that.

Before we start anything, we're going to make our first quick major point. The First Commandment of Electricity (also the Eighteenth Commandment, the Thirty-Seventh Commandment, the One Hundred and Seventy-First Commandment, and the Three Thousandth through the Three Millionth Commandment) is:

> Turn Off the Power Before You Do Any Work
> on Your Electrical System

You will *always* shut off the power. You will *never* be too lazy to shut off the power. Not shutting off power is the one and only way to get hurt fooling around with electricity. The hurt can be pretty serious. If you shut off the power, you will not get hurt.

Q. How do you see?
A. You do electrical work in the daytime.

What is electricity? Electricity is electrons moving through something — for example, a wire. Most things you see around are made of atoms. And an atom is made up of at least three things: At least two heavy things sit in its middle, or nucleus, and at least one very light thing, an electron, spins around the outside, very much in the same way that the earth spins around the sun. One of the two things in the nucleus is called a proton, the other is called a neutron. Protons are like Al Hirt or William Conrad. They like to sit in one spot. Electrons are the lightest things around, and they like to move around. They are also so little that no one has ever seen one, and probably no one ever will, except for the incredible shrinking man.

Protons and electrons have a thing for one another. Each one has

a charge, and, by definition, the proton's charge is called a positive charge, while the electron has something called a negative charge. (Neutrons have no charge at all.) Now, opposite charges, again by definition, attract each other. This means that if we can somehow separate an electron from the proton it has been circling, it will do anything it has to in order to return to that proton. The proton itself, being heavy and liking to sit around, won't go looking for the electron. It will just sit and wait, wanting an electron to come visit. These negative and positive guys love each other. They really want to get together; that's what they want to do more than anything.

It's very hard to pry protons and electrons apart, things being what they are, but there are several ways to do it. One of them is chemical. You can make chemical reactions and separate out electrons. And, of course, when you take electrons away from atoms, you have negative-charge things in one place, which are electrons, and positive-charge things in another place, which are the rest of the atoms that are left over. We've just separated out a whole bunch of electrons, and as a result we have some positive charges — that's what all those plus signs are. We're putting all these positive charges in a big jar. Now we are putting that big jar inside a still bigger jar, and at the same time we're putting all the negative-charge things produced by our chemical reaction — the electrons, represented by all those minus signs — inside the bigger jar, but outside the smaller jar. What we have here has a name: battery.

The positive charges are now just sitting and hoping. The electrons, on the other hand, are getting nervous, and they are jumping around and they want to get going. They want to find a proton, a positively charged particle, to make friends with, forever and ever. The desire of these little electrons to go over and meet their friends has a name: volts. That is to say, volts are a measurement of the strength of desire on the part of electrons to overcome separation. It can also be thought of as a measurement of the potential good times to be had. Which means the more electrons there are on hand, the greater the potential.

Now, what is going to happen? These guys can't get to each

other. They are just sitting there with all this desire and potential. We've got to find a way to get them together. And what we are going to do is: build them a road. We build a road by putting a wire here (name of wire: conductor — more about this word in a minute). These electrons over here see this wire connected there, and say, "Ah! That may be a way to find a positively charged particle." So they hop onto the wire and run along it as far as it goes. And *all* the little negatively charged guys start running around this wire to the positively charged guys, because that's what they want to do.

Our next step is to put a toll booth on the road — a monitoring device, in fact. Now we can count how many electrons are passing a given spot in an hour, and we find that about 2,260,000,000,000,-000,000,000 electrons go by the toll booth in an hour. By counting how many go by in a particular unit of time, we can monitor the effort they are putting out to get over to the positive charges. There's a name for that effort: amperes, or amps, for short. It's computed by counting the number of electrons that go past a specific point in a particular amount of time. One amp just happens to be 6,280,000,000,000,000,000 electrons per second. Not that it matters what it is. If you count them, you get some number, and you can call it amps.

If you were to multiply somebody's potential or his desire by the effort he puts out, you would wind up getting some results, or work. And work, in electrical terms, has its own name: watts. So now we know our first electrical formula:

$$\text{Volts} \times \text{Amps} = \text{Watts}$$

We will learn later on how to use this simple formula in our electrical work.

At the moment, we return to the road. There are good roads and bad roads, and so it is with wires. If you have a nice big wide wire, a lot of electrons can go by. If you have a smooth road, you get a lot more cars by; a straight road, more cars. Again, the same holds true with wires. It turns out you can measure how good a road a wire will be. This measurement is called conductivity. And anything that conducts electricity well is called a conductor. Metals, in general, are good conductors. Platinum, gold, and silver are all good conductors, and the best conductor that we can afford to use is copper. So we use copper a lot as a wire.

| Wire Size | Normal Load | Capacity Load |
|---|---|---|
| No. 18 | 5.0 amp.  (600W) | 7 amp.  (840W) |
| No. 16 | 8.3 amp. (1000W) | 10 amp. (1200W) |
| No. 14 | 12.5 amp. (1500W) | 15 amp. (1800W) |
| No. 12 | 16.6 amp. (1900W) | 20 amp. (2400W) |

Table 17.  Ability of Cord to Carry Current (2- or 3-wire cord)

Tables 17 and 18 are guides to help you select proper wire sizes for various uses. Wires are assumed to be copper, as copper is far and away the most common metal used.

| Light Load (to 7 amps) | Medium Load (7–10 amps) | Heavy Load (10–15 amps) |
|---|---|---|
| To  25 ft., use No. 18 | To  25 ft., use No. 16 | To  25 ft., use No. 14 |
| To  50 ft., use No. 16 | To  50 ft., use No. 14 | To  50 ft., use No. 12 |
| To 100 ft., use No. 14 | To 100 ft., use No. 12 | To 100 ft., use No. 10 |

Note: As a safety precaution, be sure to use only cords that are listed by Underwriters' Laboratories. Look for the Underwriters' seal when you buy.

Table 18.  Selecting the Length of Cord Set

Why are metals such good conductors? The answer requires us to look more closely at the progress of electrons on the road back to protons. And now that we are being more precise, we must say that electrons don't run from one end of a wire to another. What they do is: One electron walks along until he bumps into another electron, and then he stops. And then this other electron says, "Oops," and then he walks along until he bumps into another electron, and that's how they travel — they bump each other along. The protons at the other end don't really care which electrons they get reunited to, as long as they get some. Now, the more electrons you have hanging around in a wire to get bumped into, the more they will get bumped into. And the easier it is for them to get bumped into, the easier it will be for them to travel. It happens that metals are pretty complex atoms, and they have a lot of electrons floating around.

If you have only one proton and one electron, as in a hydrogen atom, the proton is not going to want to give him or her up, because he or she is his or her only friend. But if you have twenty-nine protons and twenty-nine electrons, as you do in a respectable copper atom, and one of these electrons goes away, the twenty-nine protons will share the twenty-eight electrons left, somehow. They'll find a way.

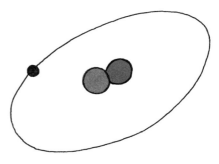

*hydrogen atom*

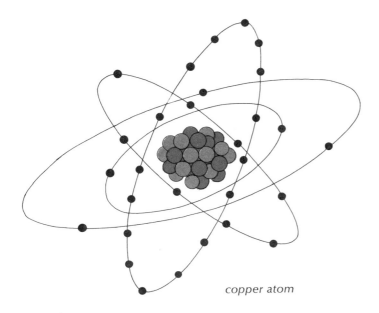

*copper atom*

Now, there are some bad conductors. Sand, for example, doesn't conduct electricity too well. Pure water doesn't conduct electricity at all. Tap water is a fairly good conductor, but that's because tap water has dissolved metals and minerals in it, and they are fairly good conductors. Concrete's a lousy conductor, and rubber's lousy, and plastic's lousy, and so is cloth. In fact, there's a name for things that don't conduct electricity too well: insulators. And insulators have their function. Getting back to that road — no road worth its onions is built without a guard rail. And neither is any road for electrons worth *its* onions. In the case of a wire, the guard rail is the insulation that goes around the wire. Electrons are very fickle guys. When they're traveling that length of wire, and they see a proton hanging around, they'll never get home to mama or poppa — they'll stop along the way. So we put insulators around them to keep their minds on business.

An ideal road would let one amp of electricity pass every second. A less than ideal road will let some fraction of that amount through — say half an amp, or 95 percent of an amp. We can measure the difference between the ideal and the less than ideal. This measure of the resistance to perfection shown by the less than ideal has a name: ohm.

Is a person a conductor or an insulator? We can answer that question by using an instrument called a volt-ohmmeter, which shows how much electricity flows through a thing by telling us how much or how little resistance that thing displays. When the needle on the dial jumps all the way over, there is no resistance, and whatever is being measured is a good conductor. If I hold both wires of a volt-ohmmeter, we can see that I conduct a little electricity. So my body has things in it that conduct electricity. Suppose I wet my fingers. Why, the meter jumps much farther. What have I done?

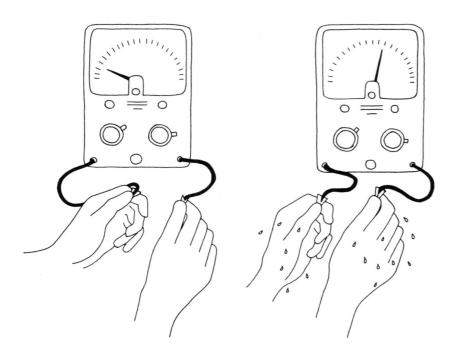

Why am I a better conductor now? It turns out that my skin is a sort of insulator. And what I have done by wetting my fingers is to dissolve all the salts and minerals sitting on my dirty fingers and turn myself into a better conductor. (I didn't get hurt by this demonstration, because it takes a certain amount of energy in the electricity to hurt. There's a very low voltage in a volt-ohmmeter — maybe .5 volts, or something like that. Ordinary house current has approximately 120 volts. It could shock me very severely, but it won't necessarily kill me. Stronger current [220 volts] could do pretty serious damage to me. It could fry me. By the way, house current voltage actually shows some fluctuation from about 110 to 120 volts, depending on how our power company is feeling, what the weather is like, whether the New York Mets lost or not. Various factors.)

Now, by introducing a resistance into our road, we can make electrons do work for us while they pursue their own activities. One of the resistances we can introduce we generally know by another name — a light bulb. The light bulb impedes the natural motions of the electrons, because the filament of a light bulb is made out of tungsten, and tungsten doesn't conduct electricity as well as copper. The electrons try to go through the tungsten in the light bulb as fast and as hard as they go through the copper in the wire, but they can't, and they bump into each other continually. Like cars backed up in a tunnel, the electrons' bumping is a frustrating experience, and it causes them to heat up. Or, to put it another way, as they bump more often they give off more energy — heat energy, in this case. The heat given off causes the tungsten to glow, and gives us light. The tungsten has to be in a vacuum or the heat produced by the bumping electrons would cause it to burn up. That was the key to inventing the light bulb — finding the right metal to glow in a vacuum.

Electricity is made by utility companies in power plants. It is made by converting one kind of energy into another kind of energy. Power plants usually start out either with heat energy or with the energy of the force of gravity, although they do occasionally use chemical energy. If a power plant is using heat energy, it will heat up steam. If it's using gravity, it will have a water wheel. Then the energy of either rising steam or falling water is converted into mechanical energy; that is to say, it is used to turn a wheel inside a machine. The wheel is a wheel of copper wire, and the machine it is part of is called a generator.

generator

A generator has these important parts: the wheel of copper wire and two to four magnets. It is an electricity-producing machine, and its job is to convert mechanical energy into electrical energy. The wheel of copper wire spins in the magnetic field between the magnets, and when that happens, forces in the magnetic field induce any free electrons in the wire to move. And — as we all now know — electrons moving in a wire is electricity.

The energy conversion that takes place in a generator is only known empirically. This means: Nobody really knows why this process releases energy. It is beyond us. But everybody knows that the process does, somehow, induce the flow of electrical current. So we harness the energy that is released, because, after all, we do what we can.

Power plants produce two different kinds of electricity: direct current and alternating current — also known as DC and AC. Which kind of electricity a plant produces is determined by the way in which it picks electrons off of its generators. Direct current is the kind of electricity we have been talking about. The electrons, having been separated from the protons, go directly to where the protons are.

DC

AC

Alternating current, however, is the kind of current we meet every day. It's the kind that flows through the house. Having been separated from the protons, the electrons start to walk from the power plant to the house, but, $1/120$ second later, before they have gone very far, they turn around and walk the other way. After another $1/120$ second, they execute another about face, and, in fact, they always alternate directions every $1/120$ second. One complete cycle of both directions takes $\frac{1}{60}$ second. Hence the phrase *60-cycle alternating current,* the standard professional name for house current.

Incidentally, a little way for an electron is in a different league from a little way for you. In $\frac{1}{120}$ second, an electron can travel from Boston, Massachusetts, to New Orleans, Louisiana, with some miles left over for sight-seeing.

*Note:* Electrons do their work by passing through things like light bulbs and toasters, not by jumping out the end of a wire into them. This is why AC works just as well as DC.

Most power plants produce mostly AC. They do this for a reason. AC can be transformed, meaning its voltage can be stepped up readily. It is efficient and economical to carry high voltage, low amperage electricity from one place to another. Amps means wire. And wire costs $$$. The higher the amperage, the bigger the wires carrying the electricity will have to be. But since watts = volts × amps, you can get still the same watts by kicking up the volts and cutting down the amps. So, if you are a power plant, it is a common practice for you to step up the volts and reduce the amps.

Let's try to clarify this with an example. Suppose we need 50,000 watts to power the speakers for a rock concert. If the electric company delivered the electricity at 100 volts they would need 500 amp wire to get 50,000 watts to you.

100 volts × 500 amps = 50,000 watts.

The copper wire manufacturer would be delighted — but not the electric company or you — as first the electric company and then you would have to pay for the wire.

*volts x amps = watts*

*wire sizes*

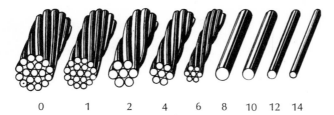

| 0 | 1 | 2 | 4 | 6 | 8 | 10 | 12 | 14 |

Table 19 and the wire size diagram show you the relationship between wire sizes and the amount of amperes they can carry.

| Wire Size | In Conduit | In Free Air |
|---|---|---|
| 14 gauge | 15 amps | 20 amps |
| 12 | 20 | 25 |
| 10 | 30 | 40 |
| 8 | 40 | 55 |
| 6 | 55 | 80 |
| 4 | 70 | 105 |
| 3 | 80 | 120 |
| 2 | 95 | 140 |
| 1 | 110 | 165 |
| 0 | 125 | 195 |
| 00 | 145 | 225 |
| 000 | 165 | 260 |

*Table 19. Ampacities of Copper Wires*

When electricity comes out of a power plant at a very, very high voltage, it is then stepped up to an even higher voltage. And then it is transmitted all the way down to some sort of a substation. The substation, in all probability, is somewhere near your house. Its job is to transform the electricity back down to something like house voltage — always somewhere between 110 and 120 volts, as we have already said — and to send it through wires to your house. The wires come in high to a suburban house, off a pole, but low to a city house, through an underground conduit to the basement. (A conduit is just a metal pipe, just like any other pipe, except that it has a wire running through it instead of water.)

High or low, the first place the electricity goes in the house is — to the meter. The meter is there so that, whatever happens, the utility company will have a record of all the electricity you have used. If your whole system blows up, the company wants to be able to measure how much electricity you used to be able to do that. Then they can bill you, or your estate. The meter measures the electricity you use in some measurement like ampere-hours or kilowatt-hours. They're all the same thing, as it turns out, because

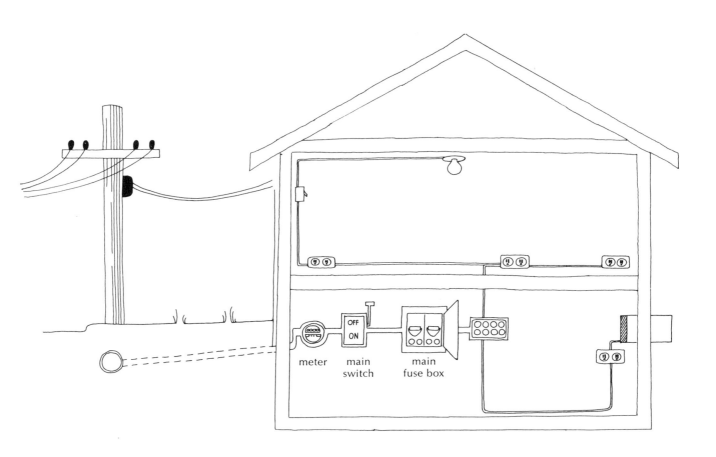

you can convert one thing to another, thanks to our most elegant
formula: watts = volts × amps.

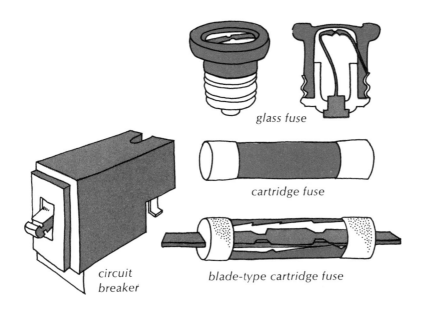

*glass fuse*

*cartridge fuse*

*circuit breaker*

*blade-type cartridge fuse*

The electricity goes from the meter into something called the
main switch. And it is — just what it says it is. It's the switch that
cuts off all the electricity in the house. You will only very rarely pull

this switch. The electricity goes from the main switch directly to the main fuse box, and if the main fuse in the house ever blew out, you might at that time have occasion to pull the main switch.

The main fuse determines the maximum amount of electricity you can ever have in the house. It tells the electricity exactly how much of it will be allowed to enter. And it lets that much in, and no more. Most houses these days have 100 amp main fuses. Some have 200 amps. Most apartments have 30 to 40 amps. It's a measure of how much electricity you have available to you.

A fuse is a safety device. There's a silver wire in it. If too many electrons try to surge through the silver wire at any one time, the friction of their effort will cause the wire to heat up. The heat will melt the silver — and that's what's called a blown fuse, or circuit.

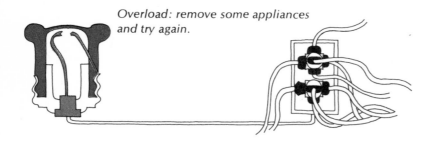

*Overload: remove some appliances and try again.*

The wires carrying the electricity into your house go from the main fuse box into an ordinary fuse box. (You may have a circuit breaker instead of a fuse box, but we have a fuse box because we want to explain a fuse box.) The fuse box farms out the electricity to various individual circuits. The circuits circulate throughout the house, carrying electricity to switches, light fixtures, and outlets (the technical term for which is receptacles). Each circuit is governed by a fuse, which controls the amount of electricity available to that circuit. Here is one circuit.

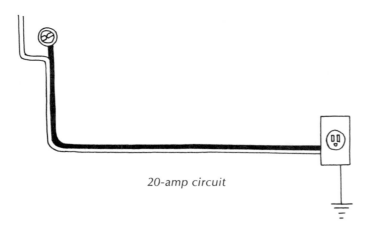

*20-amp circuit*

It's a 20-amp circuit because it has a 20-amp fuse. It's also the simplest circuit imaginable — it's connected to a one-plug receptacle (called a convenience receptacle) used by an air conditioner that requires 20 amps. The more complex circuit services several two-plug receptacles (called duplex receptacles), several light fixtures, and various and sundry switches.

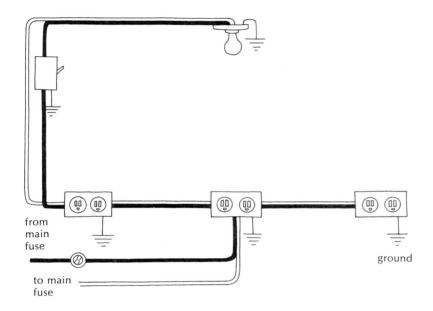

from
main
fuse

to main
fuse

ground

This circuit has a 30-amp fuse so it can carry a load of 30 amps. You can turn on any number of lights and plug in any number of appliances, provided that the total amount of electricity they all consume is less than 30 amps. If the total works out to more than 30 amps, you'll have an overload. An overload will blow the fuse governing the circuit. The circuit itself is actually a part of its own load. The wires themselves, because of friction, consume a little bit of the electricity in the circuit. So do all the connections and the switches. It is possible but unlikely to overload a circuit just by wiring it.

Table 20 is a list of common appliances and the wattages required to operate them. House current can always be taken to be 110 volts. Substitute 110 in our fancy formula (W = V × A) getting W = 110A, then pick the appropriate wattage from the charts, do a little arithmetic, and you know how many amps you have left over in your circuit . . . or how many more you need.

In both of the circuits just pictured, as you can see, *two* wires lead from the fuse to the receptacles, fixtures, switches. And . . .

Wait a minute. *Two wires?* How come *two* wires? What's that all about? Well, it's one of the curious things. It's probably one of the craziest things you've ever heard, but there it is — electricity doesn't flow unless there's a complete circuit. Without a complete circuit, nothing. And what's a complete circuit? Two wires. One wire to take the electricity to a place, another wire to take it back. If there's just one wire, the electricity goes over, but it just sits when it gets there and doesn't do anything. This holds true for all

| Appliance | Watts | Appliance | Watts |
|---|---|---|---|
| Automatic dryer (regular) | 4500 | Garbage disposer | 900 |
| Automatic dryer (high-speed) | 8700 | Hand iron | 1000 |
| Automatic washer | 700 | Home freezer | 350 |
| Automatic toaster | 1100 | Hot water heater | 2500 |
| Blender | 250 | Large grill | 1300 |
| Built-in room heater | 1600 | Refrigerator | 250 |
| Central air conditioner | 5000 | Room heater | 1600 |
| Coffeemaker | 600 | Rotisserie | 1400 |
| Deep fryer | 1320 | Stereo hi-fi | 300 |
| Dishwasher | 1800 | Sump pump | 300 |
| Dishwasher–waste disposer | 1500 | Sunlamp | 275 |
| Electric range | 8000 to 16,000 | Table fan | 75 |
| Electric shaver | 10 | Television set | 300 |
| Food mixer | 150 | Vacuum cleaner | 400 |
| Fuel-fired furnace | 800 | Water pump | 300 to 700 |

Table 20. Loads of Common Appliances

the wiring we have discussed, even though we haven't mentioned it until right now. Power plant to substation to house to receptacle — two wires. Always two wires.

There are also, while we're at it, two ways of blowing a fuse. The way we're only just now mentioning has to do with the two wires. If two wires running parallel to one another are allowed to touch one another, the electrons — an unlimited amount of them — will immediately take advantage of this shortcut and flow right from the wire bringing the electricity to the wire taking it back. The same thing can sometimes happen if two parallel wires carrying current are very close to each other but not touching.

This phenomenon is known as a short circuit. The negative charges desperately want to get to the positive charges, and they do have a certain ability to jump an air gap to do that. Sometimes when you switch a light on or off in the dark, you see a little blue spark. The little blue spark is exactly that. It's the electricity jumping the air to get from the negative to the positive. It's not really a short circuit, though, because a short circuit blows fuses.

If you are lucky enough to have a glass fuse of the old-fashioned kind, it will be able to tell you when it blows whether the problem is a short circuit or an overload. A glass fuse gives you a clear view of the silver wire inside. Either an overload or a short circuit will break the wire. If there's an overload the wire will simply separate into two pieces. If there's a short circuit, however, there will be a little black smudge on the glass itself, obscuring the wire. The reason for that is: An awful lot of heat is coming through on a short circuit, because of the unlimited surge of electrons, and the heat just fizzles the wire in the fuse and causes the black smudge.

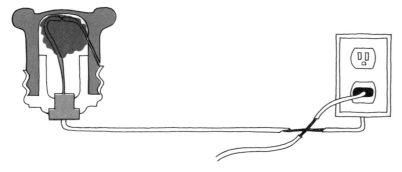

*Short circuit. Danger! Find it before replacing fuse.*

A burned-out fuse must be changed. *Caution:* The fuse blew for a reason, either a short circuit or an overload. You must remove the overload or the short circuit first. This almost always consists of unplugging the offending appliance or article. You can shut off the main switch for extra safety, but it is not really necessary. Just unscrew the glass fuse and replace it with a fuse that has the same capacity, e.g., if it was a 15-amp fuse replace with a new 15-amp fuse. *Don't* ever put in a higher amperage fuse or a copper penny.

Q. Why?
A. The fuse is a safety device. It makes sure that the electricity that goes by can be handled by the wires. Fuses are easy to change. Wires are difficult to replace, particularly if they've taken the house on their burning party.
Q. How about circuit breakers?
A. A circuit breaker is a type of switch. When it goes off simply switch it back on. *First* wait two minutes to allow it to cool, then reset by going all the way *off* and then to *on*.

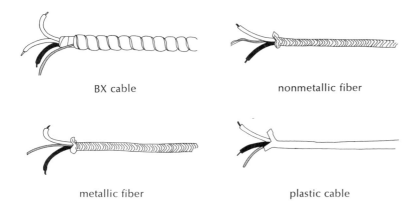

BX cable

nonmetallic fiber

metallic fiber

plastic cable

Here is a picture of the most common type of wiring, found in residential wiring. Wires in combination are called cables. The primary distinguishing factor of BX cable is a sort of metal tape wound around it on the outside. Inside it has wires. That means a wire to bring electricity to you, and a wire to take it back, and, yes, that *is* a third wire. The third wire's called a ground wire; it's an added safety feature (more about it after we talk about the first two wires).

For the sake of calling the two wires something, we'll call the wire that brings the electricity to you the hot wire. And the wire that takes it back we'll call the neutral wire. Now let us imagine a circuit. This circuit has in it one switch and one light bulb.

*correctly switched*

That's the symbol for a switch. And this is a light bulb. We close the switch, and electricity flows through the circuit, and the bulb lights up. Open it, no light. Now, suppose. Instead of putting the switch there, we put it over here.

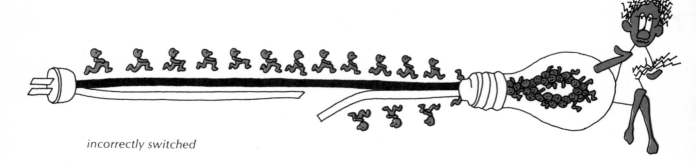

*incorrectly switched*

We open the switch, and the bulb doesn't light. So what's new? The difference is: We've made the bulb part of the hot wire instead of part of the neutral wire. That means that there's now a potential for electricity inside the bulb. "If there's just one wire," we said a couple of pages ago, "the electricity goes over, but it just sits and doesn't do anything." But if something should happen to complete the circuit, the electricity certainly will flow. The potential is in the bulb, as it could not be when the bulb was part of the neutral wire. Then there was potential only up to the switch.

It turns out to be a bad thing to let potential get in a bulb. Reason: There is one thing that conducts electricity really well, and that one thing is the ground. This means that if you were to walk over to this light bulb, and stand on the ground, and then touch either the bulb socket or the exposed metal part of the bulb, *you* would complete the circuit. Yourself and ground would become a neutral wire to take the electricity back to the power station, because the power station is also standing on the ground.

Completing a circuit like that is not very healthy for you. It's just not good for you.

Whereas, of course, if you had the switch over here (see top drawing), as you did before we made you move it around, you could come over and play with the light bulb at any time, without risk. You would be unable to complete a circuit, ever, potential having ended before it reached the bulb.

So that turns out to be the *Second Commandment of Electricity:*

> *Never* put a switch on the neutral wire.
> *Always* put a switch on the hot wire.

The Second Commandment also holds true for fuses. For the same reasons. *Never* put a fuse on the neutral wire. *Always* put a fuse on the hot wire.

How do you know if you are looking at a hot wire or a neutral wire? You look at the color of the insulation around it. The color is part of a code. The reason most codes exist is because they're safety codes, and electricity is mostly codes. The color code is one of the most important electrical codes. If the color of the insulation around the wire you are looking at is *white*, you must be looking at a neutral wire, because neutral wires are always white, and every white wire is a neutral wire. Hot wires will be red, blue, black — or any color, in fact, except white, which is reserved for neutral. *Or* except gray or green, the two colors set aside on mnemonic grounds for the insulation around ground wires. *Gray, green, ground.* Again, more about ground wires in a minute.

All wiring inside a house is done inside these metal boxes, which are called junction boxes. Junction — a place where wires are joined. There is such a thing as a switch box. It's just a junction box with a switch inside it. Then there are ceiling octagon boxes. These are junction boxes from which you might hang light fixtures. Receptacles also live in junction boxes. And a circuit is just wires from a fuse going in and out of various kinds of junction boxes.

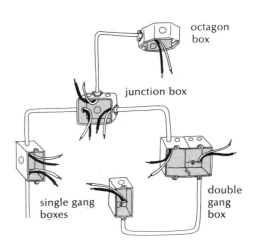

octagon box

junction box

single gang boxes

double gang box

Junction boxes are part of a code, another safety code. A junction box is a place where a person can expose a wire. Wire almost always has something around it — either BX cable wrapping, or tape, or plastic, or rubber, or things. But somewhere a person has to expose bare wire so he can make connections. Wire to wire. Wire to fixture. Wire to receptacle. He does it all in a junction box. In fact, the way things are set up, it's impossible to make a connection outside a junction box. Plug in a blender. We all know it isn't plugged in until the prongs on the plug are completely inside the slots of the receptacle. Well, where's the receptacle? Inside a junction box. So there's the *Third Commandment of Electricity:*

> All connections are made in junction boxes.

Now for ground wires. A ground wire is attached to every junction box and to the ground. A ground wire is attached to every fuse box and to the ground. Power lines are grounded. In fact, almost everything electrical is grounded as often as possible. This is another safety precaution. Should there be an electron buildup, for any reason, in a junction box, the ground wire will take the electricity back to the power plant, thus saving you the trouble of having to conduct the electricity, should you happen to touch the junction box. A ground wire is, in some cases, a bare wire — without any insulation — so that it can pick up as much stray electricity as possible.

*Fourth Commandment of Electricity:*

> All junction boxes must be grounded.

Here's how it looks all wired up.

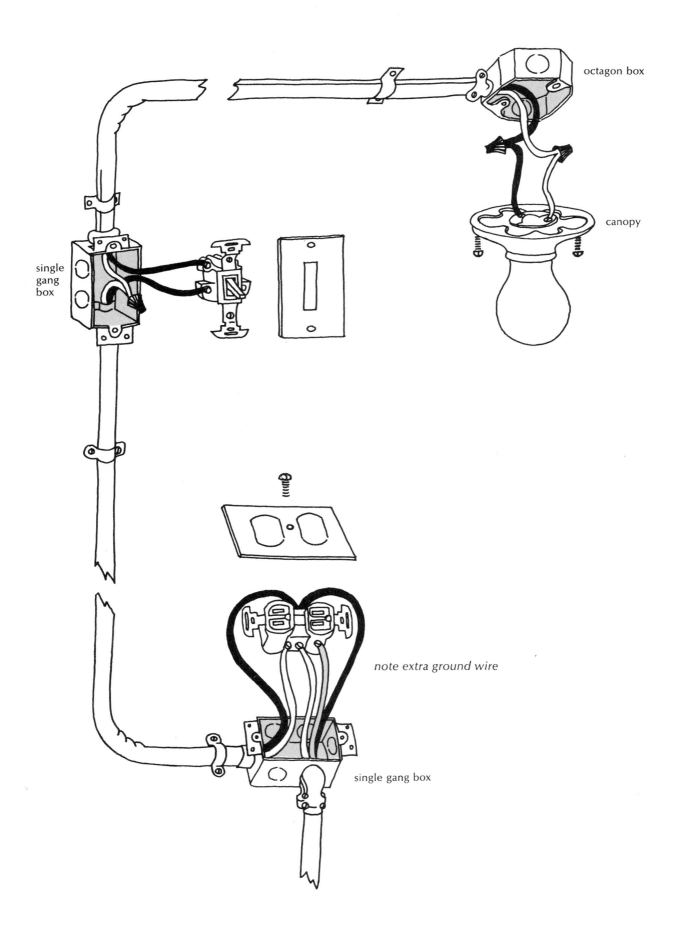

octagon box

canopy

single
gang
box

note extra ground wire

single gang box

The Basic Ingredient: 1 wire stripper.

The wire stripper is an old friend, having been on hand since Chapter One, The Basic Tools. A wire stripper costs a dollar, give or take a little. Wire strippers will be used in all the following recipes, because you can't attach a wire with insulation around the end of it to a screw and hope to make a connection. Reminder of the wire stripper's three-step M.O.: 1. Place the end of the wire that needs stripping inside the little diamond hole of the wire stripper. 2. Squeeze. 3. Pull while squeezing.

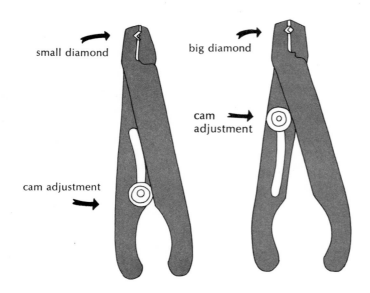

small diamond

big diamond

cam adjustment

cam adjustment

Most switches and receptacles have "strip gauges" (so labeled) on their backs to tell us how much wire must be stripped off to do the job we want to do·with them. We place the end of the wire along the strip gauge, and strip precisely that amount. 1, 2, 3.

All of these recipes are guaranteed to be simple, wholesome, nourishing, a taste treat, and easy to follow. Perfect results every time. You can't go wrong.

### Recipe for Changing a Switch

*Ingredients:*  1 wire stripper
1 screwdriver
1 circuit tester (*described below*)
several wire nuts, aka solderless connectors — if
    necessary
1 old switch

1 new switch
1 nail (optional)

1. Invoke the First Commandment of Electricity: *Turn off the power.*

    Q. How do you know at this point that the power is off?

    A. Well, the switch you're changing has to control some kind of light fixture, right? Turn the switch on, go downstairs, or next door, or wherever, and shut off the fuse. If the light your switch is controlling goes off, you have the right circuit, and the power is now off.

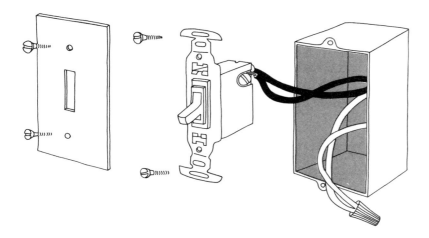

2. Remove the front plate. There are two screws connecting the front plate of the switch to the junction box. Unscrew these two screws and pull the front plate away from the junction box. The switch is connected to the junction box by two more screws, two ordinary long screws. Unscrew the two screws holding the switching mechanism, and the switch and the wires connected to it will pull out.

    *Notice:* that only black wires are connected to the switch.

    *Notice also:* that the only screws on the switch itself are brass screws.

    Which gives us a little rule: Black wires go to brass screws.

    It also invokes the *Second Commandment of Electricity.* One only switches the hot wire.

4. Now, a safety check. Take a little 59-cent circuit tester (49 cents if you're lucky). It's a little lamp with two wires coming out of it. It has a little clip so it can sit in your pocket.

    Use it to see if there is any electric power left in the switch. Put one of the probes of the circuit tester on the brass screws of the switch, one at a time, and the other probe on the junction box around the switch. The junction box is grounded. *Fourth Commandment of Electricity.* The light should not light.

*circuit tester*

5. If the light doesn't light, take off the two brass screws, take off the two black wires, and throw the old switch away.

6. *Everything in reverse:* Attach the two black wires to the two brass screws of the new switch. Attach the new switch to the junction box with the two long screws that came with it. Attach the front plate to the junction box with the two front plate screws you still have and didn't throw away after all.

New kinds of switches (and receptacles) have holes in back of the brass screws. The holes are for attaching wires without screwing. To use the holes:

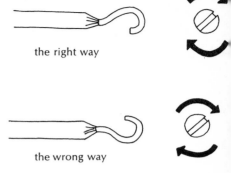

the right way

the wrong way

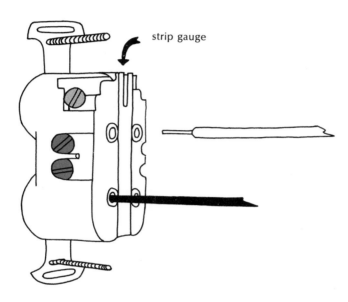

strip gauge

A. Lay the wire alongside the strip gauge on the back of the switch (*see above*).

B. Strip off just the right amount of insulation with a wire stripper (*see above*, The Basic Ingredient).

C. Push the wire into the hole. Done. The hole has a spring clip and will hold the wire. (To release the wire, insert a screwdriver or a nail into the slot next to the hole. This releases the spring clip.)

---

You will notice that there are two white wires running through the junction box. (Note that they are not always there.) These two white wires should only be wired to each other — and they must be wired together to complete the circuit, because they are, of course, the neutral wire. They are wired together with a *wire nut*, also called a *solderless connector.* It's the right way to wire things. Faster than tape. Neater. More permanent. All it is is a little plastic goody with a thread in it. In order to put it on, you put the two white (in this case) wires together and screw it on. It cuts its own thread, and the wire is wired. The medium-sized wire nut is the kind you need for most wiring. It usually says on the back of the wire nut package how many wires of what gauge will fit into the wire nut in that package.

---

## Recipe for Replacing a Switch with a Dimmer

(Dimmers are only good for incandescent fixtures of low wattage, i.e., *lamps*. Check the manufacturer's specifications on a dimmer before buying it to see what amount of wattage it can handle. Generally this will be 600W, although some dimmers can handle up to 1000W. A circuit controlled by a dimmer shouldn't be overloaded. If too much heat passes through a dimmer its internal circuits will fail.)

*Ingredients:*  1 dimmer
             1 screwdriver
             2 solderless connectors
             1 circuit tester

1. Invoke the First Commandment of Electricity: Turn off the power.
   Q. How do you know if . . .
   A. You read step 1 of "Recipe for Changing a Switch."

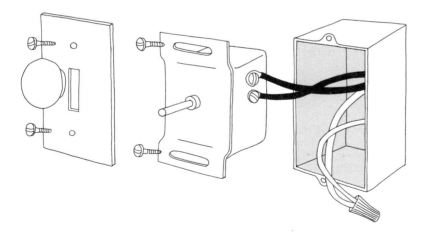

2. Remove the front plate of the switch. Unscrew the two brass screws holding the front plate to the junction box, and put them and the front plate to one side.
3. Unscrew the two long screws holding the switching mechanism to the junction box and pull the switch and the two black wires connected to it away from the junction box.

4. Safety check with circuit tester. See step 4 of "Recipe for Changing a Switch."

5. If the switch is an old switch, loosen the switch's two brass screws and detach the two black wires from it and throw it away. If the switch is a new switch, put screwdriver or nail in the holes in back of the switch's two brass screws and detach the two black wires from it and throw it away.

6. The dimmer. The dimmer has a knob on the front, where the switch on a switch is, and — generally speaking — two black wires already attached on the back. Take off the knob, and put it next to the front plate and the front plate screws. Attach the two black wires sticking out of the junction box to the dimmer's two black wires with two solderless connectors.

7. Attach the dimmer itself to the junction box with the two long screws that came with it.

8. Put the front plate back on.

9. Put the dimmer knob back on the dimmer.

---

## Recipe for Changing a Receptacle

(We are only giving out instructions for installing a new three-wire grounded duplex receptacle. *That kind.* It's our effort to help the country phase out ungrounded wiring, the one good deed you will find in this book. Grounded receptacles are now required by the National Electric Code, they're safer, and they make more sense. Many power tools and some appliances now come with grounded plugs, and more will undoubtedly do so. You *cannot* attach a three-prong grounded receptacle to an ungrounded two-wire system.)

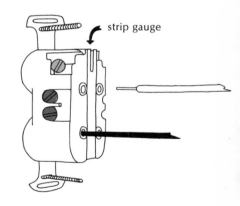
strip gauge

*Ingredients:*  1 screwdriver
1 new grounded receptacle
I gray or green or bare ground wire — if necessary
1 wire stripper — if necessary

1. Invoke the First Commandment of Electricity: Turn off the power.

2. Safety check with circuit tester. Put one of the probes of the circuit tester in one of the holes of the old receptacle and the other probe in the other hole. (If the old receptacle is a grounded receptacle, check all the slots with each other.) The light should not light.

3. Remove cover plate, as the front plate on a receptacle is called. Cover plates are attached with one screw. Put the cover plate and its screw to one side.

4. Unscrew the old receptacle from the junction box — two

screws. These are generally long screws, and this generally takes a long time. Pull the old receptacle out of the junction box and unscrew or nail-in-spring-clip the wires attached to it. If the receptacle is the only receptacle on the circuit, or if it is the last of a series of receptacles on a circuit, it will have one hot wire and one neutral wire attached to it. If it is one of a series and not the guy on the end, it will be connected up to two hot wires and two neutral wires. As you unscrew or nail-in-spring-clip the wires, you notice that (as in a switch) the hot wires are attached to brass screws, because of the little rule that black wires go to brass screws. You are also noticing that the neutral wires are attached to chrome screws. Which gives us another little rule: White wires go to chrome screws. If the old receptacle is a grounded receptacle, you are also detaching a ground wire from it, and noticing that it has been attached to a green screw. *Another* little rule: Gray/green/bare wires go to green screws. Enough noticing. Throw the old receptacle away.

5. Attach the new receptacle to the one or two hot wires and the one or two neutral wires in the junction box, remembering the little rules. Black wires go to brass screws; white wires go to chrome screws. The chrome screw on the receptacle may well be labeled White. If there is a ground wire in the junction box, attach it to the green screw on the new receptacle. If the just-thrown-out old receptacle wasn't grounded, you must now ground the new receptacle. Take a ground wire — a bare one, a green one, a gray one, you don't care — and attach it anywhere on the junction box as securely as you can. Every junction box has lots of holes in it, and usually a screw or a clip or a nut, so there's no problem here. Just remember to strip the wire, if it ain't bare, at the point where you are securely fastening it to the junction box. Then attach the other end of the wire to the green screw on the new receptacle. Ground wires go to green screws.

6. Reassemble. Push the new-and-now-wired device into the junction box, and attach it to the junction box with the two (generally) long screws that come with it. Put the cover plate back on with the short center screw laid aside with it. Done.

---

*May we recommend?* There's a recently developed product called a childproof safety receptacle. When not in use, the disk of the receptacle face is turned so that the holes are not lined up with the wires behind them and you can't plug in either an appliance or a finger. It's childproof because it takes an adult's strength to turn the disk and line up the holes.

*Ingredients:* 1 screwdriver
1 circuit tester
2 solderless connectors
1 strip of white tape — if necessary
1 circuit tester
1 new ceiling fixture

1. Invoke the First Commandment of Electricity: Turn off the power.

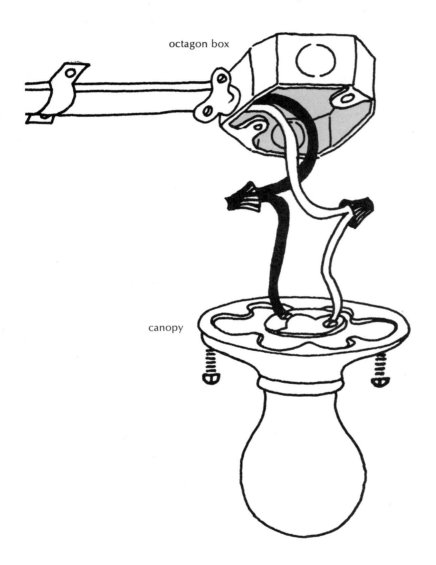

octagon box

canopy

2. Between every ceiling fixture and the junction box to which it has been wired lies a cap called a *canopy*. The canopy has been placed there for esthetic and safety reasons, and it hides the wiring. It is fastened either by two screws at its side, or by a central nut, or by one small central screw. Detach this canopy. Unscrew the screws or loosen the

nut. Pull the canopy down to reveal what's going on in there.

3. What's going on is that a black wire from the lamp is connected to a black wire from the circuit by a solderless connector or by a piece of tape. A white wire from the lamp is likewise connected to a white wire from the circuit. (There's also a ground wire in the junction box, but its only function is to ground the junction box, so it is already connected to the junction box and the ground, and you don't have to mess with it.) The problem here is that in old buildings both the black wires and the white wires are so dirty and grungy that you can't tell which is who. This is the only time a problem ever arises in any household wiring; we solve it by adopting a special procedure that demands special caution. If you can't tell which is who in your ceiling junction box, do A, B, C. (If you *can*, skip these dramatics and we'll see you at step 4.)

   A. *Make sure* you're not grounded. Wear insulated gloves or rubber boots or stand on a wooden leg or a wooden chair.

   B. Detach the old ceiling fixture from the two wires in the junction box. *Now:* Separate the two wires in the junction box, and leave them exposed, *making sure* that they are *not* touching each other and *not* touching the junction box anywhere — even where they're insulated, in case the insulation has cracked. Please be careful about this. There is a safety hazard.

   C. Turn the power on, and the switch governing the ceiling junction box. Making sure a second time that you are not grounded, take a circuit tester and touch one of its probes to the end of one of the two exposed wires in the junction box. Touch the other probe to the junction box. If the little light in the circuit tester lights up, the wire you're testing is the hot wire. If the light doesn't light, it's the neutral wire. Now you know what you need to know. Take a strip of white tape and tape it to the neutral wire for identification. Now you will continue to know what you need to know. Don't forget to turn off the power again.

4. Connect the new ceiling fixture to the wires in the junction box with solderless connectors. Black wire to black wire and white wire to white wire. Fasten the canopy of the new fixture. Put in a light bulb and have fun.

---

### Recipe for Changing a Plug

If you can find them, only buy plugs one of whose prongs is taller than the other — like the one shown at right. These are the plugs made to fit the new grounded receptacles. The

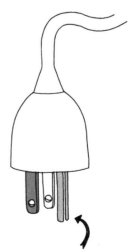

note the long grounding prong

shorter prong is the hot wire. The advantage of uneven prongs is always being able to plug something in the right way.

Changing a plug can be done in either of two ways:

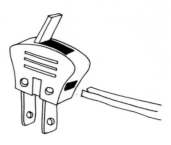

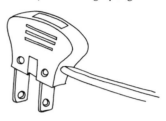

*quick change plug*

Light-duty: *For plugs on light-duty wires* — meaning lamps and small wattage appliances that use 18-to-20-gauge wire called *lamp cord* — only two ingredients are required:

> wire cutters and
> a two-prong plug with a spring-loaded clip

1. Cut the old plug off with the wire cutters.
2. Squeeze the two prongs of the new clip. This loosens the cover. Spread the two prongs apart. Insert the lamp cord, without stripping. Squeeze the prongs. Squeezing drives two spikes through the wire, making a good connection between the prongs and the wire. Continue squeezing and slip the cover over the plug.

Heavy-duty: *For plugs on heavier-duty wires,* three ingredients:

> wire cutter
> screwdriver
> three-prong plug

1. Cut off the old plug.
2. Remove the fiber washer on the new plug. This will uncover three screws: a brass screw, a chrome screw, and a green screw. Little rules tell us what to do. Strip the wire, insert it through the plug, and tie an underwriter's knot in it so that it becomes fatter than the plug opening. Then attach each

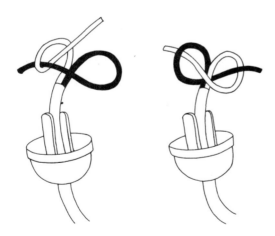

*underwriter's knot*

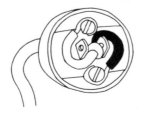

wire to the appropriate terminal (black to brass, white to chrome, ground to green). Pull the wire back so that the knot catches at the opening. Replace the fiber washer. tighten the clamp screws (if any) at the other end of the washer, and you're in business.

Recipe for Fixing a Lamp

*Ingredients:*   1 new lamp socket*
                1 pair pliers — if necessary
                1 screwdriver

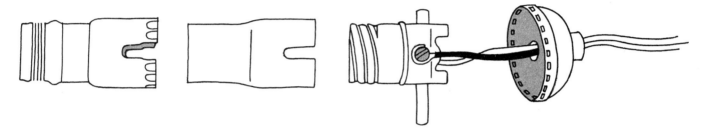

1. Lamp sockets say Press. They usually say it somewhere near the switch. Pressing here separates the old socket from the plate beneath it. If you're strong enough, press. If you're not strong enough, use pliers — but be careful not to be too strong with the pliers. Pull the plate with your other hand. It slides down and then one can remove the whole assembly.

2. We see a brass connection and a chrome connection. Unscrew the two wires, and throw away the old socket, connections, plate, and switch. It's tired. It's done its duty, and it deserves a rest. It can't be repaired — either the switch has gone bad, or the cardboard insulation in the socket has gotten tired of being cooked. The cost of a new lamp socket is nominal.

3. Slide the base plate of the new lamp socket over the wires, and attach the two wires to the two screws of the new lamp socket. Lamp cord insulation is all the same color so it'll look purty, and the only way you can tell the hot line is that the insulation around it is marked with a ridge or a series of ridges.

4. Press again, and squeeze the new lamp socket together with the base plate. You've got it.

* There are three different kinds of lamp sockets. One has a slide switch (*slide-click*), another has a turn switch (*snap-snap*), and the third has a chain switch (*zit-zit-zit-zit*). Fortunately, they are all essentially the same.

Most appliances these days are electrical, relatively sophisticated, and have a half-life of one day after the guarantee runs out. There are hundreds of types of appliances, thousands of varieties of types, and millions of parts for varieties of types. We are not going to make this an appliance repair subbook. (Or, more realistically, a subencyclopedia.) What we are going to do is tell you a magic bit of information, wisdom from all the ages of repairdom:

> When you hear hoofbeats, don't look for zebras
> (unless you're on the Serengeti Plain).

Pause here for a moment and reflect on this statement. . . . From it we will extrapolate the

---

### Universal Appliance Repair Recipe

*Ingredients:* "inoperative" appliance
1 basic tool kit
pair eyes
liberal dose common sense
1 copy of "When you hear . . ." (to be muttered
  periodically)

1. Observe plug. If out, plug in and try appliance again. This accounts for 25 percent of all inoperative appliances (personal survey).
2. Check outlet for power with circuit tester. Repair if necessary. This accounts for another 20 percent of inoperative appliances (same survey).
3. Check plug and cord for wear and tear. Replace if necessary. Thirty percent more accounted for.
4. If readily accessible replace switch on appliance. This is *not* to be done on your television set. !!!! Televisions are very high voltage appliances and they have the capacity to store voltage even when shut off. Sadly, we must bow to the TV repairman after step 3. !!!! This accounts for 10 percent more inoperative appliances.
5. If it still doesn't work — and this will be 15 percent of the time — take appliance to factory service shop, or use it for a footstool or flowerpot, or discard appliance. This decision will depend on initial cost, size and shape, or mood.

---

If you are the persistent sort and are willing to risk destruction of your appliance in the interest of knowledge, then go ahead and take the appliance apart. Very often you will see a disconnected wire, or a burned-out part, or a missing part, or a loose screw, or something very simple like that. It is very likely that this part was the culprit. If you replace the faulty part and remember to put all the things you took apart back together again, in the same manner, you will have used all the ingredients in the recipe and have repaired the bugger. This is a fairly likely outcome in most cases. Radios, stereo systems, and, particularly, *televisions* are specific exceptions. For sophisticated electronic equipment you need sophisticated electronic instruments.

Sometimes, you can take something apart, put it back together again the same way you took it apart, having repaired or replaced nothing, and believe it or not, the damn thing works. There is no explanation for this. It is analogous to the "swift-kick principle." Just thank the Fixin' Gods, stick out your chest, and smile. Happy fixin'!

Goom-bye

Dear Friends,

This book should be thrown away as soon as possible. Know-how is not something that is in a book, it is something that is in people. When you can do something — like making a bead and painting a straight line with a 3-inch brush — easily, and without thinking consciously about any of the steps involved, and without referring back to pages 125 to 127 of this book, then you will have that know-how securely in you — as securely as you already have the know-how for sitting, for talking, for reading.

All we can do, aside from listing the steps of each process, is tell you two things:

1. Know-how is not hard to acquire, because your body wants to acquire it. In fact, there's nothing to it but to do it.

2. It's OK to make mistakes, everybody does. The only function of mistakes is feedback — they tell you what you don't know yet. They do not condemn you to the heartbreak of psoriasis. How do you get to Carnegie Hall? Practice!

Now, have fun.

# Glossary

| | |
|---|---|
| Alkyd Paint | Synthetic oil is the vehicle. |
| Alligatoring | In painting, the hairline cracks that develop in an alligatorlike pattern because the paint is too thick. *See Coefficient of Thermal Expansion.* |
| Alternating Current (AC) | Electricity (electrons) flows in one direction, stops, turns around, and flows in the opposite direction. In 60-cycle AC it turns around 120 times a second. Fast, huh? |
| Ampere-hour | The use of 1 amp for 1 hour. |

$$1 \text{ volt } \times \ 1 \text{ amp} = \ 1 \text{ amp-hour.}$$
$$10 \text{ volts} \times \ 1 \text{ amp} = 10 \text{ amp-hours.}$$
$$1 \text{ volt } \times 10 \text{ amp} = 10 \text{ amp-hours.}$$

| | |
|---|---|
| Amps (Amperage) | A unit used to denote the number of electrons flowing through a conductor. Approximately 6,280,000,000,000,000,000 electrons equal one amp per second. |
| Antiknock Chamber | A device to prevent the water from rattling around in your pipes; it is an air chamber. See illustrations on pages 145 and 147. |
| Auger, or Snake | A long and tightly coiled wire with which one explores sewer pipes, finds blockages; and then by twisting, turning, pushing, and pulling, removes them. See illustration on page 153. |
| Back Fill | The soil, gravel, sand, etc., used to fill up the hole around foundation. Fill is any material used to fill an excavation. |
| Ball Float Valve | The valve inside the toilet tank that shuts off the water when the tank is full. See illustration on page 156. |
| Band | A piece of trim used to cover up the ends of joists. |
| Baseboard | The piece of wood or vinyl molding between the floor and wall. |
| Basic | See Webster. |
| Bead Technique | *The* way to paint with a brush, using the little bead of paint that forms at the top instead of the bristles to paint a straight line. |
| Beam, or Girder | A horizontal member used to support joists and therefore usually larger than joists. See illustration on page 78. |
| Below Grade | Belowground. |
| Blown Fuse | A fuse that has done the job intended for it and is now retired from the scene. |

| | |
|---|---|
| Board Foot | A piece of lumber 1 inch thick × 12 inches wide × 12 inches long. See chart page 44. |
| Bodies | See yourself. Look in the mirror. |
| Bonnet | See illustration on page 160. |
| Bowing | Deformation along the length of lumber. |
| Bricks | A little clay containing iron and other impurities. Add water and bake till hard. |
| Bridging | Crossbracing between joists to keep them from moving. See illustration on page 77. |
| Building | A pile of stones or wood or metal in which we perform our activities. Look around you. |
| Buttering | Spreading mortar on a block or brick. |
| Butt Joint | The simplest wood joint, made by butting two pieces of wood together and fastening any way you like. See illustration on page 61. |
| BX Cable | Insulated wires wrapped in metal. The most common type of cable used in house wiring. See illustration on page 181. |
| Cam | Generally a wheel that has its axis of rotation off center. (Like the driving wheels of a steam locomotive if you're old enough to remember.) |
| Carbide Steel | The hardest steel currently available. It has a high carbon content. Cutting edges last 10 to 40 times longer than high-speed steel. It is very brittle. |
| Cement | Made by burning a mixture of clay and limestone in an oven. The ashes are then pulverized into a powder known as cement. |
| Ceiling Octagon Box | A junction box shaped like an octagon. It is placed in or on the ceiling. Light fixtures are then attached to it. |
| Chatter | To oscillate like windup false teeth. |
| Check | A defect in wood. A separation across the grain. See illustration on page 40. |
| Cinder Block | Preformed blocks made from a mixture of cement, sand, cinders, and water. They are lighter and not as strong as concrete blocks, thus cheaper. |
| Cinders | Burned coal or wood. |
| Circuit | A number of conductors connected together for the purpose of carrying an electric current. |
| Circuit Breaker | A switch for making and breaking an electric current under normal conditions — and also under abnormal conditions, such as overload or a short circuit. |
| Clean Out | In plumbing, a cap nut on the bottom of a trap or near a curve in the waste line that can be removed to clean out the waste line. See illustration on page 151. |
| Clear Wood | Wood without any defects (knots, checks, splits etc.). The most expensive grade of lumber. See chart on page 41. |
| Coefficient of Thermal Expansion | The rate at which a material expands or contracts due to changes in temperature. It is found empirically. |
| Column | A vertical member carrying floors or other loads. |
| Complete a Circuit | To tap the flow of electrons to do work: light a light, drive a motor, etc. |
| Concrete | A mixture of cement, sand, gravel, and water. |
| Concrete Block | A preformed block of concrete. See also Cinder Block and Concrete. |
| Conductivity | A measurement of a material as a conductor. |

| | |
|---|---|
| Conductor | A material (usually metal) which offers a low resistance to the flow of electrons (current). The part of an electric transmission, distribution, or wiring system that actually carries the current. |
| Conduit | In electricity, a hollow pipe used to carry the wires to protect them from the elements. |
| Conifers | Softwood trees with cone-bearing needle-type leaves. They keep their leaves year round. See chart on page 43. |
| Construction Grade | A grade of lumber, which permits substantial defects. See chart on page 41. |
| Convenience Receptacle | A convenient place to plug a plug in. |
| Cupping | Deformation across the width of a piece of lumber. See illustration on page 38. |
| Curtain Wall | A non-load-bearing wall used to keep out the elements. See illustration on page 80. |
| "Cut a Tooth" | To roughen a glossy surface either mechanically (sanding) or chemically (saturated solution of trisodium-phosphate). |
| Cutting In | Painting strips around all windows, door, color changes, and painting in corners. Doing all the brushwork. |
| Dado Joint | A joint where a groove is cut into one of the pieces and the other piece is then placed into that groove and fastened any way you like. For illustration, see page 62. |
| Deciduous | Broad-leaf trees that loose their leaves in winter. They give us hardwoods. See chart on page 42. |
| Die Board | A veneer plywood using very thin, high-quality wood. Shoe heels are often made of die board. See illustration on page 48. |
| Differential Flow of Water | When water flows at different rates. *Example:* First the cold water flows at 2 gallons per minute and your shower feels great. Then it flows at 4 gallons per minute and you become a person on the rocks. |
| Dimple | To set nails below the surface in Sheetrock *without* tearing the paper. |
| Direct Current (DC) | Electrons (electrical current) flow in one direction only. |
| Door Stop | The pieces of molding running around the inside of a door frame which keep the door from opening in both directions. |
| Drag | Partially dried paint slowing down the progress of your brush. A bad time. |
| Drive Tool | A tool used for positioning and holding a drive pin. |
| Drop Forging | The process of dropping a very heavy weight on molten steel, compressing the metal, thereby making it stronger. |
| Ducts | Large pipes for air. Usually rectangular and made of sheet metal. |
| Duplex Receptacle | In electricity, a place to plug two plugs in. |
| Edge-Sawn (Quartersawn) | A type of lumber that is made by sawing the log first into lengthwise quarters and then at 45-degree angles to both flat sides of the remaining slice of log pie. See illustration on page 37. |
| Electrical Current | The flow of electrons. |
| Elevation | A full frontal view of a building or object (see Chapter Three). |
| Enamel Paint | Varnish is the vehicle. Available in flat, satin, semi-gloss, gloss, and high gloss. |
| Excavation | A hole in the ground. See illustration on page 73. |

| | |
|---|---|
| Exterior Paint | Usually self-cleaning or self-chalking, it is more elastic than interior paint. |
| Exterior Plywood | Plywood using waterproof glue. See chart on page 51. |
| Feather | In painting, to thin out the edges so that a ridge is not formed. |
| Female Threads | Treads on the inside of anything (nuts, fittings). Female threads accept mal threads. |
| Ferrous Metals | Iron, steel. |
| Ferrule | Metal ring around the handle of a chisel, saw, paintbrush, etc. Used to fasten the business end to the social end. |
| Fir Core | Plywood having thin layers (veneers or plies) of Douglas fir as its core. See illustration on page 48. |
| Firring Strips | $1 \times 2$ or $1 \times 3$ lumber nailed over an existing wall to act as proxy studs. |
| Fixed Glass | Windows that don't open. |
| Flags | Split ends at the end of bristles (natural or nylon) on good quality brushes. |
| Flat | Paint that is not shiny. |
| Flat-Sawn (Plain-Sawn) | Growth rings of tree form an angle of less than 45 degrees to wide face of board. See illustration on page 36. |
| Floor Tile | Nine- or 12-inch-square material used to cover floors (see Chapter Four). |
| Flush Valve | A high-pressure-fed valve or diaphragm- or piston-type used to flush toilets. See illustration on page 155. |
| Foot | 12 inches. |
| Footing | Concrete feet for house usually 8 inches thick and 16 inches wide on which the foundation walls stand. (Legs need feet for balance, so do buildings.) See illustration on page 74. |
| Footing Drain | A drain around the footing to keep water from building up and destroying the footing. See illustration on page 81. |
| Foundation Walls | The leg bone's connected to the foot bone is to people as the foundation is connected to the footing. A load-bearing wall below grade level. See illustration on page 74. |
| Fresh Air Intake | A vent at ground level to take fresh air into the waste system to prevent noxious gas buildup. See illustration on page 151. |
| Fuse | A device used for protecting electrical apparatus against the effect of excess current. Types are: Blade type, above 60 amps; cartridge, 30–60 amps; glass type 10–30 amps. |
| Fuse Box | A box where fuses reside. |
| Gasket | A piece of goo (usually rubber) which lives between two pieces of metal and makes them fit together well and not leak. |
| Gate Valve | A valve in which a metal door (gate) comes down to shut off the flow of water. These valves are found along the piping and are designed to be turned on and off sparingly. See illustration on page 146. |
| Generator | A machine that transforms mechanical energy into electrical energy. It works by moving a conductor through a magnetic field. See illustration on page 173. |
| Glazier's Points | Little nails that hold glass panes in window frames. |
| Glazing Putty | Goo that holds some windows in and seals out drafts. |

| | |
|---|---|
| Globe Valve | The kind of valve that is frequently turned on and off, such as a faucet. See illustration on page 146. |
| Grade | Level of the ground. |
| Grit Number | Refers to the number of grits per square unit for sandpaper. The more grits per square unit, the smoother the sandpaper. See sandpaper chart on page 54. |
| Ground Wire (or Line in Electricity) | The safety line that at some point is securely connected to the ground (earth, terra firma, etc.). |
| Grout | Mortar to which enough water has been added to make pourable. Has been added in mortar joints. It is used for filling cracks and spaces between tiles. |
| Gypsum Block | Cast block of gypsum, aka plaster. |
| Gypsum Board or Gyp Board | Gypsum between two layers of paper. Also called plasterboard, Sheetrock, wallboard. |
| Half Lap | Overlapping the paint swatches the roller makes. See illustration on page 119. |
| Hardwood | From deciduous trees, i.e., the trees that lose their leaves in winter. |
| Header | A board (usually a 4 × 8 or larger) to which joists are fastened. Usually used around openings, such as stairs. |
| Head Pressure | The height to which water will rise — the phenomenon of water seeking to reach its own level, the level it came from, by pushing. Also refers to the force of the push. See page 143. |
| High Gloss | The shiniest kind of paint. |
| High-Speed Steel | A hard steel used in metal cutting because it retains its hardness at a low red heat. |
| Hollow Ground | Grinding that gives a concave surface to saws, chisels, and other cutting tools. Found in the best-quality tools. *See also* Taper Ground. |
| Hollow Tile Walls | Walls made with thin hollow clay bricks. Plaster or glazed tile is usually applied. |
| Hollow Wall Anchors | See illustration on page 100. |
| Hollow Walls | Generally a wood or metal stud wall that does the work, to which wood or Sheetrock or plaster is applied. See illustration on page 91. |
| Hot Line or Wire in Electricity | The line that is switched or fused. It is usually red or black or blue. |
| House | A building in which we live, love, and suffer, and that is worth fixing. |
| House Trap | The last trap on the waste line before it exits from your house to the septic tank or main (city) waste line. See illustration on page 151. |
| Inch | $\frac{1}{12}$ of a foot. |
| Insulator | Material that offers a high resistance to the flow of electrons. |
| Interior Paint | Paint suitable for interior use only. |
| Interior Plywood | Plywood using moisture-resistant glue. See chart on page 51. |
| Iron Coat | A special paint with iron chips in it that grow into rust and waterproof foundation walls. |
| Jamb | The side of a door frame. |
| Joint | The juxtaposition of two or more pieces of wood so as to accomplish the joining of said pieces of wood. |

| | |
|---|---|
| Joist | The horizontal beam that holds up floors and ceilings, usually a 2 × 8 or larger. See illustration on page 77. |
| Junction Box | In electricity, the box where wires are joined together or bent asunder. |
| Kerf | The cut made by a saw. |
| Kiln-Dried Lumber | Lumber dried in an oven to reduce its moisture content. |
| Kilowatt-Hour | 1,000 watts used for one hour. |

$$1{,}000 \text{ watts} \times 1 \text{ hr} = 1 \text{ kw hour}$$
$$10{,}000 \text{ watts} \times 1 \text{ hr} = 10 \text{ kw hours}$$
$$20{,}000 \text{ watts} \times \tfrac{1}{2} \text{ hr} = 10 \text{ kw hours}$$

| | |
|---|---|
| Lacquer | A mixture of a volatile (fast-evaporating) liquid with resin and/or cellulose ester. An on-the-surface finish. See chart on pages 57–58. |
| Lacquer Paint | Pigment in a volatile (fast-evaporating) liquid. Usually sprayed on because of this trait. |
| Lap Joint | A joint in which mating sections are cut out of both pieces that are then overlapped and joined together as you like. For illustration see page 62. |
| Latex Paint | Paint to which rubber has been added as the binding agent. Usually (but not always) these are water-thinned paints. |
| Level | True horizontal. |
| Limestone | Chalk. |
| Load-Bearing Walls | Walls that carry other walls and floors. |
| Lumber Core | Plywood with thin layers (veneers or plies) of wood as the bread and kiln-dried pieces of lumber stacked side by side as the peanut butter and jelly. See illustration on page 48. |
| Main Clean Out | See illustration on page 151. |
| Main Fuse Box | The home of the main fuse. |
| Main Switch | The switch just after the meter that shuts all the power off on that circuit so that the system can be worked on. |
| Male Thread | Thread on the outside of anything. Male threads go into female threads. See illustration on page 159. |
| Masonry | Stone or any combination of stone, clay (bricks), sand, cement, water. |
| Metal Lath | A metal mesh screen attached to wood or metal studs to which plaster is applied. See illustration on page 92. |
| Meter | A passive device used for counting electrons as they go by. |
| Mil | $\frac{1}{1{,}000}$ of an inch. |
| Miter Box | See illustration on page 13. |
| Miter Joint | A joint where the two pieces are each cut at a 45-degree angle and then joined together any way you like. For illustration, see page 61. |
| Mixing Valve | A valve that mixes cold and hot water and gives us comfortable water for showers. See illustration on page 162. |
| Mortar | Used for holding masonry together, usually brick or stone. A mixture of cement, lime or lime putty, sand, and water. Add the maximum amount of water that will still give the consistency of a stiff, thick frosting (as in cake!) |
| Mortar Joint | The mortar between blocks or bricks. It's what holds them together. |

| | |
|---|---|
| Mortar Mixture | (Using masonry cement)<br>General Use — Type N<br>    1 part masonry cement, 3 parts sand. Add enough water to make it good and sticky. Use within 2 hours.<br>High Strength — Type M<br>    1 part masonry (type 11) cement, 1 part Portland cement, 6 parts sand. Add enough water to make it good and sticky. Use within 2 hours.<br>Medium strength — Type N (most often used)<br>    For parapet walls, exposed exterior walls.<br>        1 part Portland cement, 1 part lime or lime putty, 6 parts damp sand, and enough water to make it good and sticky. Use within 2 hours.<br>High-strength mortar — Type M<br>    For foundation walls and ground contact.<br>        1 part Portland cement, ¼ part lime or lime putty, 3¾ parts damp sand, and enough water to make it good and sticky. Use within 2 hours. |
| Morticing | Cutting of slots (usually in wood) to accept hinges or other pieces of wood and make them fit nice and neat. |
| Movable Sash | A window that opens. |
| Mullion | A vertical member of a window frame separating adjacent windows. |
| Muntins | The vertical and horizontal bars separating adjacent panes of glass in a window. |
| Nap | In painting, the length of the roller fiber. |
| Neutral Line or Wire | In electricity, the line that is *never* switched or fused. Its color should always be white. |
| Nonferrous Metals | Aluminum, bronze, copper, gold, lead, platinum, silver. Everything but iron or steel. |
| Non-Load-Bearing Walls | Walls that only carry their own weight. |
| Number Two | A grade of lumber between clear and construction that allows a limited number and type of defects. See chart on page 41. |
| Ohm | A measure of the resistance to the flow of electrons. In an ideal conductor all the electrons would flow, but in the real world there are no ideal conductors. The higher the ohms, the higher the resistance to the flow of electrons through a conductor (or insulator). Ohms are measured with an ohmmeter. |
| Oil Paint | Any paint with oil (usually boiled linseed oil) as a vehicle. |
| On Center | From the center (point or line) of one object (stud, bolt, etc.) to the center (point or line) of another. |
| Overflow Tube | The tube sticking up inside a toilet's tank through which water flows slowly in order to seal the toilet trap. See illustration on page 156. |
| Overload | When a circuit uses more amps than it is wired or fused for. |
| Packing | Goo (usually some sort of plastic) that lives under a faucet bonnet and keeps the faucet from leaking around the bonnet when the faucet is on. |
| Paneling | Any rigid sheet or plank used as a wall covering. |
| Pecks | Decay and insect damage in wood. A defect. See illustration on page 40. |
| Perspective | A drawing of a building or object as the eye actually sees it (see Chapter Three). |
| Pigment | Generally a metallic oxide that forms a paint when mixed with a suitable liquid (vehicle). |

| | |
|---|---|
| Section | A vertical slice through a building (see Chapter Three). |
| Self-Cleaning Paint | Exterior paint that breaks down at a set rate due to exposure to the elements. good quality to have for paint used on the exterior as it prevents excessive pair buildup. |
| Semi-Gloss | Paint that is fairly shiny. |
| Septic Line | Any pipe used to take away the water you have dirtied. |
| Septic System | The system of pipes that takes away your dirtied water and purifies it (sup posedly) before dumping it into our waterways. |
| Septic Tank | A tank (usually concrete) in which solid organic sewage (we all know what tha is!) is decomposed and purified by anaerobic bacteria (did you ever see an aerobic bacteria?). |
| Set | In saw blades, the process of bending one tooth left, the next one right, then lef and so on. Makes for a wider kerf (cut) and helps to prevent rest of saw fror binding in wood. |
| Sewer System | The gravity system for getting rid of liquid wastes. |
| Shakes | 1. Splits off the edges of a board along the grain. A defect. See illustration o page 40. 2. Shingles. |
| Sheathing | Generally 4 × 8 sheets of plywood ⅜″ to ¾″ thick attached to exterior walls o roofs. See illustration on page 79. |
| Sheet Flooring | Linoleum or sheet vinyl in 6-, 9-, or 12-foot-wide rolls used to cover floors. |
| Sheetrock | Gypsum between two layers of paper. Also called gypsum board, gyp board plasterboard and wallboard. |
| Shellac | Shellac is the mixture of alcohol with the resinous substance deposited on twig by the female lac bug common to southern Asia. Honest. An on-the-surfac finish for wood. See chart on pages 57–58. |
| Short Circuit | In electricity, when the hot line comes in contact with the neutral line or groun |
| Shut-off Valve | Valve used to turn the water supply system off so that it can be repaired. |
| Sill | The lumber or board on which the first floor joists rest. See illustration on pag 77. |
| Sledgehammer | A soft metal heavy-duty hammer, usually weighing 2 pounds or more. |
| Sloan Flush Valve | A flush valve of diaphragm or piston type. See illustration on page 155. |
| Snake | See Auger. (A picture is worth 1,000 words.) |
| Softwood | Wood from conifers, i.e., cone-bearing trees. They do not lose their leaves ir winter. |
| Solid Wall | Walls, generally brick or concrete, with no spaces inside them. See illustration or page 91. |
| Solvent | Cleaner and thinner for paints, etc. See chart on page 116. |
| Spackling Compound | A mixture of plaster and lime usually used for filling cracks in plaster walls. The addition of lime slows down the drying time. |
| Splits | Lengthwise cracks in lumber similar in appearance to checks, but usually man made. |
| Spring Steel | Steel that is flexible and springs back to its original shape. Used in quality hand saws. |
| Spud Wrench | A wrench for tightening and loosening large nuts, especially union nuts. Se illustration on page 154. |

| | |
|---|---|
| Pipe Joint Compound | A puttylike substance used to seal metal to metal connections to prevent liquid or vapor leaks. |
| Plain-Sawn (Flat-Sawn) | Growth rings of trees form an angle of less than 45 degrees to wide face of board. See illustration on page 36. |
| Plan | A horizontal slice through a building (see Chapter Three). |
| Plaster | A mixture of gypsum (a natural mineral) and sand and water. |
| Plasterboard | Gypsum between two layers of paper. Also called gyp board, gypsum board, Sheetrock, wallboard. |
| Plate | 1. A thin sheet of metal or wood. 2. Various horizontal boards laid flat across studs, or floors, or foundation walls, or whatever. See illustration on page 78. |
| Plumb | True vertical. |
| Points | The teeth on a saw. A 6-point saw has 6 teeth per inch of blade. |
| Polyurethane | A varnish made of synthetic resins. See chart on pages 57–58. |
| Portland Cement | A mixture of clay and limestone varying in the ratios of 1 to 3 parts clay to 4 to 7 parts limestone, then burned in a kiln. *See* Cement. |
| Pressure Side | The side of a valve the water is coming from. |
| Prime Coat | A thinned-down paint used to seal porous surfaces such as wood, plaster, etc. |
| Quartersawn (Edge-Sawn) | A type of lumber that is made by sawing the log first into lengthwise quarters and then at 45-degree angles to both flat sides of the remaining slice of log pie. See illustration on page 37. |
| Rack | To move before the wind. It's what your table does when it spills your coffee while you're cutting your meat. |
| Rafter | A sloping joist, used to hold up the roof. See illustration on page 79. |
| Rail | The top or bottom edge of a door. |
| Ratchet | A clever arrangement of a gear and lever that permits the gear to turn freely in one direction only. Used in wrenches so that loosening or tightening in close quarters becomes a little less troublesome. |
| Receptacle | In electricity, a place to plug the plug in. |
| Reciprocating Saw | A power saw that cuts with an up-and-down motion. |
| Resin | A product from the sap of certain plants and trees. It is hard, fusable, and more or less brittle, insoluble in water; soluble in some organic solvents. |
| Ridge Beam | In roof construction, what the rafters lean against. See illustration on page 79. |
| Riveting | Use of metal studs (rivets) to fasten sheets of metal together. The rivets are rounded at one end when inserted; then the straight end is hammered until it also is rounded and thus holds the sheets of metal together. |
| Saddle | The piece of wood under a door which keeps spilled drinks in the room in which they were spilled. |
| Satin | Paint that is not so shiny. |
| Saturated Solution | A liquid solution in which the maximum amount of an additive is dissolved. Stir sugar into a cup of tea until no matter how much you stir you cannot get any more sugar to dissolve (it settles to the bottom). You have just made a saturated solution. |

| | |
|---|---|
| Stile | The vertical edge of a door. |
| Stud | Vertical structural lumber, usually a 2 × 4 which is commonly placed 16 inches on center. See illustrations on pages 78 and 79. |
| Subflooring | The structural floor that is nailed directly to the joists. A finish floor of wood, tile, carpet, etc., goes over the subfloor. See illustration on page 77. |
| Surface Preparation | To prepare a surface prior to finishing. |
| Switch Box | A junction box where a switch lives. |
| Tack Rag | A rag, usually cheesecloth, impregnated with varnish to make it sticky. Used for picking up dust. |
| Tape | A perforated paper used with taping compound to make smooth joints between Sheetrock panels. |
| Taper Ground | Specifically, saws: thin at the top, thick at the bottom. On hand saws, the bottom is where the teeth are; on power saw blades, the top is where the teeth are. |
| Taping Compound | An easy-to-use ready-mixed plaster. |
| Tempering | The heating and rapid cooling of steel or other metals to change its qualities, usually to make it harder. |
| Tool | A specialized, durable, long-lasting hand. |
| Tool Steel | Steel that is harder and tougher than ordinary steel. Suitable for cutting and shaping wood and metals after it has been properly treated. (*See* Tempering.) |
| Torque | Twisting power. |
| Transform | In electricity, to change by stepping up or down the voltage. |
| Trap | In plumbing, the place that usually gets clogged. Its purpose when not clogged is to prevent waste gases from entering a room. See illustrations on pages 150 and 151. |
| Trisodium Phosphate | A fat. The business end of cleaning agents. Used in large quantities it helps pollute streams, rivers, lakes, oceans. |
| Twist | Turning along the long axis of anything. A lost dance, much to our joy. |
| Undercut | To make a hole bigger at the bottom than at the top so that the plaster or other filler one stuffs into it won't fall out. |
| Underlayment | A layer of plywood or hardboard used to level a floor prior to applying a floor covering. |
| Union Nut | A special nut that tightens around one pipe without loosening its grip on an adjacent pipe. Must be seen to be believed. |
| Universal Box | The building block for all wood construction. See the whole section on it. |
| Valve | A device for turning the water (steam, gas, etc.) on and off. Without valves there could be no plumbing. |
| Valve Seat | The resting place of the stem washer when the faucet is off. See illustrations on pages 158 and 160. |
| Valve Stem | The metal cylinder that connects the stem washer to the faucet handle. Analogous to the way your leg connects your foot and thigh "or the valve stem connected to the stem washer." See illustrations on pages 158 and 160. |
| Varnish | The mixture of oil with a resin (copal or lac). An on-the-wood finish. *See* Shellac. See chart on pages 57–58. |

| | |
|---|---|
| Vehicle | The liquid (oil, alcohol, water, etc.) that carries the pigment in paint. |
| Veneer Core | Plywood made up of thin layers (veneers or plies) of wood. See illustration on page 48. |
| Vent | A pipe that lets gases out of the house. |
| Volt-Ohmmeter | A device for measuring volts and ohms. |
| Volts | A measurement of the strength or desire of electrons (negative charges) to re-unite with protons (positive charges). |
| Wallboard | Gypsum between two layers of paper. Also called gyp board, gypsum board, plasterboard, Sheetrock. |
| Wallpaper | Any thin rolled sheet of material used as a wall covering. |
| Water-Base Paint | A paint that uses water as the thinner for the vehicle instead of turp, or mineral spirits, or other organic solvent. The pigment and vehicle (polymers) along with stabilizers and preservatives are combined with water. After the paint is applied (exposed to air), the emulsion (pigment, vehicle, stabilizers, preservatives) coalesces (blends together) and allows the water to evaporate and the pigment and vehicle are left on the surface. Neat trick, eh? |

Water base paint types:
Latex — rubber vehicle or binder
Vinyl — vinyl vehicle or binder
Acrylic — acrylic vehicle or binder
Polyvinyl Acetate (PVA) — PVA vehicle or binder

| | |
|---|---|
| Water Supply System | The system of pipes and valves that bring fresh (supposedly) water to you. |
| Watts | A unit of work; what you get when you multiply: |

| | VOLTS | × | AMPS | = | WATTS |
|---|---|---|---|---|---|
| | 120V | × | 10A | = | 1200W |
| Is the same as — | 240V | × | 5A | = | 1200W |
| Is the same as — | 1200V | × | 1A | = | 1200W |

| | |
|---|---|
| Wood Lath | Thin rough wood slats usually 1 by 3 inches, which are nailed horizontally across the studs and to which plaster is applied. Metal lath is more commonly used these days. See illustration on page 92. |
| Yard | Three foots (feet). |

# Index

*Numbers in italic denote illustrations.*